MW00812716

IN SEARCH OF
ULSTER-SCOTS LAND

In Search of Ulster-Scots Land

The Birth and Geotheological Imagings of a Transatlantic People 1603–1703

BARRY ARON VANN

THE UNIVERSITY OF SOUTH CAROLINA PRESS

© 2008 University of South Carolina

Published by the University of South Carolina Press
Columbia, South Carolina 29208

www.sc.edu/uscpress

Manufactured in the United States of America

17 16 15 14 13 12 11 10 09 08   10 9 8 7 6 5 4 3 2 1

Library of Congress Cataloging-in-Publication Data

Vann, Barry.
  In search of Ulster-Scots land : the birth and geotheological imagings of a
transatlantic people / Barry Aron Vann.
     p. cm.
  Includes bibliographical references and index.
  ISBN-13: 978-1-57003-708-5 (cloth : alk. paper)
  ISBN-10: 1-57003-708-6 (cloth : alk. paper)
  1. Scots-Irish—Southern States—History. 2. Protestants—Southern States—
History. 3. Immigrants—Southern States—History. 4. Ulster (Northern
Ireland and Ireland)—Emigration and immigration—History. 5. Southern
States—Emigration and immigration—History. 6. Dissenters, Religious—
Scotland—History. 7. Protestants—Scotland—History. 8. Protestants—Ulster
(Northern Ireland and Ireland)—History. 9. Ulster (Northern Ireland and
Ireland)—Church history. 10. Southern States—Church history. I. Title.
  F220.S4V36 2008
  270.0975—dc22

                                                            2007033324

This book was printed on Glatfelter Natures, a recycled paper with 50 percent
postconsumer waste content.

Contents

ILLUSTRATIONS

ACKNOWLEDGMENTS

Many people knowingly and unknowingly contributed to my knowledge, skills, and dispositions to undertake this project. First, I appreciate my mother, Dorothy Jones, and my father, Henry Vann Jr., and Rufus and Vernedith Voiles, my maternal grandparents, for encouraging me to read and talk about places and events that none of us had ever seen. As people born and raised in the impoverished mountains of western North Carolina, they invited me to listen to their stories of long-dead loved ones whom they had known when they were children. They described a world fresh with mist rising out of its hollows and dew still on its cool grass. I could smell the wood burning in their fireplaces, the taste of moonshine, and the agony of losing family to untimely deaths. The world they then described to me was foreign, for they were raising me in Detroit, Michigan.

Through their reflections, I got to know people I never met in person, but they were real to me. I suppose their stories helped me to see the need to re-create the thought worlds of people whom I could never meet. As a boy, I often lay in bed at night after hearing my mother's or grandparents' stories, and more often than not, their reflections filled me with wonderment. I began thinking about southern mountain pioneers such as Daniel Boone, Davy Crockett, and those who sailed across deep, dark oceans in ships filled with smells and conditions most of us would not like and would certainly find alien. I often asked myself a number of questions: "What were they thinking when they set out on their journeys? Why did they leave their homes for places unseen? Did they leave loved ones behind? Were they missed? Were these folk like my grandparents? If so, did they long to see the places where they once felt at home?"

My career as a geographer has taken me many places, always perhaps in pursuit of answers to those childhood queries. Along the way, I developed respect and love for a number of people who helped me find answers to those questions. Here are just a few of the people to whom I owe a debt of gratitude for helping me.

Thanks are owed to geographers Dr. Frank L. (Pete) Charton and Dr. Conrad T. Moore. Both men shaped my basic understanding and love of geography. Special thanks are extended to Les Hill, whose cartographic skills sharpened my feeble attempts at map-making, and my friend and mentor Professor Chris Philo at the University of Glasgow, who made many contributions to my understanding of the methodologies employed by historical geographers. I cannot adequately express my appreciation of Chris Philo. There are simply too few adjectives to describe his work as a geographer and educator. Professor Richard Smith at Cambridge University and Professor Ian Whyte at the University of Lancaster were early supporters of this work. Their encouragement pushed me forward more than they will ever know. Professor Brian Graham of the University of Ulster offered solid ideas on the manuscript, especially some of the terminology I eventually employed.

I would be remiss if I did not thank some key historians and theologians who helped me along the way. Dr. John Stodghill, formerly of Grenada, Mississippi, ignited my passion for Scotland, and Rev. Colin Williamson of Perthshire, Scotland, shared his knowledge, family, home, personal library, and time with me as I sought to make interesting discoveries. Only my grandmother and he truly know the significance of "life's railway to heaven." Professor Ian Hazlett at the University of Glasgow gave me a great deal of his time and a great many of his thoughts on the manuscript; Professor David George Mullan of Cape Breton University is appreciated for his mountain of scholarship on Scottish Puritanism. I was blessed to have his keen eye and structured comments on the manuscript, for he read through it twice. I also need to say a word of thanks to Dr. Tony Parker, who hired me as an honorary teaching fellow at the University of Dundee, and to Professor Jane Ohlmeyer at Trinity College–Dublin. Jane's descriptions of the Tudor-Stuart policies on sixteenth- and seventeenth-century Ireland are superb and well worth reading. I am also indebted to educators and social scientists like Dr. Barbara Hinton at the University of Arkansas and Professor Ron Dodge, formerly of Cleveland, Mississippi.

As any author of an academic work can attest, colleagues are also important in supporting one's resolve to finish undertakings of this kind. Specifically I would like to acknowledge the encouragement and support I received from Professors Colum Leckey, Earl Hess, and Joanna Neilson, all stalwart historians at Lincoln Memorial University, Harrogate, Tennessee. Professors Loren Rice III and David Worley lent me their ears on many occasions. I also need to acknowledge the help provided me by the staff of the library at Lincoln Memorial University. Though few in numbers, their hard work and persistence in locating materials were amazing.

Perhaps the most thanks are owed to students who have suffered through many of my lectures and discussions about topics related to this book. In particular, I thank Lindsay (Heather) Benton, Tracey Brooks, Gilbert (Buddy) Butler, Jim Callahan, Mathew Campbell, Cody (The Codeman) Fritz, Jeremy Garnett, Leigh Ann Garrison, Ginger Hatfield, Nikkie Hatfield, Kelly Jerrell, Melody Jones, Markita Kiser, Wesley Lee, Michael McMurray, Mathew Meachem, Joshua Nantz, Miranda Overton, Quinton Rogers, Chris Sherman, Joshua Southerland, Natalie Sweet, Alicia Tyler, Adam Wolfenbarger, David (Why Not) Wyatt, and hundreds of other students, both past and present, whose bright eyes and sharp minds helped keep the fire of curiosity burning in me.

This book would certainly not be possible without the strong support of Alexander Moore at the University of South Carolina Press. He is especially appreciated for the kind and thoughtful manner in which he helped me bring this book to life.

Finally I must thank those closest to me. Leslie Foley's friendship and encouragement are also appreciated. My wife, Amy; Sarah Vann; and Preston Vann know the full cost of this project.

I am grateful to these people for their support. Any errors contained in this book belong to me alone.

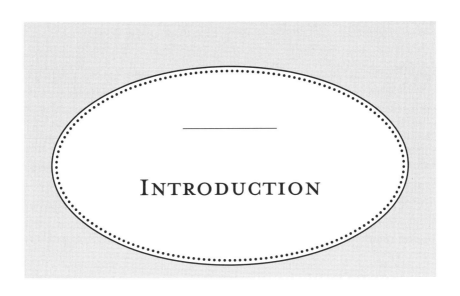

INTRODUCTION

America's citizens who are descendants of Irish people, whether Catholic or Protestant, continue to be affected by political and religious events that existed or took place centuries ago and thousands of miles away across the cold, deep waters of the Atlantic. In recent years, a number of writers have produced both popular and academic books on the historical links connecting Ireland, Scotland, and America. Some of these works are profoundly informative and imaginative, and others are little more than romantic myths written for the edification of people interested in genealogy. Of all the groups who came to America from Great Britain and Ireland, perhaps more is known about Irish Catholic families who came over when the Potato Famine struck the Emerald Isle in the 1840s and 1850s. They settled mainly in the urban areas of the Northeast and in Midwestern cities situated on the shores of the Great Lakes. More than a century before them, streams of more obscure Irish Protestant families began arriving farther south in port cities such as Philadelphia and Charleston. Most of these folk were Presbyterians with Scottish ancestry.

Their Scottish ancestors began arriving in Ireland in the early seventeenth century. They made up a significant and defining part of the Protestant community in Ulster, the historic province of Ireland comprising three Ireland counties and the whole of Northern Ireland. But they were not the lone Protestant group. Smaller numbers of dissenting English, French, German, and Welsh Protestants also settled in the north part of the island and became part of the dissenting Irish Protestant population in Ulster, but the hegemony of the Scottish element of that community left an indelible mark on Irish Protestantism. In the eighteenth century, these same groups, made up of families such as Adair, Boone, Collins, Crockett, Duncan, Graham, McKamey, Morgan, Rogers, Sevier, and Voiles, formed the tide of humanity that spilled over the Appalachian Mountains in search of life-sustaining lands on which to build homes for themselves and their children. By the end of the nineteenth century, their homesteads, churches, and colleges were scattered across the upper South.

Irish Protestants have made important and lasting impacts on the political landscapes of Northern Ireland and the southern United States.[1] Irish Protestants, sometimes called Scots-Irish or Scotch-Irish, make up a substantial part of the American South's ethnic mosaic, but few articles and books have attempted to show the genesis of the educational, political, and religious institutions, including their ancestors' religious thought worlds, that helped create the region's staunchly conservative belief system, political ideology, and landscapes. Their institutions and thought worlds have colored the image of the upper South, giving it the vernacular title of the Bible Belt.

The story of the Irish genesis of the Bible Belt is incomplete. Admittedly, writing a history of a transatlantic people is difficult. The distance between the homelands of the people written about and the residential locations of the scholars doing the writing clearly creates a significant problem. Some of the people that scholars want to study lived in another country made up of complex regional cultures that may or may not continue to exist in their earlier forms. It is perhaps too inviting to think of seventeenth-century countries in Western Europe as singular nation-states plagued only by lingering tensions between rising Protestant merchants who supported a more participatory government system and the Catholic nobility clinging to old regimes. Such a view leads scholars to underestimate the role played by regional cultures or the depth to which subtle differences in religious beliefs had an impact on a host of so-called secular actions such as migration and political dissension. Hence, there is a need for more concentrated scholarship on the genesis of dissenting Irish Protestantism. In doing so, it is necessary to consider its founders' regional and ethnic peculiarities that clearly had effects on life in certain parts of seventeenth-century Scotland and Ireland.

The distance across the Atlantic has also led some Americans to accept broad and perhaps inaccurate generalizations about the community's founding people and their institutions. For example, the Scottish Kirk is sometimes treated by Americans as a homogeneous body composed of populist Scots eager to establish democracy on their soil, regardless of whether the land is in Caledonia, Ireland, or America.[2] What many American writers understandably miss here is that for over three-quarters of the seventeenth century, which saw the birth of Protestant Ireland through the Plantation of Ulster, the Kirk was more often controlled by Erastian-supporting Episcopalians than by populist Presbyterians.[3] They also seem to miss that John Knox, though arguably the Calvinist leader of the Scottish Reformation, was not the founder of Scottish Presbyterianism. He was actually indifferent to that form of church government. His desire for a theocracy, however, was vividly clear.

Popular writers also sometimes do not realize that most Protestants in Great Britain and Ireland, at least up to the eighteenth century, were Calvinists of varying degrees, despite their preferred polity. There were, however, small and growing communities of Arminians and Quakers that were viewed quite negatively by the larger Calvinist community, but the real issue of contention in the Stuart kingdoms centered on who should wield political and ecclesiastical power. Was it to be the magistrate or the Church? The absolute separation of the Church from the state, as some understand it in a modern American context, was a concern only for small groups of Quakers and perhaps some Baptists[4] focused on eschatology but not for the much larger groups of Episcopalians and Presbyterians.

Many North American scholars also mistakenly believe that Puritans composed an exclusively English social and political movement and that their impact on America was only in New England.[5] Recent research by David George Mullan, on whose fine work part of this research is built, quite effectively attacks that myth.[6] The group of ministers that introduced Presbyterianism into Ireland, which made it the first region in Great Britain and Ireland to have a truly Presbyterian polity, was certainly composed of members that functioned as sort of an ecclesiastical intelligentsia.[7] After an examination of their beliefs, practices, and social ties, which are presented in the middle chapters of this book, I agree with sociologist James G. Leyburn that the bulk of Scots living in Ulster in the later decades of the seventeenth century were Puritans. Unlike my colleague of older vintage, I also argue that these immigrants were participants in a chain migration process, so those that set it motion were likewise Puritan in their leanings. Their letters suggest that they considered their English counterparts, including John Winthrop and others who settled in New England, to be their brothers and sisters in Christ.

Puritans, whether they were English, Irish, or Scottish, viewed all secular events through their theological thought world. As this book shows, their religious ethos certainly influenced their perceptions of people, places, and events, including external factors that when filtered through their ethos provided them with a justification to fight or move across both land and sea in search of a place blessed by their sovereign God. Irish Puritans came to America a century after their English counterparts who settled in New England, but unlike their predecessors, their imprint on America was and indeed continues to be in the South.

From the Isles to America

Recent books that discuss the spread of Irish Protestants' culture across the American South are generally good and well-received writings, but a review of them suggests that there is room for a more thorough explanation of where and why this ethnic group was created and how their thought worlds and institutions continue to affect the United States. By adding new information on these substantive areas, we can better appreciate connections between the old and new parts of their Ulster-Scots Land[8] community. This is an important concern because without fully understanding the genesis of this group, it is easy to misunderstand and inaccurately describe the culture of the uplands of the American South, for since colonial times, Irish Protestants have maintained a dominant role in that politically influential part of the country. The demographic factors, political events, and religious thought worlds that created the roots of the recent problems in Northern Ireland are the same as those that gave birth to America's Bible Belt. A brief review of some of the recent writings provides support for the argument that more research is needed.

Among the books that show with varying degrees of success these Ulster-Scots Land connections are David Hackett Fischer's *Albion's Seed: Four British Folkways in America,* James Webb's *Born Fighting: How the Scots-Irish Shaped America,* and Richard Blaustein's *Thistle and the Brier: Historical Links and Cultural Parallels between Scotland and Appalachia.* Kerby Miller has produced a significant body of work on Ireland and Irish migrations, including some valuable writings on identity formation in America. His *Emigrants and Exiles: Ireland and the Irish Exodus to North America* is unequaled in transatlantic studies focusing on Ireland; moreover, his *Irish Immigrants in the Land of Canaan: Letters and Memoirs from Colonial and Revolutionary America, 1675–1815* is well-received and won the James S. Donnelly prize in 2004 for the best book on Irish or Irish American history (awarded by the American Conference on Irish Studies). As good as these works are in their overall contributions to the body of knowledge on Scottish and/or Irish culture and migration, each reveals some of the problems plaguing research on these topics. Specifically the problem is in their lack of an accurate description of the historical religious geography that set the stage, and in many instances, contributed to the creation of immaterial (thought worlds) and material factors that led to migration decisions and the spreading out and manifestation of culture. Such an effort, I argue, requires a deeper and more thorough grounding in sixteenth- and seventeenth-century Protestant theology and its relationship to secular events. A better understanding of regional cultures and distinctions within Scotland, Ireland and America is also needed. In short, because we are considering the spread of culture and people across national boundaries, the discipline of geography can add depth to our understanding and appreciation of the events and forces that continue to shape our world. This is a topic that is discussed in greater detail later. For now let us return to an analysis of the literature.

Fischer certainly contributes a great deal of information on Irish Protestants in the backcountry of colonial America. He chooses to call them "the border British" because he assumes that most of the Scots-Irish people were actually from the Scottish and English border counties. He then goes on to provide a list of the various names by which these people have been known, an idea that Patrick Griffin picked up and extended in his book *The People with No Name: Ireland's Ulster Scots, America's Scots-Irish, and the Creation of a British Atlantic World, 1689–1764*. Fischer does well in identifying the origin of some place names or toponyms such as Cumberland, but his identification of the main source region for immigrants is inaccurate. For example, he places Wigton, Dumfries, and Ayr in the border region. The southwest of Scotland, though arguably a part of the Lowlands, was certainly a distinct ethnic and physiographic area apart from the Borders.[9]

He then offers his readers some inaccurate statements about the roles played by politics and religion in Scottish migrations between Britain and Ireland as well as the formation of a distinct, trans–Irish Sea culture area: "In New England a group of about 140 Irish Calvinists had arrived from Belfast as early as the year 1636, on board a ship nicely named the *Eagle's Wing*."[10] In truth the *Eaglewing* (the spelling used by Robert Blair in his autobiography) carrying that passenger list never made it to New England.[11] A storm, which the members of the party agreed was an act of God, turned them back to Ireland. Among the leaders of the failed voyage were the ministers Robert Blair and John Livingstone. Upon their return to the isles, they helped to create the dissenting culture area, Ulster-Scots Land, that stretched across the Irish Sea. For his part Blair participated in the Scottish assembly that approved the National Covenant of 1638, which Charles I strongly opposed. The movement that produced the covenant was partly inspired by the vitriolic sermons of Blair, Livingstone, and others deposed from Irish pulpits. The staunchest supporters of the movement went against other Scots, including many who were Calvinists, by fighting their monarch in the Civil War. It is clear that Fischer places this extremely important group of leaders and their followers in New England, so it must be construed that he does not recognize the real community from which immigrants to the backcountry were drawn. Fischer also does not point out that the leaders of the group sailing on the *Eaglewing* were deposed ministers from the Church of Ireland. Their depositions were not caused by their adherence to Calvinism, which was widespread in the Anglican Church as well as the Churches of Ireland and Scotland, all of which concurrently had Episcopalian polities during the Stuart dynasty. Instead, these church leaders were the victims of the ever-changing political climate in Ulster and Great Britain that exemplified the tensions between Erastians and theocrats. Put together, Fischer provides a history, at least as far as the eastern shores of the Atlantic is concerned, that does not capture and communicate facts about the distinctive historical geography of the people before they left the isles.

Meanwhile, James Webb shows a great deal of passion trying to weave together a history of a people with which he proudly declares his kinship.[12] Much of his work hence relies on his readers' sense of Scottishness to accept their connection to events, which were mostly of a military nature, to themselves in this modern age. Ethnic groups are tied to and even shaped by events that took place in their community's history, so it is important to connect the pieces across time to give modern readers a clear picture of the past and perhaps a glimpse into the future. Webb's book gives the impression that Scots Calvinists were genetically predisposed to be rebellious fighters in the name of Scottish populism, when in reality many of them accepted government-controlled religion, especially in the northeastern areas around Aberdeen, and supported Charles I during the civil war. He mentions William Wallace, the celebrated champion of Scottish independence, on over fifteen pages, and then Webb shows the military brilliance of Robert the Bruce at Bannockburn in 1314. Interestingly he then leaps three hundred years ahead and into the Ulster Plantation. Along the way he devotes only two pages to the Scottish Reformation of 1560 and makes a critical mistake by assuming solidarity in the Kirk about its preference for a democratized and Presbyterian polity. He clearly associates that movement with the establishment of Presbyterianism, but he never mentions Andrew Melville, the founder of Presbyterianism. It was adopted in Ireland in 1642, nearly fifty years before it was modified and accepted as the polity of the Scottish Kirk in 1690.[13]

Theology and religious practices were important aspects that defined the character of Irish Presbyterians in the seventeenth century, yet recent work on colonial America, absenting the fine contribution of Marilyn Westerkamp, who effectively connects them to the Great Awakening, steer clear of the religious thought worlds of immigrants and the retention of them in the Southern Uplands.[14] Although Griffin makes some geographical errors on the origins of the Scottish immigrants before their departure to Ulster, his work on Presbyterian diffusion from Ulster to America is solid.[15]

With respect to cultural diffusion to the South in general and Appalachia in particular, geographical problems also plague the body of work, although scholars such as Michael B. Montgomery and Cratis Williams effectively show linguistic connections between Ulster and Appalachia.[16] In his book *The Thistle and the Brier,* sociologist Richard Blaustein provides an extensive bibliography of the history of Appalachian studies programs, and in so doing, he shows contrasting views of the strength of some transatlantic relationships. In terms of his being able to separate Ulster from Scotland in making comparisons with Appalachia, he is less effective. He, it appears, relies heavily on Fischer's idea that America's Scots-Irish people were equally drawn from three regions: Ulster, the Scottish Borders, and northern England. I, too, made the same mistake in *Rediscovering the South's Celtic Heritage.* Although the border regions did produce some population flows into Ulster, a close reading of Raymond Gillespie's *Colonial Ulster* vanquishes that myth.[17] As a result, unfortunately, regional distinctions in Scotland were dismissed. Although Blaustein seems to agree with John C. Campbell in *The Southern Highlander and His Homeland* that religious repression and politics played key roles in causing Ulster migrations to America, he virtually ignores how monarchical policies encouraged migrations into Ireland in the first place.[18] Finally and most troubling, Blaustein seems to ignore the Scots-Irish people's religious thought worlds. Many of their descendants in America have certainly maintained their ancestors' strong beliefs about sacred land and people. Even recent voting patterns reveal a regional preference for presidential candidates who have an ear for what has mutated into an American geotheology (aspects of place linked to worship and the divine). As Blaustein suggests, a weakness in the scholarship connects the Lowlands of Scotland to America.

Kerby Miller also writes about Irish Protestantism, but he minimizes the Scottish influence on it.[19] He recognizes the role played by covenants in facilitating social bonding among the members of the Ulster Presbyterian society, but he does not show how political and religious events in Scotland, such as the signing of the National Covenant, had an impact on the formation of the dissenting Irish Sea culture area that served as the source region for Protestant immigrants to America. He is correct in his conclusion that political oppression was a factor in the *Eaglewing*'s attempt to reach New England, but he, like Fischer, fails to explore how the leaders of the party of dissenting Irish families and their ministers interpreted the storm. He also does not see a connection between the leaders of the party and the formation of the dissenting culture area that produced so many immigrants to America.

Clearly there is a need to add to the scholarship that connects the Lowland people of Scotland to America, for little has been added since the seminal work of James G. Leyburn, who published *The Scotch-Irish: A Social History* in 1962. The "missing link" seems to be the Ulster sojourn. Following is an assessment of the writings on that important leg of their journey.

Scottish Migrations to Ulster

The emigration of Lowland Scots from their homeland to the north of Ireland in the seventeenth century, which included the formation of the first permanent Presbyterian denomination,[20] no doubt involved an abundance of interesting reasons beyond an analysis of policy and political decisions, yet the causes of their resettlement lack an adequate investigation. As T. C. Smout, Ned Landsman, and Thomas Devine describe the body of research on the post–James I plantation movement in Nicholas Canny's collection of studies on European migration, "The main destinations were now Ulster, possibly England, to some extent America, with a continuing component to the Netherlands. Unfortunately little sustained study has been undertaken of any of these movements, except that to America."[21] Notwithstanding their conclusion about the work on the migrations between Scotland and Ireland, Philip Robinson's *Plantation of Ulster*, like *Colonial Ulster*, the seminal piece by Raymond Gillespie, offers valuable insights into life in Plantation Ireland. Even though these works deal specifically with the formation of a Protestant Ulster-Scots community, they make a number of assumptions about Scotland and the difficulties associated with crossing the Irish Sea. In doing so, they exaggerate the push forces, which were the events and conditions that caused people to leave Scotland. In doing so, the journey across the Irish Sea itself is depicted as a hazardous, even epic journey. The life and policies on the other side of the Irish Sea in this phase of the formation of the

Protestant Ulster community are the subject of *Scottish Migration to Ulster in the Reign of James I* by Michael Perceval-Maxwell. The work of W. MacAfee and V. Morgan in "Population in Ulster, 1660–1760" provides little elucidation on the years before 1660. The policies that created the plantation movement and its initial settlers, on the other hand, have been heavily scrutinized by scholars.[22] Because the Ulster-Scots removal to America began as the Scots migration to Ireland ended, the events of that time period have likewise received intense analysis. The same can be said of the scrutiny given to the exodus of Highland Scots and the Catholic Irish to colonial and nineteenth-century America. Their migration has attracted scholars from both sides of the Atlantic.[23] Some Presbyterian historians, regardless of their nationality, have endeavored to make martyrs out of the immigrants as well as of those who died during the "killing times" (1680s), and others have portrayed them as "frontiersmen" in the service of God.[24]

Ian B. Cowan has produced a significant body of work on the Covenanters, who dominated the southwestern landscape during the years 1660 to 1688.[25] In his book, Ireland is mentioned, and he writes about two Scottish Covenanters who were apprehended in Ireland and about two Irish ministers who were killed at the Battle of Rullion Green in December 1666.[26] Cowan does not show any other connections between the two places. David Stevenson, who has also produced quality scholarship on the Covenanters, seldom mentions the Irish connections or the existence of social ties between southwestern Scotland and Ulster.[27]

Much is known about the undertakers,[28] including where they held land in Scotland, that during the reign of James I, they were motivated by economic gain,[29] and that those undertakers recruited settlers and ministers, presumably from their estates or nearby areas.[30] It is also generally agreed upon that in the middle and late decades of the seventeenth century, political strife over Oliver Cromwell's Commonwealth as well as the Covenanter problems during the Restoration served to precipitate emigration.[31]

About the typical migrant living in the middle of the seventeenth century, less is known. Limited explanations do exist, and they are often reflections of pull factors, which, put simply, were events and conditions that made Ulster settlement appealing. Because land was comparatively cheaper in Ulster, there was a greater chance that a person could become socially and economically mobile there. It logically follows that poorer economic conditions back home helped to cause emigration.[32]

In addition to political policies, it has been argued that the weak economic conditions in the southwest of Scotland in the seventeenth century were caused by overpopulation. This specific explanation is widely accepted among historians, including Raymond Gillespie,[33] Ian D. Whyte,[34] Griffin,[35] Simon Schama,[36] and Smout, Landsman, and Devine.[37] Theoretically that explanation fits well into Wilbur Zelinsky's mobility transition construct that is popular among demographers.[38] There is a need to synthesize theories about mobility with a distinct cultural group (for example, dissenting Presbyterians) in southwestern Scotland and Ulster.

The recently published work of editors William Kelly and John R. Young, *Ulster and Scotland 1600–2000: History, Language and Identity,* provides essays by leading scholars on the relationship between Ulster and Scotland. With respect to the migration of Puritan-Presbyterians from Scotland and Ulster, however, the collection offers little new insight into the perspectives that shaped the world views of the leaders of that community. These worldviews and ethos are important because they were filters on external events and may have led to decisions to migrate. The book includes three chapters on seventeenth-century migrations, including a chapter by Steve Murdoch, who offers a Scandinavian perspective on Scots and Ulster and challenges the notion that Ulster was the primary choice of immigration for Presbyterians from the Scottish Lowlands. Murdoch argues that Scandinavia and the Baltic offered a more lucrative destination for Scots than Ireland, pointing out, "This could either lead to Scots from Ireland being drawn to the Baltic or vice versa."[39]

Unlike Murdoch, who focuses on Scots and Ulster-Scots in Scandinavia, Young provides a summary in his chapter of some of the political events associated with nonconforming ministerial migrations between Scotland and Ulster. Specifically he focuses on the plantation scheme as a policy-and-migration phenomenon resulting from persecution over the Five Articles of Perth (1620s and 1630s), the conflicts associated with the National Covenant, the Catholic rising in Ireland (1641), the Civil War (1637–1651) and the Restoration.[40] Though he clearly sees major political events as a causal factor in the migration of dissenting Scots divines, his analyses of the roles of their larger community, individual perspectives, and the function of transportation infrastructure linking together southwestern Scotland and Ulster is weak.

Patrick Fitzgerald also contributes a chapter on the Scottish migrations to Ulster in the late 1690s. His principal concern is with economic conditions that served as push-and-pull factors in Scottish migration flows, arguing, "The pattern of migration [between Ulster and Scotland] clearly bore a strong correlation with fluctuations in the agricultural economies of Britain and Ireland."[41] Fitzgerald's chapter helps bring into focus the rural-to-rural migration pattern formed across the North Channel during this time, but it does not explain why Ulster was chosen as a place to settle over other high-growth areas such as those found in and around Glasgow.

The collection of essays in *Ulster and Scotland* reinforces the established explanation that economic and political factors were the primary reasons for the movement of Scots in the seventeenth century. It provides little insight into how the community of Puritan-Presbyterians formed and functioned in the context of this movement to and from southwestern Scotland and Ulster. As Young astutely admits, a national-regional model is needed because national policies had an impact on the communities and individuals in the southwest.[42]

None of those works features any discussions on the social dynamics within the community, its ethos, or how its members understood secular events. It is difficult to find any discussion on the trans–North Channel nature of the ties that bound Irish Presbyterians to their Scottish counterparts, including among ministers. As geographers have generally neglected research on the Plantation of Ulster, there have been few substantive studies on the use of mobility infrastructure during the seventeenth century in southwestern Scotland and Ulster.[43] The research of the current volume seeks to provide an important contribution to building a model that recognizes that the community of Puritan-Presbyterians in the southwest of Scotland was linked to a Scots community in Ulster. This seventeenth-century expansion of community into an existing culture area has had a lasting impact on the Irish and Scottish landscapes. Nonetheless, the research thus far on the Plantation of Ulster lacks an examination of the religious climate in Scotland with respect to its political and economic linkages. In addition research needs to include a delineation of the physical features of the land- and seascapes that helped form the centuries-old Irish Sea culture area, for mobility infrastructure was well established and used by the seventh century. By including religious thought worlds and the geographical features of the Irish Sea and its coastal environs in analyses of mobility on the Irish Sea and the Ulster Plantation, a solid foundation can be built on which to reconstruct the Puritan-Presbyterian community that rose out of it.

Other Factors of Mobility in Southwestern Scotland

Despite the widely accepted explanation of overpopulation (which led to economic deprivation), social institutions and situations that had the capacity to serve as push-and-pull factors in creating migration scenarios between southwestern Scotland and Ulster are difficult to separate from each other in causal explanations. When viewed in the context of an expression of political freedom, the restriction of religious practices, for example among dissenting Presbyterians in the southwest after the Restoration in 1660, arguably provided a political impetus to migrate.[44] The same can be said for political decisions that debarred dissenting Protestants in the southwest from full participation in the nation's economic life.[45] One could reasonably argue that much of the migration from Scotland to Ireland over issues of economics and religion after the ascension of Charles I, including the decades up to the Glorious Revolution, were actually caused by political and religious factors.

Relevant non-Plantation migration studies of the era have implications for Plantation research. Rab Houston has studied internal migrations in seventeenth-century Scotland, specifically, migration mobility in the late seventeenth century by analyzing testimonials of people who moved from one parish to another. Testimonials, in effect relocation passports, were issued by an officer of a Kirk session. Migrants presented those testimonials to the sessions in the parish of their proposed new Scottish homes. As Margo Todd points out, testimonials were so important that active trade in counterfeit versions was common.[46] Houston concludes that people were moving within the most populous counties and that employment was a factor.[47]

What is significant about Houston's work in the context of the Plantation of Ulster is the near absence of testimonial records from southwestern Scottish parishes, although nearby Hutton and Corrie parishes yield records as do Melrose in the east and Wiston and Roberton in the southern periphery of the central belt. The Lothians and the central-belt parishes yielded virtually all of the testimonials.[48] In light of what is known about the militant Covenanter movement in the southwest during the reigns of Charles II and James VII, the migration pattern as depicted by those testimonials suggests that formalized religious practice outside of the Church of Scotland prevailed in the southwestern region, making most of the population that was prone to migrate unable to relocate within Scotland. The pattern could also have meant that no members of the established church were migrating to, within, or from southwestern parishes.[49] The implication of Houston's study for plantation scholarship is that the economic activity in the Lothians and central belt was compelling enough to cause intraregional and interregional migration, but that the inability of dissenting Protestants in the southwest to obtain Kirk-issued testimonials may have blocked their settlement in those areas that offered gainful employment.[50] In that case, it is reasonable to argue that better economic conditions in Ulster presented a more realistic option for those who were hard pressed by poor economic conditions at home.[51]

Huw Jones has cleverly constructed a model that incorporates economic structure or niches into migration decisions.[52] He argues that scholars with Marxist interpretations of population change have paid little attention to migratory events. His model attempts to delineate the conformity between Scottish migration patterns and the broad sequence of the mobility transition but framed by changes in modes of production. In other words, the type of industry in a given area requires a correspondingly similar type of worker. This can be seen in a contemporary context. For example Silicon Valley, California, requires large numbers of technically trained workers, so it will attract persons fitting that economic niche. On the other hand, it will not attract pastoral farmers. Informed by Jones's model and by recognizing that the flows were primarily from rural-to-rural places, it is reasonable to argue that Ulster attracted pastoral farmers from the southwest of Scotland because that was an economic niche it offered.[53] However, such an explanation is reductionistic and excludes other factors that may have influenced their decisions and ability to migrate between Southwestern Scotland and Ulster. As discussed next, southwestern Scotland and Ulster formed a culture area as early as the Mesolithic era (8000 to 3000 B.C.). Mobility on the Irish Sea in the seventeenth century was relatively easy when compared to the overland movement of groups of people and bulky items sold in commerce.

Travel on the Irish Sea

Transportation and sailing capability on the Irish Sea in the seventeenth century is generally an overlooked area of interest in plantation-era migration studies. It is important because the capability to travel at sea affected the direction of the expansion of community and the formation of a new dissenting culture area. Scholars, however, have disagreed on the difficulty of travel across the North Channel in the seventeenth century. To some migrants, the sea was a hindrance to migration, and to others, it was little more than an inconvenience in relocating to Ulster. Here again, the role played by the sea is important. Writers who characterize travel across the North Channel as a difficult and lengthy undertaking are more likely to magnify conditions that may have pushed people to migrate. The reverse seems to be true for those scholars who regard such travel as relatively easy. In this section, the evidence is examined to determine which position is nearest to the truth.

The geographer H. J. Mackinder, in a manner consistent with the historical scholarship that was common during the twentieth century, described the North Channel of the Irish Sea as the "insulation of Ireland," or an intervening obstacle to migration and communication.[54] It was archaeology that found evidence to demonstrate that the Irish Sea was not such a divide or intervening obstacle during premodern times. Based on the scholarship of archaeologists, O. G. S. Crawford published an article in 1912 that recognized the importance of western sea routes as a means of distributing gold lunulae of Irish origin.[55] In his and Lily F. Chitty's *Personality of Britain,* published in 1932, Cyril Fox identified sea routes off Western Europe, categorizing the routes into three sections that included the waters of the Irish Sea.[56] Building on the work of those scholars and others, E. G. Bowen, a Welsh historical geographer, commented, "No longer do we consider that in ancient times the sea divides and the land unites, but on the contrary, that the sea unites and the land divides."[57] In his observation, Bowen identified ancient sea routes among Belfast Lough, Iona, and the Solway Firth (see map 1).[58] These routes were established during the Mesolithic period.[59]

Clearly transportation improved over the centuries and would have had an impact on migratory events. With the work of Bowen, it is feasible to piece together statements from primary sources and maritime histories to establish that by the seventeenth century (at least) it was possible to extend an interactive Scots community across the Irish Sea. As Bowen's scholarship suggests, sea transportation was used by merchants, farmers, and fishers as well as saints (ministers) who lived in settlements scattered along the seacoasts of Scotland, Ireland, and England. This was especially true for those who traded goods with markets in London, Dublin, Glasgow, and Edinburgh.[60]

The migration of Scots to Ulster needs to be set in the ecological context of the Irish Sea and its coastlands. As discussed later, the comparatively low population density in the southwestern Scottish Lowlands during the period relative to areas, such as the Lothians and the central belt, raises some questions about relying too heavily on the overpopulation thesis. However, when one considers the impact of the inland topography of the Southern Uplands, it becomes clear that the population was socially, culturally, and economically oriented to the coast. No doubt human population was, as the location of burghs suggest, highly concentrated near the sea. Coastal departure points such as the one at Port Patrick most likely attracted a wide assortment of people intending to relocate to Ulster. The Irish Sea, like a modern highway, provided an avenue for extending the Puritan community westward across the North Channel and into Ulster. Aside from this research, recognition and analysis of the role of seaways on the Plantation of Ulster are absent from the literature.

Framing a Geographical Perspective

This book inserts a new perspective about the formation or genesis of the community from which thousands of its members, within a century of its inception, left for North America and especially to the South. A religious historical geography perspective offers a framework to better appreciate the immaterial and material aspects of a people who formed a dissenting Irish Sea culture area, Ulster-Scots Land. An in-depth look at how the defining attributes of Ulster-Scots Land, that is, its geotheological beliefs, religious higher education institutions, and political attitudes, joined together in the American South to give the region its vernacular title of the Bible Belt, which is also a culture area.

To explore the creation of Ulster-Scots Land, it is important to delve into Robert Blair's world view and his explanation for being thrust over to Ireland against his will[61] and then to join together insights from geography, history, social psychology, sociology, and theology. The body of work conducted thus far on topics related to the Plantation of Ulster has been completed primarily by academic historians. Although somewhat dated, the work of James G. Leyburn represents a compelling departure from the literature compiled by historians because he provides a sociological perspective in *The Scotch-Irish: A Social History*. Historical geographers with interests in migration and religion have paid little in-depth attention to the settlement of Protestant Scots in Ulster during the seventeenth century. Lindsay Proudfoot and David Livingstone, geographers at Queen's University in Belfast, insist that the paucity of work by historical geographers on population flows and Presbyterian diffusion during the Plantation of Ulster is attributable to a lack of archival material on which to base research on large population flows.[62] Along this line of thought, a distinction drawn by Jaqueline Beaujeu-Garnier between the disciplinary perspectives of history and geography is revealing: "The content of history is limited to particular objects, namely human actions which are the consequences of conscious thought."[63] Beaujeu-Garnier points out that academic geographers have long tended to concern themselves with material objects that humans can see, instruments can detect, or statistics can analyze, encouraging the selection of projects appealing to current temporal contexts that yield data sets that are more concrete and that can be used.[64]

My contention, however, is that geographic and historical methodologies can coalesce to provide scholars with a clearer impression of the formation of a seventeenth-century Presbyterian community that stretched across the Irish Sea. This sentiment that geography and history can unite is shared by a number of other scholars, including Carl O. Sauer and E. G. Bowen. For them the issue was not just combining a sensitivity to time (history) and space (geography),[65] it was also about bringing into one inquiry both the material and the immaterial, meaning both the observable landscape and the more "invisible" forces that arguably shape that landscape.

Although massive data sets on Scots settlers and their precise geographic settlement areas in Ireland escape detection, information on ministers is available for study. As articulate and well-connected leaders in ecclesiastical communities, ministers often had followers who moved with them. In 1636, for example, ministers John Livingstone and Robert Blair attracted 140 members of their Ulster communities to accompany them on a failed Ulster-Scots relocation to New England in the *Eaglewing*. The group, though, returned to Ulster. As William Row pointed out, within two years, circumstances, which they regarded as of divine origin, enabled them to move back to Scotland.[66] Forces that caused the ministers to migrate may have influenced a substantial number (although difficult to enumerate exactly) of their followers to move with them. Although also difficult to determine, ministers may also have been influenced by certain people within their congregations to relocate.[67] A thorough understanding of how the leaders of the expanding Puritan-Presbyterian community in southwestern Scotland and in Ulster interpreted secular events and circumstances as well as the geographic space involved provides a more complete delineation of the creation and spreading of that community. This, then, suggests two issues warranting further consideration: the spatial basis of the community, in which case it is proposed to deploy (and to rework) the concept of "culture area," and the role played by the likes of leaders' understandings as an influence on the creation of this community and its spatial dimensions. In order to reflect upon these issues, it is possible to draw some themes from studies of historical geography and religion.

On the first issue, Alan Baker points out that any historical region or area being studied (for example, America's Bible Belt, which is a spatial extension of the dissenting trans–Irish Sea entity that is the focus of the present work) "often did not have boundaries that were clearly defined at the time being studied; and such boundaries as were defined were often not static but themselves changed through time."[68] Baker explains that attempts to accurately identify regions of the past are plagued with difficulties because historical actors and modern observers define the same area or region differently according to the criteria being employed, and these criteria may vary.[69] In this respect, attention can be paid to Sauer: "The geographer is engaged in charting the distribution over the earth of the arts and artifacts of man, to learn whence they came and how they spread, what their contexts are in cultural and physical environments."[70] Sauer's writings demonstrate that cultural diffusion and the formation of culture areas are fluid. Normally, diverse groups and complex group-learning processes are involved.[71] Although seeming to dismiss Sauer, Chris C. Park identifies Wilbur Zelinsky as an important alternative influence in the development of the geographical study of religion.[72] In particular, Park points to Zelinsky's 1961 empirical study on church affiliations in the United States, which included a well-received map showing different religious (albeit Christian) regions.[73]

More particularly inspiration can be drawn from Bowen, who, it has been argued, was influenced by Sauer and gratified by the historical and cultural turn in the Sauer's famous 1941 paper.[74] Bowen held a strongly cultural conception of regions, discussing culture areas in his work, and it is revealing that in his 1959 presidential address to the Institute of British Geographers, he explored "Le Pays de Galles," or Wales, as a highly unstable spatial construct varying in response to all manner of cultural influences coming and going across the centuries.[75]

The current research argues that sea routes between Galloway (southwestern Scotland and bordered on the south by the Irish Sea) and Ulster helped form a dissenting Scottish culture area. This area, like Bowen's construct, is used as a means to express a sense of spatial extent of interconnectedness in lieu of neatly delimited, sealed-off territories conveyed by much regional-geographical thinking. Bowen causes the culture area to leap off the page and into his readers' eyes and is especially true with his maps. He plots the locations of early Christian-inscribed funerary stones. He does not use lines to demarcate a region but the historical context (Christianity during the time of Roman withdrawal from Britain), and the specific locations of funerary stones along the Irish Sea coasts then suggest interconnectedness among places.[76] Bowen considers that areas rarely have spatially correlated cultural traits, certainly not in any straightforward fashion. The map lines should be regarded as zones of transition and not necessarily abrupt changes in the cultural landscape.[77] Bowen's identification of a western seaways culture area is much more extensive and diverse and indeed more Catholic than what is discussed in the research in the current volume.[78]

More recently, yet arguably very much in the vein of Bowen, Miles Ogborn states in his excellent work on historical geographies of globalization that cultural interdependence had an impact on early modern Europe (1500 to 1700) through intricate networks that reached across vast bodies of water, including to Asia and the Americas.[79] He takes issue, however, with the singular economic logic of scholars such as Immanuel Wallerstein, who advanced a "world systems theory" to explain interconnectedness and globalization. On the contrary, Ogborn wants to underline global connectedness (or relatedness) in present and past times by arguing that such relations are pieced together through all kinds of diffusing, including through migrating people, practices, documents, and devices, and coordinated by an eclectic assortment of human institutions, including empires, corporations, religions, families, composed of people with equally diverse visions, wishes, and desires (among them, for "promised land"). Ogborn also argues that each interconnected network necessarily requires its own delineation with respect to its nature and extent.[80] In his two seminal works,[81] Bowen anticipated such a broad perspective on the networking of "culture areas."

Informed by Bowen's use and identification of vaguely demarked culture areas, this work does not purport to show a neatly sealed-off ethnic and/or political space for any group now or in the past. It is arguably true that colonial Scottish Presbyterians wanted to carve out a distinctive place in the world in line with their underlying geotheology, and some today might want to spot simple historical continuities or delimit simple geographical shapes in "identifying" a distinct, well-defined Ulster-Scots Land. But the ideas of Bowen and indeed the entire emphasis and approach in this current volume absolutely cannot and should not lend themselves to such simplistic political appropriation. This is especially true for Ulster, for spatial discontinuity characterized much of the Scottish, English, and indeed, Irish settlement patterns during the seventeenth century. *Ulster-Scots Land* is used only in reference to the creation of a dissenting Protestant culture area that straddled the North Channel of the Irish Sea during the plantation era.

It is worth reflecting upon this focus with respect to existing work on the interface between geography and religion. Through the 1990s, studies in the specialty area of cultural geography dealing with religion reveal a body of work best described as lacking coherence and in a state of disarray.[82] More recently, however, a resurgence of interest has occurred in this subfield. Julian Holloway and Oliver Valins insist that geographers of religions are now providing fresh insights into religious and spiritual topics ranging in geographic scale from the corporeal to the institutional to the geopolitical.[83] Such studies are important to the body of geographic scholarship, for, "religious and spiritual matters form an important context through which the majority of the world's population live their lives, forge a sense of (indeed an ethics) of self, and make and perform their different geographies. Religious beliefs are central to the construction of identities and the practice of people's lives."[84] They did not, however, mention that most studies fit nicely into the area-studies tradition, which seeks to demonstrate unique expressions of social structure, religion, politics, economics, and topography in particular places defined as a region or perhaps even a spatially less-structured construct as a culture area. As succinctly put by William D. Pattison in 1964,

> The area-studies tradition (otherwise known as the chorographic tradition) tended to be excluded from early American professional geography. Today it is beset by certain champions of the spatial tradition who would have one believe that somehow the area-studies way of organizing knowledge is only a sub-department of spatialism. Still, area-studies as a method of presentation lives and prospers in its own right. One can turn today for reassurance on this score to practically any issue of the *Geographical Review*, just as earlier readers could turn at the opening of the century to that magazine's forerunner.[85]

Pattison's observations are valid in this century as well. Fraser MacDonald, for instance, offers us his observations on "the micro-politics and social relations of space in the context of worship" among Presbyterians in Scotland; however, his observations are "largely based on fieldwork undertaken on the island of North Uist during 1998 and 1999."[86] Simon Naylor and James R. Ryan also published a study that applies to what might be conceived as a restricted space, maybe a "culture area" of sorts, mosques in the suburbs of South London.[87]

Taking a longer-term view of the subfield, it is perhaps easier to construct an argument about the approach taken by this present study. In his 2005 paper, Michael Pacione noted that studies that tend to be cast as "geography of religion" studies were made popular in the United States through the work of Sauer and the Berkeley School, which emphasized the influence of "cultural landscape," including religious belief and worship, on the "material culture" (in the built forms, say, of churches or other structures with symbolic importance).[88] Though Sauer was particularly concerned with the origin and diffusion of material culture in the creation of cultural landscapes, he was open to new and well-organized approaches to study.

[There] has been the tendency to question, not the competence, originality, or significance of research that has been offered to us, but the admissibility of work because it may or may not satisfy a narrow definition of geography. When a subject is ruled, not by inquisitiveness, but by definitions of its boundaries, it is likely to face extinction. This way lies the death of learning. Such has been the lingering sickness of American academic geography that pedantry, which is logic combined with lack of curiosity, has tried to read out of the party workers who have not conformed to prevalent definitions. A healthy science is engaged in discovery, verification, comparison, and generalization. Its subject matter will be determined by its competence in discovery and organization.[89]

Encouraged by Sauer's admonition to ask new types of geographical questions, the present study does not really follow up on his material-culture-landscape approach, although some mention is made to the material places where ecclesiastical elites held services. On many occasions, these were outdoors, indicating a religiously inspired use of natural landscape rather than the creation of a distinctive cultural landscape.[90] This difference of approach can be clarified by reference to R. W. Stump, writing in 1986, who contrasted *religious geography* with the objective, spatial delineations of scholars doing work described as the *geography of religions*. Stump proposes that the latter, including Zelinsky's inquiries, is a somewhat different perspective than religious geography. He argues that religious geography "focuses on religion's role in shaping human perceptions of the world and of humanity's place within it; its primary concerns are the role of theology and cosmology in the interpretation of the universe."[91] Here it is easy to see that the "world" includes secular forces that influence migration decisions and attitudes toward the occupation and use of profane and sacred spaces. This view is arguably consistent with the school of *humanistic geography* advanced by Y. F. Tuan.[92] Given the researcher's interest in these immaterial (belief-based) dimensions of diffusion, the research appeals more to Stump's description of religious geography, although it should be admitted that Lily Kong sees religious geography as a perspective shaped by the thought world of the researcher and not the object of study per se.[93] She writes that such a study does not constitute a "geography of religion, but belongs instead to the realm of religious geography. This religious geography was what Stump (1986) classified under the rubric of geosophy, the study of geographical knowledge."[94] *Geosophy* is a concept associated with John Kirkland Wright, another senior figure in the history of American geography, who, in his famous address to the Association of American Geographers in 1947, outlined what it entailed.[95] The discussion will return to Wright later.

Ronald L. Johnston succinctly describes religious social organizations, with clear application to the Scottish ecclesiastical intelligentsia,[96] as "providing divine sanctions for behaviour that society defines as normative . . . [and that] strengthen their sense of unity."[97] A point missed by Johnston and by the nineteenth-century French sociologist Emile Durkheim, however, is the notion of imagined communities and the construction of noninteracting reference groups gleaned from the pages of Puritan writers as well as from biblical text.[98] Because Andrew Melville's highly literate ecclesiastical intelligentsia filled many important pulpits in the southwest of Scotland and Ulster, their thought world should not be divorced from a study on the expansion of community during the Ulster Plantation. They possessed a high regard for learning and fed ravenously on the writings of their English and Continental counterparts, creating an imagined community of like-minded Puritan brothers and sisters. This is an important characteristic to ascribe to the Scottish divines because in effect their reading selections expanded their "imagined geographies" as well.[99] Although it is customary for geographers and historians to conceptualize imagined communities and imagined geographies as recent phenomena prompted and enlarged by modern communication structures made up of wires and roads, the social networks and reference groups of educated members of the Puritan divines in Scotland and England were members of an imagined community that possessed both apocalyptic and social dimensions. M. Savage points out, "While people's actual community identification may have declined, their imagined identification may have increased."[100] As observed by Nigel Thrift, "Through the nineteenth century, Western society developed more conscious levels of community identification with places, based primarily on the growth of media and travel."[101] Because of high levels of literacy and the availability of printed material espousing their beliefs, it is necessary to apply the concept of imagined geographies back in time to include social structures such as the body of Scottish and English divines in the seventeenth century who subscribed to the tenets of Puritanism. The diffusion of Puritan Presbyterianism into Ireland was the result of intellectually generated social movements within highly literate segments of English and Scottish societies who saw themselves as parts, if not the conjoined head, of the "true Church of Christ."[102]

These perceptions among seventeenth-century divines reveal a major limitation with both the Sauerian and Zelinskian geographical orientations to religion, for in effect they require the geographer to focus on either concrete manifestations of religion on the landscape or spatial patterns of denominations. Indeed it might by argued by some that cognitions and emotions associated with "religion" itself should be ignored.[103] Little is said of the "interior" (the imaginings and perceptions central to religion as felt and thought) dimensions of belief systems. Within the discipline of geography, older scholars such as Wright and William Kirk have given considerable attention to the interconnections between geographies "real" and "imagined."[104] Kirk's work drew upon the field of Gestalt psychology. More recently Chris Philo has drawn heavily on the work of French historian and philosopher Michel Foucault and has added to a growing body of literature embracing behavioral geography by turning attention to the discourses' organized bodies of thought that cannot but be central to all manner of "locational" decisions.[105] With respect to the present study, political forces created a variety of human behaviors. For instance, the return to Scotland of Irish ministers and some of their flocks during the "crackdown" of Charles I in the 1630s clearly had a profound impact on the religious culture of southwestern Scotland. This contributed to subsequent flows of Southwesterners to Ulster, while on the other hand, many covenanters who stayed behind during the reign of Charles II were polarized from their more moderate Scottish neighbors.[106] This community's ethos certainly borrowed from sacred history, and like the Israelites before them, they were willing to take refuge in the wilderness.

As the eighteenth century entered its second decade, "Ulster as a wilderness" was replaced by Ulster as a tightly controlled province of an imperial power.[107] A good many Puritan Presbyterians began to see America as a real wilderness in which to achieve a Christian commonwealth. Large numbers of them, whether they were residents of Ulster or Scotland, joined the flood of their English brothers and sisters who were establishing communities in America.[108] This transition in characterizing the settlement of the north of Ireland has many geotheological implications, for, as Perry Miller discusses with respect to the Puritan settlement of America, the movement of this population "was an organized task force of Christians, executing a flank attack on the corruption of Christendom. These Puritans did not flee to America; they went in order to work out that complete reformation which was not yet accomplished in England and Europe, but which would quickly be accomplished if only the saints back there had a working model to guide them."[109] Miller's seminal work on the "errand into the wilderness" sparked quite a debate among historians who have an interest in colonial North America. As Theodore Bozeman shows in his important work, some scholars completely deny the existence of a "founding errand" among Puritans.[110] Other scholars, including Peter N. Carroll, Alan Heimert, George Williams, and Avihu Zakai, have explored and support the concepts of errand and wilderness as a means of understanding how Puritans in the seventeenth century coped with external forces.[111] However, as these sources show, the concepts of wilderness and errand have been restricted to studies of English Puritans and their migration to and within the North American continent. Buoyed by the comments of the seventeenth-century English Puritan John Cotton, who wrote, "The principal cause of all passages in the world: which is not mans weaknesse, or goodness, but chiefly the wise and strong good providence of God: who presenteth every age with a new stage of acts and actors"[112] and the fine work on Scottish Puritanism by Mullan, the present volume introduces the notions of imagined geographies and communities into plantation research. In so doing and taking seriously the kinds of imaginings integral to statements such as those by John Cotton, the present volume turns to another geographer of older vintage, John Kirkland Wright.

Indeed, most of the terms and concepts used in this study were coined by J. K. Wright to identify the nuances of religious geography, and the research reported later in the present volume owes much to the distinctive, if neglected, coming together of Wright's geosophy and Stump's identification of religious geography.[113] Specifically terms such as *geotheology* (the general relationship between space and the worship of God), *geoteleology* (the relationship between space and the unfolding of Providence), *geopiety* (the religious, emotional attachment to terrestrial space) and *geoeschatology* (the role of space in the outcomes of Providence) are all significant in what follows in the present volume.[114] Wright's approach and his useful lexicon precisely call for consideration of such interior imaginings in geographical research because of the role that imaginings, feelings, and thoughts have in molding human behaviors, which often affect the landscape with visible patterns and structures.[115] The current volume embraces aspects of Sauer and Zelinsky, but then it moves on to a position more closely akin to Wright as a way of deepening the explanation that is offered for the religion's landscape effects, spatial patterns, and links to demography as well as to politics.

This work argues that the thought world of seventeenth-century Presbyterians in the southwest of Scotland is particularly important to consider because it provided community members with lenses through which they interpreted secular events as push-and-pull factors. Their under-standing of those events influenced their perceptions of land- and sea-scapes as well as decisions to take action (fight, conform, or migrate) that affected both southwestern Scotland and Ulster. Geotheological beliefs of Scottish Presbyterians diffused to Ulster and eventually to the American South along with other aspects of their faith. In doing so, two dissenting culture areas were formed—one along the North Channel of the Irish Sea and, through relocation diffusion, another stretched across the Upland South of the United States. The hope in this book is principally to illuminate these substantive questions and to contribute a novel example of what can be most logically cast as "historical religious geography" building upon the still-valuable examples set by Bowen and Wright.

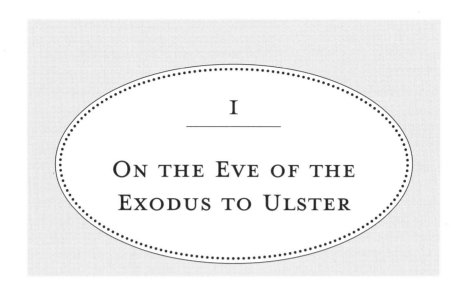

I

On the Eve of the Exodus to Ulster

Religious conflicts and political upheavals in the seventeenth century certainly made life in the southwest of Scotland uneasy, but they were not the only problems facing lowly farmers traditionally tied to the feudal system. By 1600 the once-forested soils in the region were too shallow and infertile to support an economy based solely on agriculture. In his travels from Glasgow to Ayrshire early in the Plantation of Ulster, Sir William Brereton observed, "We passed through a barren and poor country, the most of it yielding neither corn [grain] nor grass; that which yields corn is very poor, much punished with drought."[1] William Shakespeare, whose geography of the imagination was based presumably on Scotland's reputation, likened its Lowland landscape to the barrenness of the palm of the hand.[2]

Adding pain to misery, the feudal system was dying. Poor farm families unable to pay money-rent to stay on the lands occupied by their families for generations were told to leave their homes and traditional way of life. Meanwhile in a broad Scottish context, social and cultural developments during the century ushered in a better business climate in some areas, especially in Glasgow, the central belt, Edinburgh, and border counties (see map 1).[3] Modest expansion in employment in those places encouraged growth and movement in the country's population. People who conformed to the standards of religious life established by the Kirk when it was governed directly by the monarch through an Episcopalian polity could chose to move to any of the country's high-growth areas. On the other hand, nonconforming Presbyterians, especially after the Stuart Restoration in 1660, were not allowed to move into areas of the country experiencing growth. Because Presbyterianism was popular in the south-west, the situation left a surplus of labor there. With land now centered on pastoral practices, there was little demand for labor. Religious oppression, declining environmental conditions, and changes in economic relationships pushed the regional population coastward and eventually across the narrow waters of the Irish Sea. With few employment positions outside of coastal burghs experiencing growth resulting from the Plantation of Ulster, there can be little doubt that such places appeared overpopulated to outsiders.[4]

Until the beginning of the seventeenth century, Scotland experienced little sustained population growth.[5] Evidence does suggest that as the seventeenth century unfolded, population grew for the country as a whole. The southwest seems to be no exception.[6] Brereton, who gave the description of the landscape mentioned above, noted that the beleaguered economic condition of that part of Scotland was the primary reason for causing people to relocate across the Irish Sea.[7] In 1597 Timothy Pont described the Ayrshire Barony of Cunningham with "one may wonder how so small a bounds can contain so very many people."[8]

In 1624, Sir William Alexander observed, "Scotland by reason of her populousnesse being constrained to disburden her selfe (like the painful bees) did euery yeere send forth swarmes."[9] Alexander's comments may have been biased because he was interested in promoting colonial ventures, but, as one critic of Alexander put it, those "swarmes" were an occasional embarrassment to Edinburgh.[10] In the 1620s, a Venetian ambassador made a similar observation of Scotland: "[The] kingdom is populous . . . the women being prolific, showing how much more fruitful are the northern parts."[11] An anonymous author described Scotland in the 1580s as a place where the "Beggars & vagrant poore [exist in] infinite numbers, and the same by reason of their extreame wants and misery [are] very bold and impudent."[12]

Taken together, those sources provide compelling evidence to argue that coastal burghs in the southwestern region were overpopulated. However, overcrowded conditions would have been more apparent during certain times of the year, for market days brought in especially large crowds.[13] Nonetheless and despite the obvious complexity of life in the region, overpopulation and changes in land tenancy are often centralized in explanations for the migrations from Scotland after the early 1600s.[14] These generally accepted arguments, which offer little depth to the understanding of the conditions that caused an excess of population relative to the carrying capacity, have made their way into recent histories of Britain. According to Smout and his colleagues, Ayrshire, Wigtonshire,

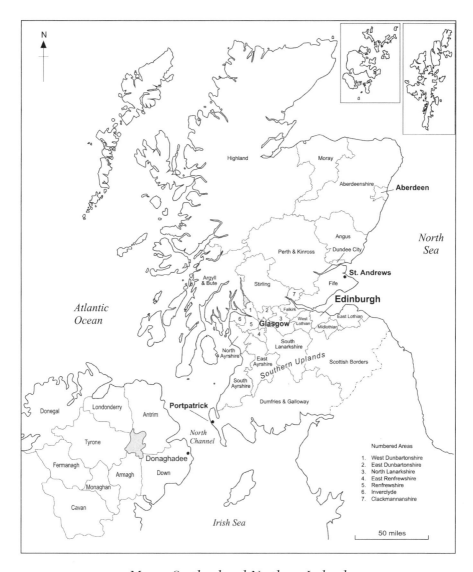

MAP 1: *Scotland and Northern Ireland*

and Galloway were overpopulated by the year 1600, and by 1650 the resulting poor economic conditions there had forced between twenty thousand and thirty thousand Lowland Scots to immigrate to Ireland.[15] Simon Schama writes, "By 1620, large numbers of poor farmers had been transplanted from the overpopulated, over-zealous Calvinist southwest of Scotland to a place where they could really get their teeth into a challenge."[16] Importantly most of the English and French settlers in Ulster were also Calvinists. Simply stating that the southwest was overpopulated and giving some attention to economic hardships fail to describe the precise conditions as they developed in that part of the country.

As an example of the complexity of the region, it is important to recognize that it was a hotbed of Puritan-Presbyterian activity, signifying a dissenting polity. It was indeed the home of charismatic ministers, such as, Robert Blair, Richard Cameron, Donald Cargill, David Dickson, John Livingstone, James Nesbit, James Renwick, Samuel Rutherford, and John Knox's son-in-law John Welch. The region's Puritan community viewed all events, whether of a political, economic, or environmental nature, through its belief system.[17] Because of their emotional connection to the glens and moorlands of the region that was reinforced by the belief that Scotland was a covenanted land, John K. Wright would have described the southwest as a "geopious" region.[18] A minister's power to influence people to relocate had to have some secular basis, and overpopulation, if it was an issue for him, would have given him fertile material for his sermons and letters.[19] An examination of sermons and letters, presented later, supports Margo Todd's assessment that famines and plagues that may be related to overpopulation in Scotland were believed to be the result of sinful behavior, that even the sins of one individual could provoke God's wrath, which might be directed at an entire community. Those who migrated in the name of economic survival were often seen as sinful and in need of repentance. Repentance, church attendance, and public apologies to the congregation and God were required of sinners who were deemed responsible for the calamity, not emigration.[20] Emigration was not seen as a way to escape God's wrath, for Puritan Scots believed that his nature as a sovereign, omnipresent deity made his justice inescapable.[21] Migration as a response to "persecution" was another matter, however, for even baby Jesus was taken into the spiritual wilderness of Egypt to escape the sword of Herod.

With the religious environment in mind, it is worth examining the overpopulation rationale for seventeenth-century Scottish migrations to Ulster in four areas: the evidence demonstrating demographic and economic changes in the region; the immaterial aspects of social and economic growth; whether ministers perceived economic conditions in such a way as to encourage others to relocate to the less-populated environs of Ulster; and the carrying capacity in Scotland's regions with special attention given to the southwest and its well-established relationship to the Irish Sea, which invited expansion into Ulster. The overpopulation explanation for the migration of southwestern Scots to Ulster has some merit. The reasons for the conditions that caused their plight are complicated, varying through the century, and could be interpreted as being the result of political persecution or the result of God punishing a sinful magistrate or Kirk. Some of the migration could simply be the result of people taking advantage of the region's orientation to the Irish Sea and the new opportunities afforded to them by the investment of surplus wealth in the king's plantation scheme.

Challenges to Economic Growth in the Lowlands

Despite intermittent outbreaks of bubonic plague (1644 to 1649), smallpox and dearth (1670 to 1689), and the ravages of famine during the last half of the 1690s, the growth in urban population outpaced that of the rural hinterland.[22] Economic indicators, particularly the prices paid for crops and burghal taxes to the national government, suggest that the seventeenth century was a time of perceptible economic growth and diversification of manufacturing in Scottish cities. This was especially true for the areas in and around Glasgow, Aberdeen, the central belt, and Edinburgh. Still, the Lowland hinterland, especially in the southwest seems to have been besieged by the pressures of having too many people and too little opportunity. Episodes of plague were not the only impediments to the southwest's economic growth and its ability to feed its people.

One of the primary reasons for the vulnerability of the masses was their reliance on a restricted diet that featured the oat crop. Any failure of the crop on a local scale pushed the peasantry from their normal position of rough plenty into a deep trough of deprivation and possible famine.[23] There were years of plenty, however. For example, the first fifty years of the seventeenth century were times of good to acceptable harvests, although a few seasons after 1630 saw prices for crops that were higher than normal.[24] The production of 1623–24 was bad, however,[25] and the effects of shortage were felt most among the poorest areas of the country. From 1660 to 1695 there were mostly bountiful crop yields, so food prices were high during only four harvests.[26] Prior to this period, poor harvests had been often followed by starvation among the poorest people as well as by widespread dislocation of farm families. The army of vagabonds, which had always existed in Scotland, "was enormously swollen during times of bad harvest, and emigration to Ireland and Scandinavia always ran highest in these years."[27] The period of relative plenty in Scotland from 1660 to 1695, for instance, was followed by a three-year period of famine during the closing years of the seventeenth century.[28] The Kirk's policies on relief of the poor undoubtedly reduced the number of deaths from famine during that time, but the Kirk and the state could do little to find meaningful occupational positions for the estimated two hundred thousand beggars who roamed Scotland in 1698.[29] Scotland as a whole was therefore besieged by the consequences of overpopulation as the eighteenth century arrived with its estimated population of one million people, a possible 100 percent increase since 1600.[30]

In order to study Scottish population, including population pressures and migration flows to and from the southwest during the seventeenth century, relying on varying estimates reported by scholars and contemporary authorities is necessary and includes the work of Alexander Webster, who conducted the first reliable estimate of Scotland's population in 1755.[31]

> The pattern of population distribution in 1755 is probably a reasonably accurate reflection of that of earlier times. The growth of many burghs in the late sixteenth and early seventeenth centuries, and the expansion of Edinburgh and Glasgow in the later seventeenth and early eighteenth centuries, would have increased the contrast between population densities in central Scotland and other areas but otherwise the pattern of population densities was probably not much different at least as far back as the late sixteenth century.[32]

Informed by Whyte's observations above on the static nature of Scotland's population distribution, it is possible to use Webster's data in a regional context. In 1600 Scotland had an estimated population of five hundred thousand.[33] Most of its people, according to Leyburn, lived on the northeastern coastal strip and in the Lowlands, roughly two-fifths of the country's land area (approximately 12,162 square miles).[34] A population estimate of 1,048,000 was made at the time of Union in 1707.[35] Although there is no way of knowing precisely how the population was distributed in 1707, the coastal region and particularly the Forth, Clyde, Tayside (Perth to Dundee), and Aberdeen areas were probably the more densely populated. Leyburn contends that the largest urban area, Edinburgh, had a population approaching ten thousand inhabitants in 1600, but Michael Lynch and Todd provide a larger figure of twelve thousand for 1560.[36] Assuming that 90 percent of the population lived in the Lowlands, population density there would have been thirty-seven people per square mile.[37]

Webster concluded that 1,265,000 Scots were living on the land in 1755. Webster did not, however, use a Highland-Lowland dichotomy. He used a three-way division that separated the Lowlands and Highlands with a central belt. Webster's use of a trichotomous regional comparison does accurately portray the country's cultural and physiographic regions, but he makes some peculiar assignments of places into those respective regions. For example, he places Perthshire in the Highlands, but the southern part, including population centers such as Auchterarder, the Bridge of Earn, Dunning, and Perth are situated in the Lowlands. Moreover, he places the comparatively low-lying costal strip from Dundee through Montrose to Aberdeen with its high population density in the Highlands. In 1755, the northeastern coastal strip had a population density of more than sixty people per square mile as compared to zero to nineteen people per square mile in the Highlands, yet Webster saw fit to include the coastal strip in the same category as the Highland villages of Fort William, Inverbroom, and Achanalt.[38] The central belt had a population density in excess of ninety people per square mile. On the other hand, the southwestern Lowlands, excluding south Ayrshire, had a density of between twenty and thirty-nine people per square mile, the lowest in Scotland with the exception of the northwestern Highlands.[39]

Webster's study offers a limited but valuable spatial perspective on seventeenth- and eighteenth-century population in Scotland. It must be kept in mind that the comparatively low population density in the southwest perhaps reflected a post–plantation era people whose numbers had already been depleted by emigration. However, high-growth areas such as those found in the Lothians and the central belt likewise sent away emigrants.[40] Given that by the end of the seventeenth century, 40 percent of the population in the Lothians lived in urban areas, population density in the southwestern Lowlands was comparatively lower.[41] In the early years of that century, many of the villages in the Lowlands were small. Only a few settlements had as many as two thousand inhabitants.[42] If Scotland was a gemeinschaft society, as suggested by Leyburn, then it is reasonable to assume that towns such as Irvine, Anwoth, and Dumfries were small enough for native residents to know nearly everyone who lived in their settlement. Economic and demographic changes in those settlements arguably upset the residents' sense of gemeinschaft.

From these informed sources, it is possible to argue that between 1600 and 1755 Scotland's overall population increased by a factor of 2.53.[43] In

Edinburgh the number of residents had climbed from ten thousand to fifty-seven thousand,[44] a factor of 5.7. Other population estimates calculate a factor of 4.75.[45] The population living in cities (of more than ten thousand) increased by a factor of 3.31.[46] Unlike England, Scotland did not have a primate city. In the 1690s Edinburgh's population accounted for only 4.7 percent of the country's population, whereas London accounted for 10 percent of England's population. This is important to note because given Scotland's rural past, the relatively greater rate of growth in Edinburgh as opposed to the country as a whole suggests that urban growth resulted from population flows from the hinterland and not through natural increase.[47] The comparatively low population density of the southwestern area relative to the southeastern and central-belt regions does little to support the contention that overpopulation as caused by relative changes in the birth and death rates for the population was the main push factor in the emigration of southwestern Scots.

As the seventeenth century progressed, Edinburgh, and Glasgow, and their hinterlands were gaining in economic importance: "While the economy was still essentially rural, burghs were becoming more conspicuous and the changing pattern of the economy had its effect on the prosperity and relative importance of the burghs."[48] They provided attractive residential and work options for impoverished rural peasants who were becoming disaffected by the feuing of farmland in the Borders and by the raising of rents in the southwest.[49] The growth in Glasgow, like that of Edinburgh, suggests that its rate of increase in population between 1600 and 1755 was faster than for the country as a whole. Rural to urban shifts were also occurring in other parts of the country. Aberdeen, for instance, grew by 50 percent from 1695 to 1755 while its rural hinterland declined in population.[50] In 1612 Dundee paid 11 percent of the burghal taxes in Scotland, but as a result of economic growth in the central belt, especially in the east, its share of the tax burden by 1705 had declined to only 4 percent of the nation's total. Meanwhile, Glasgow's burghal tax share rose from 4 percent to 20 percent.[51] This is important to recognize because the redistribution of burghal tax payments shows that internal population flows coincided with regional economic growth, which expanded the carrying capacity of areas adjacent to the Southwest.

Smout calls the period from 1690 to 1780 the prelude to the takeoff that,

> by contrast, inaugurates a more or less inevitable and self-sustaining progression towards a modern economy. . . . The take off's most obvious feature is fast industrialisation, though it is frequently characterised by a previous, or near-simultaneous, transformation in

agriculture. Nevertheless, farming and rural life inevitably decline in importance before the explosive vitality of the urban and industrial sectors, and the force of this rupture may produce social confusion so great that many intelligent observers in all ranks of society will deplore the fact that it ever happened. In the long-run, however, as self-sustained growth becomes the norm, very great benefits accrue from the industrial revolution.[52]

The available data and Smout's description of the demographic and economic transitions occurring in the late seventeenth century all suggest that the country was indeed in stage two of the demographic transition model. It is quite possible that Scotland was experiencing a "prelude to the takeoff" earlier than 1690.

From a geographical standpoint, the data on demographic growth and economic shifts suggest that segments of the population were moving from rural to urban places decades before 1690; thus many people were experiencing a stressful shift away from their familiar social settings associated with rural communities to the uncertainties of a new life brought about by the externally generated goals of urban society. It would also appear that based on regional population patterns and absenting the influence of topography and land-use capacity, the southwestern region was not the most likely area to experience emigration resulting from population pressures. On the other hand, the ruggedness of the southwestern Lowlands and the coastal-settlement patterns of the residents suggest that the ecumene for the population was quite reduced or spatially restricted. Moreover, the feuing of farmland and the requirement of possessing Kirk-issued testimonials of good conduct for relocating to another parish kept southwestern nonconformists out of the midst of high-growth areas. As Rab Houston discovered, this would have certainly been the case after 1660.[53] A displaced Presbyterian farmer in the Restoration period would not have been able to relocate to the areas in Scotland that offered opportunities for employment, for the Kirk, which was subjected to an Episcopal polity under Charles II, would have denied him a favorable testimonial. No doubt the movement of people in and around coastal burghs, where trans–Irish Sea commerce and employment opportunities existed, made the small settlements seem overcrowded to visitors such as the Venetian ambassador[54] and Sir William Brereton.

Changes in Land Tenancy

Rory Fitzpatrick combines both population increase and closed economic niches in the Lowland's dying feudal society as the impetus for emigration among Lowland Scots. No doubt the economic expansion in the coastal burghs on either side of the Irish Sea attracted many of them. The changes started when:

> the expectations of the nobles and lairds were raised by the unaccustomed prosperity . . . they had seen on the Continent. . . . To break free and achieve a more luxurious standard of living they imposed money rents, changing tenancies over to a feuing system, whereby a tenant made an initial payment and thereafter an annual fixed one.[55]

As Fitzpatrick assessed the situation, the "Lowlands, an area with the largest population and the one most affected by social changes, now had a large pool of potential emigrants, people desperate for land or work."[56] The Hamilton estates of the western shires raised rents during the 1640s by as much as tenfold, and the rents in the border region were similarly raised because of increased trade with England after 1603 and the Union of the Crowns. For instance, the rental of Ettrick in the eastern Borders rose from £2763 in 1586 to £22,760 by 1650.[57] As Fitzpatrick's research demonstrates, geographies of the imagination, in this case perceptions of conditions on the Continent, led landowners to raise rents, which in turn dislocated large numbers of people. However, Fitzpatrick's explanation fails to consider how the Lowland religious culture, with its emphasis on pious, hardworking, self-reliant lifestyles, may have actually accelerated the feuing of lands. That topic is taken up in the next section.

Religion and Economic Change

Ideas and religious beliefs can influence the interpretation of political, economic, and/or environmental events. Overpopulation, which was actually a failure of the economic structure to accommodate disaffected rural farmers, may have facilitated an environment in which the ideas and beliefs of Puritan-Presbyterian Scots, as the heirs of the chosen and wandering Nation of Israel, came alive with ardent joie de vivre.[58] With many Scots already settled in Ireland and their religion widely expressed in Ulster, exile across the narrow Irish Sea was thinkable during times in which environmental, political, or economic conditions at home were unpleasant or potentially life-threatening.[59] While the belief system of the Puritan-Presbyterian community in southwestern Scotland made many members ready for migration in the face of oppression, it also contributed to the social infrastructure that supported, if not encouraged, economic growth.[60] Ironically the emphasis on productivity and prosperity as signs of eternal election helped to undermine the tenancy system in the region. Not only did the Puritan belief structure encourage hard work among lowly tenants, landowners also sought evidences of God's favor.

Collecting money-rent in lieu of the man-rent exchange of the feudal system was certainly in unison with the prevailing religious ethos that placed responsibility on the individual for earning God's blessings.[61] Unfortunately for a number of tenants, they were unable to pay their rents and were forced to migrate. Because having money to pay rent was a sign of God's benevolence, not having enough to cover living expenses could raise concern about one's salvation.[62] Being displaced from a position as a tenant may also have been seen as evidence of God's displeasure about unrepented sins.[63] Either way, the displaced farmer bore the burden of conscience and responsibility for finding a way out of poverty.

Nonetheless a portion of the economy's expansion and its capacity to generate surplus wealth to make speculative investments in the plantation scheme was arguably the result of the efforts of the Kirk at the parish level to bring about change among the members of its congregations, who apparently inculcated the Protestant ethic, for such was the catalyst for the kind of profit and investment pattern that made it socially permissible to dislocate tenants whose family had lived on the laird's estate for generations. This belief system and its relationship to capitalism are described by Max Weber.[64] In discussing Weber's thesis, sociologist Gordon Marshall notes that idleness, wasting of one's time, and ostentatious living were considered to be extreme vices in Scotland during the seventeenth century. On the other hand, he observed that industry, long-term economic planning, diligence in one's vocation, saving, and reinvesting were highly regarded behaviors. According to Marshall, a social by-product of the Calvinist-based ethic in Scotland was pressure on Calvinist Scots to

> invest in industry and set themselves up as manufacturers, rather than as "country squires," wasting their time and inheritance in the useless and unprofitable pursuit of easy or "gentlemanly" life; that tradesmen, mechanics, and manufacturers should be encouraged in every possible way; that increased productivity was self-evidently a "good thing," and that where this was at all possible, increased profits should be sought via better management, improved techniques, rationalisation of the productive process, the use of better-quality raw materials, proper training of the labour force . . . which in turn would yield even greater sums for further reinvestment and expansion.[65]

However, empirical analysis of Weber's thesis is difficult because of the scarcity of data and the effect that other political and economic forces undoubtedly had in expanding Scotland's economy in the wake of the

Scottish Reformation. Although a direct link between religion and the rise of capitalism in Scotland is difficult to make, Marshall found that 106 new manufacturers were established in Scotland between 1560 (the time of the Scottish Reformation) and the Act of Union in 1707.[66]

In contrast to the assessment made by Marshall, Weber's thesis concerning religion and economic growth is dismissed by Smout.[67]

> Max Weber's classic thesis suggests a close link between the rise of Calvinism and the rise of a capitalist economy in European societies. The Calvinist ethic with its stress upon man's calling and on the virtues of hard work and frugality, in its destruction of medieval taboos against money lending and in its belief that the successful acquisition of wealth is a sign of God's blessing, is said to provide the ideal soil for the rooting of economic individualism. Few countries were more completely Calvinist than Scotland, yet it is hard to see how any support can be found for Weber's thesis from the situation in this country between 1560 and 1690. . . . The Reformation cannot be shown in any way to have favored the rise of economic individualism.[68]

While little can be said in direct opposition to Smout's point concerning "economic individualism," his argument misses the central thesis of Weber's work, which advocates the idea that sustainable economic development is predicated on significant community and social development. Smout does acknowledge the Kirk's role in facilitating improvements in education as a positive contribution to social infrastructure that contributed to the rise of the conditions that encouraged industrialization.[69] Yet Weber's thesis is not on institutional initiatives relative to the establishment of economic individualism; rather, its focus is on beliefs and expectations (spirit) that result in pious behavior that reveal manifestations of signs of God's election in the life of the individual. This notion is in harmony with the rise of the doctrines of prior and predestinarian decrees and bilateral covenants in Scottish religious thought in the seventeenth century.[70] As Marshall rightly points out, Weber further contends that because the "truly faithful" in Christ abhorred worldliness and materialism while still believing in the moral virtues of hard work, the income derived from their labors was not spent on mere worldly things. The money saved by not buying nonessential items was, according to Weber, an act of pious asceticism, and the resulting surplus income was invested in solid and productive ventures that, they believed, would reveal God's blessings through the accrual of profits and long-term financial security.[71] This belief was expressed by members of the southwest's ecclesiastical intelligentsia such as David Dickson.

> 1. That some Professoures in the visible Church, may make defection, and not persever to the ende. 2. That such as make finall Defection here-after, are not a parte of GOD's House, for the present, howsoever they bee esteemed. 3. That true Believers must take warning, from the possibilitie of some Professoures Apostacie; to looke better to themselves, and to take a grip of CHRIST, who is able to keepe them. 4. That true Believers both may, and should, holde fast their Confidence, unto the ende; yea, and must ayme to doe so, if they persever . . . 6. That the more a man aymeth at this solide Confidence, and gloriation of Hope, the more evidence hee giveth, that hee is of the true House of God.[72]

Dickson taught that it was God's will that true believers would manifest visible signs of internal election and justification in their lives. Such a belief would, it could be argued, place upon the individual a "psychological imperative" to be productive in his or her calling. Dickson and his colleague James Durham admonished their readers, "That the way to be sure both of our effectual calling, and election, is to make sure of our faith in new obedience constantly: *for if ye do these things, (saith he), ye shall never 'fall,'* understanding by these things, what he said of sound faith, and what he had said of the bringing out of the fruites of faith."[73]

Dickson and Durham were not alone in writing letters and sermons suggesting a psychological imperative that encouraged social behaviors that could have increased economic productivity or a sense of responsibility for unrepented sin. Robert Rollock, who in 1596 encouraged the absorption into Scottish theology of the Puritan construct of bilateral covenants,[74] exhorted his readers to be diligent in their labors because "Alas, it is a shame when a stranger sets his foot in Scotland to see this great misorder, and that shame-lesse begging. Then there is the remedie, labour . . . thou glories God in thy doing & labouring: but in idleness, thou glorifies not God."[75] Rollock also made it clear that occupations, regardless of their status, were to be pursued diligently and that failure to do so would not be good: "If thou be going at the pleugh, Thou glorifies God. Eate thy bread with the sweat of thy browes, otherwise it shall not do thee good."[76]

Those attitudes and behaviors, though perhaps not universally shared, provided the foundation for social development amongst ardent Puritan-Presbyterians, which created a favorable environment for the institutionalization of sound business practices and ventures, including raising rents on poor tenants who felt that their sins caused their own plight. Additionally the literacy programs of the Kirk, as Smout points out, as well as a general increase in the value of learning encouraged by the Kirk Reformers, all added to the development of social infrastructure.[77] In other words, in a logic suggested by Weber, over a period of perhaps several generations, these pious attitudes led to ascetic, work-oriented behaviors that produced modest amounts of surplus wealth with which investments in human capital and economic activity could be made. This process arguably gave rise to capitalism and to the creation of institutions to sustain it.

These changes, however, did not produce immediate, quantifiable data such as that which would be depicted on bank balance sheets if they existed during the early and middle parts of the seventeenth century. It did, however, produce the social conditions necessary for the creation of modest monetary surpluses for the establishment of a national bank in 1695.[78] Sufficient funds and surplus products were also available for making investments in ventures such as the Ulster Plantation and the Company of Scotland Trading to Africa and the Indies (1695) and its ill-fated Darien Scheme (1698).[79] By 1695, the agricultural economy thus showed signs of diversification. The potato, a New-World import, was being cultivated in Scotland and the western Isles. Also in that same year, leisure activities, such as public concerts, were appearing in Edinburgh.[80] In part because of religious forces influencing social and economic conditions to become more stable, modest expansions in the carrying capacity occurred and theoretically accelerated population growth to such an extent that surplus populations formed again as economic niches quickly filled while further religiously influenced economic decisions involving land tenancy caused the primary employment niche in the southwest to close.

Religious beliefs and economic change were intertwined in southwestern Scotland and Ulster. The next section shows that although Puritan leaders in southwestern Scotland and Ulster encouraged hard work and pious behavior, they arguably had little sympathy for those migrating because of poverty.

The Interpretation of Overpopulation

The consequences of overpopulation include susceptibility to starvation and death from disease that are caused by malnutrition, but there is scarce evidence that divines used conditions brought on by overpopulation, such as famine, as a reason to encourage others to migrate to Ireland. Political repression, though, made palatable silage for those Puritans who saw themselves as chosen heirs to persecuted and beleaguered biblical saints, for as Samuel Rutherford wrote to John Nevay, "Suffering for Christ is the very element, wherein Christ's love lives, and exercises itself, in casting out flames of fire and sparks of heat."[81] To Puritans, symptoms of overpopulation were the result of idleness and/or Sabbath breaking and were regarded as sinful. The culture of Scottish Protestantism regarded "Sabbath observance as the solution to a multitude of ills, from plague and famine [divine judgment on Sabbath breach], to sexual promiscuity and violence: it was the means to the end of a godly and well-ordered community, and a principal mechanism for establishing the new culture of Protestantism."[82] Regardless of the reason, being poor was a sign of God's disdain for sinful behavior.[83] Those who migrated because of being victims of overpopulation were certainly not encouraged to leave by religious leaders. On the contrary, to migrate to Ireland for basic survival needs was regarded as evidence of having lived a scandalous life.

Conditions such as regional famine that were caused by the population exceeding the carrying capacity were, in the minds of Protestants in Scotland, God's way of dispensing just punishment for sins, including those of an individual.[84] Rollock declared, "It is a shame when a stranger sets his foot in Scotland to see this great misorder, and that shame-lesse begging."[85] He thought there was one solution to this problem, and that was that idle people needed only to do labor. Blair, who served as a minister in both Ireland and Scotland, wrote that for the most part those who immigrated to Ulster were escaping poverty and scandalous lives.[86] The Reverend Andrew Stewart echoed this idea, "From Scotland came many, and from England not a few, yet from all of them generally the scum of both nations, who, from debt, or breaking and fleeing justice, or seeking shelter, came hither, hoping to be without fear of man's justice in a land where there was nothing, or but little as yet, of the fear of God."[87] That there were economic, social, and political forces acting against residents of the southwest was of no concern to Stewart because a sovereign God would have made it possible for a truly righteous, Sabbath-observing man to make a living through employment or provide for a bountiful crop to feed himself and his family.[88] Durham and Dickson held similar views.[89] In light of the negative social sanctions against those who migrated because of poverty resulting from overpopulation, the conditions they experienced in their Scottish homeland must have been exceptionally difficult.

According to the regional descriptions of population made by Webster, the most likely areas to experience emigration resulting from high population growth would have been the central belt followed by the Dundee-to-Aberdeen coastal strip. Whereas the carrying capacity of the interior of the southwest was restricted by thin soil and uneven topography, as well as by reliance on agriculture that was changing from a man-rent to money-rent arrangement, the region's coastal settlements, the neighboring border region, the central belt, and the east coast were undergoing economic expansion that made employment opportunities more readily available. Population estimates, census data, and observations by travelers show that some but by no means all out-migrating rural people relocated to those high-growth areas.

If overpopulation was a factor in the migration scenario in the southwest of Scotland, then, it does not by itself explain why Ireland was more attractive than the central belt and the areas in and around Glasgow. As laid out earlier, written testimonials from parish officials from the established Church were required for entry into a new Kirk parish, for those who did not possess a testimonial were thought of as subversive. It is likely that this situation deflected Presbyterians emigrating from the southwest away from areas in Scotland experiencing growth.[90] Ireland arguably became an attractive option for many of them, although, as implied, there is little evidence that ministers saw the conditions associated with overpopulation as sufficient reason to encourage their congregations to emigrate to Ulster. On the contrary, to Puritans, idleness and the failure to work diligently at one's calling or vocation were viewed as sinful. As such, economic factors may have prompted many to migrate from southwestern Scotland to Ulster, but they may not have felt empowered to acknowledge these economic causes. The political climate in Scotland certainly allowed many to use political reasons to justify relocating to Ulster. As the next section shows, however, the geography of the southwest and the ease with which people could cross the narrow North Channel made moving to Ulster less difficult than perhaps some scholars had said.

Southwest Orientation to the Irish Sea and Ulster

Scotland in 1600 was an impoverished yet varied land that had been subjected to intense resource exploitation.[91] The shallow soils of the Highlands in the north gave way to the fertile, arable lands of the central belt and eastern Lowlands.[92] Socially the feudal system that was introduced by the Normans had dominated the Lowland landscape for several centuries while the resilient clan system of the Gaels prevailed in the Highlands.

However, the southern and eastern Highlands were not devoid of feudal influence, and neither were the Lowlands absent from the social impact of the clan system.[93]

In terms of land use, the southwestern Lowlands were virtually denuded of trees. Whereas the Lothians and Border regions have landscapes and climates suitable to deep-plough and pastoral farm practices, the landscape west of the Borders becomes rocky, reflecting the resilience of the regional features of the lithosphere.[94] In this region and especially to the north or the interior of the Lowlands, high prominences and moorland dominate the landscape. This region, known as the Southern Uplands, is best suited to grazing but not to deep-plough cultivation (see map 1). Upland areas that exceed 700 meters (2,275 feet) are common in Galloway. Given that the Solway Firth and Irish Sea are but a few miles away from those high prominences, the local relief is dramatic in places. With the exception of a few settlements, most circa 1600 were located near or on the coast. Ayr, Castle Douglas, Dumfries, Girvan, Glenluce, Irvine, Newton Stewart, Portpatrick, Stranraer, and Wigton, are the region's largest settlements, located between the Southern Uplands and the coast.

The rugged upland areas were also not conducive to the overland transport of produce and livestock or to the importation of needed goods. Taking advantage of western sea routes, the southwest developed a culture oriented to the Irish Sea.[95] In addition to the physical setting of the region that encouraged its western orientation, Scottish regions have traditionally demonstrated a strong element of localism.[96] Those facts taken together no doubt caused the region to orient its external economic contacts away from Edinburgh and toward the west across the Irish Sea. The North Channel provided an effective transportation medium for both products and people.

Aside from the site and situation advantages of coastal settlements, the carrying capacity in the interior of the region must have been as low as for many Highland areas in the northwest.[97] Overpopulation, which is relative to environmental and cultural factors, especially with respect to economic structure, could have caused pastoral farm residents to emigrate under adverse conditions. On the other hand, the Plantation of Ulster increased economic activity in the southwest of Scotland, causing a growth and diversification in the region's industries. Shipping and other forms of trans–North Channel commerce were certainly encouraged by the Plantation: "Trade with Ireland, easily overlooked, provided a valuable boost to the west-coast burghs, particularly after the Ulster Plantations in the early seventeenth century."[98] Growth in those forms of commerce absorbed some of the pastoral labor force of the hinterland while increasing the population density of coastal settlements. Perhaps the observations on population made by Pont, Brereton, and Webster were influenced by this shift in the regional population. Clearly the Plantation of Ulster and the economic growth in and around Glasgow would have increased the region's carrying capacity, thus reducing the impact of the consequences of overpopulation and the impetus to emigrate. Beyond the environmental factors influencing the carrying capacity of the region, the immaterial aspects of culture, which included economic decisions as well as religious beliefs and expectations for "Godly behavior" among the faithful, also played a role in affecting its capacity to absorb more people.

Dumfries, Irvine, Newton Stewart, Portpatrick, Stranraer, and Wigton are of modest size today by today's standards, and they were much smaller in the seventeenth century. Each had fewer than two thousand people during the plantation era:[99] "Much of the Lowlands, outside the central belt, were served only by small settlements, barely urban, with populations of a few hundred, and the occasional larger town with perhaps 2,000 inhabitants."[100] Many of the residents were fisherman who sold their catch to urban markets, including the growing population in and around Glasgow. Across the Lowlands, people relied heavily on Atlantic herring, especially during times of scarcity.[101] Residents of both the open country and the small towns were accustomed to relying on the sea.

Coastal burghs were tied together by western sea routes that were followed by navigators who knew them well. Sea transportation in the seventeenth century, unlike in the Mediterranean basin, relied more on traditional methods of navigation. Navigators on the Irish Sea depended on their memories of coastline features and their sense of direction to follow the routes. Mediterranean seafarers, on the other hand, benefited greatly from the work of Venetian, Genoese, and Catalan draftsmen who compiled widely used harbor books, which described coastlines, ports of call, and the amount of time required to travel between ports.[102] A harbor book or *portolano* was written by seamen for seamen.[103] The seafarers who plied the waters of the Irish Sea in the sixteenth century called the manuals "sheepes skinnes" and held those who used them in contempt.[104]

Navigators on the Irish Sea likely understood that the most favorable time to travel the North Channel was after the passage of a cold front. The Irish Sea and its coastal areas are subject to frequent low-pressure centers or depressions that bring misty, rainy weather. When comparatively cold, northerly air pushes into the basin, the "resulting visibility can be quite outstanding."[105] For navigators who relied on coastal landmarks, clear skies associated with high-pressure centers made sailing easier and safer. Night travel, as experienced by Blair,[106] was likewise affected by the passage of a cold front, especially with an emerging bright moon shining against a star-filled night.[107] The coastline is in plain view on those nights.

In recognition of the sea orientation of the culture area, ministers used metaphors with which their flocks could easily relate to their situations. Samuel Rutherford, who held a charge at Anwoth near the Solway, is noted for the imagery used in his writings.[108] He employed fishing and seafaring metaphors in his letters and sermons. The way in which he described fishing activities suggests that the practice was a means of making a good living: "I think I see them fishing for baronies, and thousands setting their lines and making all their might for a draught of fish, and to make up a fair estate to them, or theirs."[109] Alas, many come back with empty nets, and he consoled Lady Cardoness:

> When Christ hides Himself, wait on Him, and busy yourself till He returns; it is not a time to be careless. It is a good thing to be grieved when He hides His smiles. Yet believe His love in a patient waiting and believing in the dark. You must learn to swim and hold up your head above the water, even when the awareness of His presence is not with you to hold up your chin. I trust in God that He will bring your ship safe to land. I counsel you to study sanctification, and to be dead to this world. Urge kindness on Knockbrex. Labour to benefit by his company; the man is acquainted with Christ.[110]

Rutherford's use of metaphors involving the sea, fishing, or swimming to show the futility of works without faith or to underline the need to have faith in times of trouble was evidently set within the context of an activity that he felt his flock would understand.

Despite the seafaring orientation of the culture area, historians' comments on the North Channel as a facilitator of transportation are not uniform. For instance, Raymond Gillespie holds a different view from that of James G. Leyburn.[111] Immigration to Ulster, according to Gillespie, meant travel across the Irish Sea. Sea travel at the time, he reckons, was often dangerous and uncomfortable. Leyburn, on the other hand, regards the North Channel as much less of an obstacle, with the lands of Ulster "visible across the Channel from the shores of southwestern Scotland. Any Scot who had the inclination might now take the short journey across to Ulster."[112] In contrast, Gillespie argues that Ulster's economic and social contacts lay to the south toward the Pale and not to the west or east toward Scotland and England. Gillespie further notes that the Irish Sea posed many difficulties for both transporting goods and for delivering correspondence: "The North Channel was frequently rough and crossing it in a small, open boat was uncomfortable as Sir William Brereton discovered when he crossed in 1636 and was violently seasick," and to make matters worse, he had to swim ashore.[113] Brereton also complained about the expensive costs of crossing the Channel—he paid £1 for his sickening journey.[114] Gillespie also notes that Blair became seasick when he crossed the Channel. Because of the high frequency of rough seas, adds Gillespie, it was necessary for trips to be well planned yet flexible. Crossing the Channel could take up to twelve hours.[115] Twelve hours, however, was within the travel time of most migrants during the era, for, as Rab Houston found in his study, people relocating in seventeenth-century Scotland rarely ventured beyond one day's travel from their old homes.[116]

Gillespie's argument is based on comments made by men with little known experience in boats, except of course for Robert Blair. It is doubtful that the typical farming and fishing family living along the coast would have held the same view, as is evidenced by the extensive use of the Portpatrick-to-Donaghadee sea route.[117] At a minimum distance of twenty-one miles, southwestern Scotland and Ulster are close, and for a seafaring folk, that distance made for a fairly easy voyage, and one that was not beyond the reach of most local people.

In practice, the travel time was usually much shorter than twelve hours. The twenty-one miles of sea Channel that separate Portpatrick and Donaghadee, which was a common route as far back as the early days of the plantation, was manageable in less than half that time. In 1747, the itinerant minister John Wesley made the crossing in rough seas, and it took his boat five hours.[118] On a later trip it took Wesley only three hours to make the journey.[119] Drawing upon the Montgomery manuscripts, Bardon writes that a journey across the Channel between Donaghadee and Portpatrick was a three-hour trip in fair weather.[120] According to MacHaffie, "By 1607 it was not uncommon for Scots, when the weather was favorable, to go on horseback from Stranraer to Portpatrick with wares for sale, cross in a passage boat, hire horses at Donaghadee, ride to Newtownards, sell their produce in the market, reverse the journey and be home the same day."[121] Sea traffic between the two places was so common that complaints made their way to the Scottish Privy Council in 1615 regarding shipments of stolen goods upsetting the plantation. In response and in an effort to control shipping and travel between Scotland and Ireland, the Privy Council awarded Scottish planter Hugh Montgomery a charter for a ferry service along the route in 1616.[122]

Blair wrote that many people came over from Scotland, and cattle were brought as well.[123] The earl of Abercorn, a Tyrone settler, brought large shipments of cattle over from Scotland for the express purpose of providing manure for his estate.[124] The cattle business in Ulster was robust, and shipping was good enough in Bangor and Donaghadee that by 1628 those ports handled a quarter of all Irish beef exports.[125] Cattle from all parts of Ireland as early as the 1630s were shipped from those ports because of the "aptness of transportation" offered by them.[126]

The relative ease with which members of the Puritan-Presbyterian community could cross the North Channel enabled them to make visits to see acquaintances and others to whom they felt special affection or allegiance, including ministers such as John Livingstone. After he was deposed from his charge in Killinchy for nonconformity, he relocated to Stranraer on July 5, 1638.[127] On one occasion, five hundred members of his former congregation in Killinchy came over to take communion from his hands.[128] Also on one occasion, twenty-eight Ulster children were brought over to Stranraer to be baptized by Livingstone.[129]

On the eve of the Famine, Kerby Miller notes, as many as sixty thousand poor people from the remote reaches of northwestern Ireland, mainly Connaught, Tyrone, and Donegal, made annual trips to find work in England and Scotland. By the end of the plantation era, Irish fishermen regularly made excursions to the Newfoundland fisheries.[130] Merchants dealing in textiles and grains operated on both shores of the North Channel during the plantation.[131] In addition to regular deliveries of mail, livestock, and coal, it was common for ministers and military personnel to cross the Irish Sea.[132] The notion that the Irish Sea was an intervening obstacle, as suggested by Gillespie and argued by Mackinder, seems not to consider the possibility of a shared cross-Channel culture area. Clearly these facts illustrate that Channel crossing was within reach of many Ulster settlers, and it is difficult to agree with the argument that the North Channel was an intervening obstacle. On the contrary, it served as a transportation artery. The ability to cross the North Channel made moving there an attractive option, especially because throughout the seventeenth century, Ulster was under a different parliament that welcomed even dissenting Protestants who would aid it against possible rises among the resident Catholic population.

The Anglicization efforts of the monarchy's plantation scheme relied heavily on religious institutions, so while economic need pushed many across the Irish Sea during the first decades of the seventeenth century, the political policies of the government helped to justify movement between southwestern Scotland and Ulster. Such religious and political circumstances arguably favored a context in which migration across the North Channel did become acceptable to and was even promulgated by the Puritan-Presbyterian intelligentsia. It is to such matters that much of the remainder of this book turns.

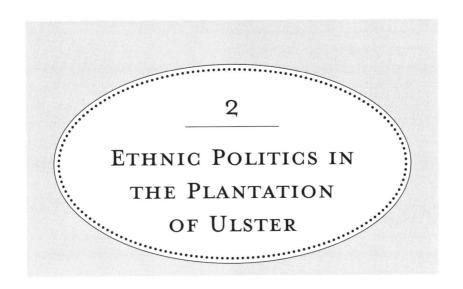

2

ETHNIC POLITICS IN
THE PLANTATION
OF ULSTER

The Plantation of Ulster was an economic venture with a distinct mission to create cultural change among Irish Gaels through socialization with loyal British subjects.[1] The established Church of Ireland with the monarch as its supreme governor was to be the primary institution through which the native Irish were to learn their new roles as responsible, civilized citizens of the realm.[2] The monarchy's house of worship on the Emerald Isle needed resident members as agents of social change, so the recruitment of Protestants from the loyal parts of Great Britain began in 1608.[3] However, before the seventeenth century was concluded and from the standpoint of the monarchy, the coming together of English and Scottish Puritan-Presbyterianism, because of Scottish nonconforming nature, spawned more problems than it originally had with the Gaelic Irish.

The Plantation Scheme

The Scots' migrations to Ulster were hence set in motion by the policies and actions of James VI and I, but the resistance of the native Irish to his plan manifested itself in sometimes fierce and persistent political resistance, including that which found a home and outlet in the institution of religion. The ethnic dimensions of the plantation scheme discouraged social integration with the native population. The policies also encouraged Protestants in Ireland to maintain ties with institutions, friends, and relatives in Scotland and Great Britain.[4] It is important to stress that limited religious conflict, in the spirit of creating lasting social change among the "rude Irish," was an intended result of the monarchical plantation policy. That conflict, though, was to subside under strong social pressure reinforced by persistent political might. What was not foreseen by the Tudors, the Stuarts, and the Lord Protector was the institutionalization of conflict through the politicization of religion there. Furthermore, it was the extension of political and economic discrimination against dissenting Protestants in Ulster that began with the passage of the Woolens Act in 1699 and the Test Act in 1703, despite decades of the government paying their ministers a stipend called the *regium donum*. This result was not envisaged by James VI and I and his successors because they thought the native Gaels of Ireland would become Anglicized through social interaction and instruction delivered by loyal Church clergy and that, as a result, the problems with the "rude Irish" would fade away.[5]

Prior to the reign of James I, it was the policy of Tudor monarchs either to crush the rebellious Irish or to force them into adopting English culture.[6] Neither Queen Mary's plantation in mid-Leinster nor Queen Elizabeth's more ambitious efforts in Munster achieved their goals. Still, Elizabeth's Nine Years' War against Irish chieftains Hugh O'Neill and Hugh O'Donnell left the land ravaged and depopulated. Adding to the misery of this war was famine across the bogs, hills, and mountains of the north of Ireland.

Ulster's population was literally reduced by terror and famine. Sir Arthur Chichester summed up the role of his forces when making a strike into Ulster, "We spare none of what quality or sex soever and it hath bred much terror in the people who heard not a drum there or saw a fire of long time."[7] An English settler wrote in 1610 that Ulster "presents herselfe in a ragged sabled robe, ragged there remayneth nothing but ruynes and desolation, with very little showe of humanitie."[8] Concerning the absence of farmers in the once-cultivated region, a situation that rejuvenated the soil, the minister Robert Blair observed, "The wolf and widcairn were great enemies to these first planters; but the long rested land yielded to the labourers such plentiful increase, that many followed the first essayers."[9] As a result of its aim to obliterate an indigenous culture of a nearly destroyed people, an effort initially resisted by widcairns, the Jacobean Plantation initiative created a social situation that institutionalized cultural/political conflict.

In about 1600, military leaders of the English forces in Ulster estimated that the native Irish could muster an army of 8,592 men.[10] By multiplying that figure by four to account for nuclear families, Perceval-Maxwell provides a population estimate of between twenty-five thousand and forty thousand native Irish at the turn of the seventeenth century.[11] The population density would have ranged from 1.13 to 1.80 people per square kilometer (2.93 to 4.68 per square mile), depending upon which total population figure is used (twenty-five thousand and forty thousand, respectively, or 22,126.4 square kilometers, or 8,543 square miles, for the nine counties of Ulster). To show the impact of the Tudor campaigns on Ulster's people, it is necessary to compare population density for all of Ireland. Whyte estimates that Ireland had a population density of 33.89 per square kilometer in 1600 (87.78 per square mile), so Ulster's population was almost eliminated.[12]

The ravages of war and famine left a population vacuum in Ulster. The population in the Scottish Lowlands, which was concentrated in the Lothians and the central-belt regions and along the coastal areas, was 14.29 people per square kilometer (37 per square mile).[13] Population density in the farming hinterland of coastal burghs was much greater than for inland areas. For the farming and fishing population pressed against the Irish Sea in the Scottish Lowlands, the openness of lands in Ulster was attractive. That openness was certainly used by James VI and I to lure Anglicized settlers into the nearly exterminated lands of Ulster. With respect to the later years 1652 to 1672, Whyte points out, "Tenant farmers from the southwestern Lowlands . . . who immigrated to Ulster enjoyed better tenurial conditions than they had at home."[14]

The number of people who settled in Ulster after the establishment of a Presbyterian polity in the Kirk in 1690 reveals the role played by established sea routes and the process of chain migration in the plantation. By the close of the plantation movement in 1715, the figure of an estimated thirty thousand Scots immigrants in 1650 had increased by more than eight-fold through natural increase and continual Scottish immigration.[15] From its founding on June 10, 1642 with five ministers and four elders, by 1660 the Army Presbytery in Ulster had grown to include five presbyteries that employed seventy ministers. Also by 1660, the Army Presbytery, which had been renamed the Presbytery of Ulster in 1646, served eighty congregations with one hundred thousand communicants.[16] Even as late as 1714, observed Bishop MacMahon, Calvinist immigrants "from the neighbouring country of Scotland . . . are coming over here daily in large groups of families."[17] Edward Synge, bishop of Tuam, estimated that between 1690 and 1700 fifty thousand Scots families settled in Ulster.[18] Apparently to meet the heavy demand for its ministries, the Presbytery of Ulster, which was renamed the Synod of Ulster in 1690, was reorganized in 1702, and nine presbyteries were formed. At that time, there were nearly 120 congregations and more than 100 ministers serving an estimated 250,000 Scots immigrants.[19] The number of Presbyterian congregations at the Restoration in 1660 was doubled by 1715.[20] The most recent of the arrivals had been Covenanters, so "the tone of Ulster Presbyterianism, already prevailingly Puritan, took on the added strictness and rigidity of that persuasion."[21]

The genesis of the dissenting culture area along the shores of the Irish Sea occurred because James believed he understood the principal reason for the failure of earlier attempts to Anglicize Ireland. He reasoned that the Tudors' efforts to solve the "Irish problem" of rebellion and backwardness failed because there simply were not enough British settlers.[22] For centuries, English settlers, including Normans, had assimilated into the dominant Irish population and became part of the so-called problem. As Robert Bell observes, many Anglo-Norman families after the invasion of 1172 became "hibernicised," and "by the sixteenth century they were counted by the English as among the 'wilde Irishe.'"[23] When he ascended the English throne in 1603, James enthusiastically inherited the Tudors' scheme to Anglicize the native Irish.[24] The Plantation of Ulster was a project that he attacked with intense personal interest, declaring its objectives "worthy always of a Christian prince to endeavour."[25] As king of Scotland, James was already experienced at trying to settle Gaelic areas with Anglicized colonists; from 1597 to 1607 he tried unsuccessfully to plant Protestants on the Isle of Lewis and Kintyre.[26] The establishment of permanent Scottish settlements in Ulster was the direct result of the experience and perspicacity, though short-sighted, of the king himself.

Being intensely interested in changing the culture of Gaeldom, James envisioned a major role for the monarch's Churches of Ireland and Scotland to play, for he wanted the Gaels to adopt an Anglicized way of life.[27] He felt that this situation was best accomplished through the homogenizing of religion and the creation of civil order and government amongst a "godles, lawles, and disordered" people.[28] His policy and method were based on his belief in the superiority of British culture. According to his plan, Protestant settlers from England and Scotland would provide the Gaelic-speaking Irish Catholics with cultural and political role models to envy and emulate, for, as Jane H. Ohlmeyer points out, the king and his officials in Dublin, Edinburgh, and London viewed the peripheral regions in the realm with worry: "Their inhabitants were classified as barbarians, rebels, and subversives intent on destabilizing the peripheries of the British monarchies."[29] In the king's way of thinking, as reported by Smout, the west Highland MacDonalds and their kinsmen in Antrim formed a troublesome clique composed of barbaric people with little show of civility,[30] with "not much difference between a MacDonald of the Isles and a MacDonnell of Antrim."[31] To deliver a death blow to these troublesome cliques and Gaeldom generally, the Privy Council in 1609 authorized advertisements to solicit applications for Protestant planters who would in turn recruit Protestant settlers.

The king's ability to carry out his scheme of planting Ulster with Protestants was made possible by the seizing of lands vacated by the fleeing Catholic Earls of Tyrone and Tyrconnell (the vanquished O'Neill and O'Donnell). Their lands occupied six counties in Ulster, and with them, James had sufficient area to plant large numbers of Protestants from Great Britain. The king had in previous years granted large tracts of land on the northeast coast of Ireland to the Hamilton and Montgomery families, mainly in Counties Down and Antrim. Those grants of land, along with the six counties escheated by the fleeing earls, gave James the opportunity to plant most of the nine counties in Ulster.[32] This situation was unique for an English monarch bent on socially and culturally transforming the native Irish. James was proud of his plantation scheme, which he dedicated to the "settling of religion, the introducing [of] civility, order and government amongst a barbarous and unsubdued people, to be acts of piety and glory, and worthy always of a Christian prince to endeavour."[33]

Despite the king's pious intentions, native Irish guerrilla groups called *wood-kerns,* to which Blair made reference, resurfaced in 1610 to harass Protestant settlers. Before the plantation era they were a thorny problem to their rival Gaelic lords. Small bands of wood-kerns would come out of the forests to pillage the farms of new settlers, before retreating once again to the safety of the trees. Laws were passed to curb their Robin Hood–like activities. A wood-kern could be shot without trial, but it was common for them to be taken alive and paraded through a local village to the place of execution before being hanged. Chichester eventually permitted the guerrillas to leave Ireland to enlist in the forces of Gustavus Adolphus, the king of Sweden, so they could be used against James's Spanish opponents.[34]

Irish Gaels who stayed out of the ranks of the wood-kerns were not immune from the king's social-engineering plans. The institution that James conceived as his vehicle for changing Ulster society was a loyal church body based on the Church of England's Episcopalian polity. James believed his very survival as king depended on such an arrangement. Chichester, who helped to destroy Ulster's population during the Tudor Wars, served as James's Lord Deputy of Ireland.

Although Chichester was an important aide to his superior, his allowing the recruitment of Puritan ministers into the Church of Ireland created significant problems for James's successors. A number of Scots ministers were brought over to serve in the Church of Ireland, and a large portion carried with them a deep and abiding wish to serve God and Christendom under the auspices of an ecclesiastical body that was structured along the lines of Presbyterianism.[35] These ministers and their English compatriots, such as John Ridge and Henry Colwart, built the foundation, through instruction, for a laity hungry for their own dissenting Presbyterian Church, unfortunately for the king.[36] Perceval-Maxwell metaphorically describes the king's policy and its result: "He used Scottish earth for his purpose, in which the seeds of Presbyterian doctrine lay buried. Even some of the Scottish gardeners he employed preferred Presbyterian weeds to Episcopalian flowers. Thus what grew . . . bore little resemblance to that image envisioned by the designer."[37] *In Search of Ulster-Scots Land* demonstrates that the Scottish Presbyterian seed in Ireland was fertilized and watered by the theology of Calvinists in Geneva and Puritans in England, who were also members of this imagined community, and pruned by their lack of uniformity on issues of polity, moving the Ulster-Scots further away from the ideal immigrant imagined by the king.[38] The result among Irish Presbyterians was a hybridized church structure that empowered the congregation relative to that of church officers. The nonconforming, dissenting, and voluntary congregation in Irish Presbyterianism emerged from a cultural mixture with power exceeding that held by its counterpart in an established Scottish Presbyterian Kirk parish. This, in contrast to Scottish Episcopacy, was more participative, especially when compared to the polity stressed by Charles I and William Laud.[39] As the Scottish Presbyterian divine David Calderwood, Samuel Rutherford's spiritual mentor, wrote, "If anie thing was amisse in the lifes, doctrine, or anie part of the office of their pastors, everie man had libertie to shew wherin they were offendit."[40] The idea of congregational mutual accountability, which was based in part on the doctrine of the "priesthood of all believers," was a theological seam that sewed together generations of Scottish Puritan divines, including Calderwood, to form a religious ideology guided and held together by Puritan dogma.[41] Church discipline, therefore, extended to everyone. They believed that the sins of the community may provoke the judgment and wrath of God and hence their concern with "purity" of the body of Christ (the Church). The sources of this idea were John Calvin's Geneva and the Old Testament.

Certainly if the church and its offices were not above reproach, as described by Calderwood, the Melvillian notion of two kingdoms kept the state within reach of a similar reprimand based on moral grounds as interpreted by God's ministers.[42] Andrew Melville (1545 to 1622), the Kirk leader who spoke of two kingdoms with Christ as the head of the universe, argued that James VI was a "silly vassal" of Christ's kingdom, relegated to the role of magistrate of a lesser earthly realm.[43] However, since the Kirk was the institution responsible for interpreting God's will, the king as head of the civil jurisdiction (in Melville's way of thinking) should seek advice from the Kirk on matters involving moral and ecclesiastical dimensions.[44] James did not agree with Melville's assertion about polity.[45]

The Melvillian notion of two kingdoms was at the root of tensions over governance and religion in seventeenth-century Protestant Scotland and Ireland, because it represented a depiction of society and Christendom that was in direct opposition to the monarchy's vision of society and the role of religion in it. While the monarchy desired a directing, Erastian relationship with the Church, Puritans sought the opposite arrangement in theocracy that was based on the resilient Calvinist doctrine of the sovereignty of an omnipresent, omniscient God who reveals himself to earthly believers through his spoken and written word.[46] As expressed in the Scots Confession, Knox and his colleagues claimed,

> This is not the universal Kirk of which we have spoken before, but particular Kirks, such as were in Corinth, Galatia, Ephesus, and other places where the ministry was planted by Paul and which he himself called Kirks of God. Such Kirks, we the inhabitants of the realm of Scotland confessing Christ Jesus, do claim to have in our cities, towns, and reformed districts because of the doctrines taught in our Kirks, contained in the written Word of God, that is, the Old and New Testaments which were originally reckoned canonical.[47]

While the Kirk was charged with teaching doctrines consistent with scripture as interpreted through the Spirit of God, the magistrate was responsible for providing civil government that protected good men, punished all evildoers, and worked to preserve and purify religion.[48] In other words, the magistrate was to support the work of the Kirk. Ecclesiastical authority, as expressed by the doctrine of two kingdoms, was held strongly by Presbyterians. It survived numerous administrations as it made its way across the north of Ireland, and 123 years after Knox and five others wrote the Scots Confession, the Presbytery of Ulster planted the first presbytery in America, for instance.[49] With that American planting also went the beliefs that supported the divine right of the Kirk to police its ministers in all respects.[50] Its founding minister, Francis Makemie of the Laggan district in Donegal, maintained this sixteenth-century understanding of ecclesiastical jurisdiction, saying his work as a minister was performed "in the sight of an all-seeing and omnipresent God"[51] and that his service to God, as reflected in his writings a decade later, was delivered

with the "continuing satisfaction to godly, learned and judicious discern-
ing men" in mind.[52] The theological beliefs and social bonds held by
Makemie and his colleagues, for whom he spoke, were inculcated by others before them who subscribed to Melville's concept. The community
that they helped to build in southwestern Scotland expanded into Ulster,
with echoes back across the Irish Sea, with the polity and sovereignty
doctrine attributed to this ecclesiastical community eventually being diffused to America.

The Stuart policies on Catholicism in Ulster were manifestly similar to
those followed with respect to the Scottish Gaels: "The essence of Crown
policy . . . was to seek social reform rather than promote wholesale social
dislocation."[53] This policy replaced James VI's initial, failed attempt in
1598 to plant Lowland Scots on the Island of Harris. Under the king's
cousin the Duke of Lennox, colonists called the Fife Adventurers were
under no illusions about their mission. They were to put Lewis residents
to the sword, clearing the way for further settlement of colonists from
the Lowlands. The adventurous settlers and agents of social change attempted to build a small town called Stornoway but soon became dis-
mayed by the wet climate and the persistent harassment by locals. The
Gaels proved to be strong opponents, forcing James to rethink his strategy
to Anglicize them.[54] To him, it seemed more prudent to bring about social
and cultural change through education, so he developed a plan to use the
established Protestant Church for that purpose. The king ordered Lord
Deputy Chichester to bring about Anglicization through church instruction and to refrain from imposing oaths of ecclesiastical supremacy or
allegiances on the Irish natives.[55]

Perhaps the king wanted only to exclude biological genocide from his
methods because the plan he chose was clearly intended to bring about
the death of his realm's Gaelic culture, for he loathed it. James wrote in
Basilikon Doron, "[Those] that dwelleth in our mainland, that are barbarous for the most part, and yet mixed with some show of civility; the
other, that dwelleth in the isles, and are utterly barbarous, without any
sort or show of civility."[56] "The court of James VI," writes Michael Lynch,
"had little sympathy for Gaeldom."[57] James's ideas about the Scottish and
Irish Gaels (the Irish included all Gaels, whether they were in the isles,
Scottish highlands, or in Ireland) are shown in the manner in which he
treated the chiefs from the Isles. In 1608, he asked Lord Ochiltree (presumably James Stewart, who purchased Andrew Stuart's lordship in 1615
and thus was the fourth Lord Ochiltree) to help him to bring about cultural change among the Gaels in a scheme that called for tricking the
chiefs into a literal snare from which their release was contingent upon

their agreeing to certain conditions dictated to them by Andrew Knox, bishop of the Isles. In 1609 those conditions, spelled out in a document known as the Statutes of Iona, were forced upon the chiefs.

The statutes, renewed in 1616,[58] affected the traditional lifestyles of future generations by requiring leading families in Scottish Gaeldom to send their children to the Lowlands for instruction in English. Under the king's actions, the chiefs were responsible for the conduct of every member of their respective clans. Limits were established on the size of their households, the number of war galleys they could own, drinking, feasting, and carrying firearms; bards (troublemakers whose heroic orations were liable to incite violence) were to be suppressed.[59] The king was arguably more concerned more about their loyalty and what he saw as their wild lifestyle than he was with their religion, although a purely secularized education did not exist in the Lowlands at the time. James intended to plant Anglicized settlers in Ulster to drive a wedge between the Gaels in Scotland and their friends and relations in Ireland. It so happens that many of these Gaels whom the king regarded as "wolves and wild boars" were also Roman Catholics and those he chose to serve as an anglicizing wedge were mostly Calvinist Protestants still celebrating their Reformation and liberation from the "evils of papacy."[60] With obvious antipathy among the Protestants for Roman Catholics, conflict was inherently built into the plantation scheme even if other aspects of cultural genocide could be removed from the scenario.

Even so, the Statutes of Iona actually encouraged Catholic migration to Ulster. This migration was made possible by clan ties and the well-established western sea routes. The MacDonalds of Kintyre lost political ground to the Protestant Earl of Argyll, Archibald Campbell, who had the support of the king's court. The numerous septs of the MacDonalds were also politically discredited, so they, too, crossed the North Channel to the seemingly receptive MacDonnell lands in Antrim, although Catholic migration was severely dampened after the 1641 rising was quelled.[61]

The rising was facilitated by Charles I, Archbishop William Laud, and Lord Deputy Thomas Wentworth. The lord deputy had assembled and trained an Irish Catholic army to fight Calvinist supporters of the National Covenant in Scotland in 1638. Charles also ordered Randal MacDonnell, the Earl of Antrim, to assemble an army of his Catholic kinsmen to aid in the suppression of the upstart supporters of the National Covenant.[62] With a body of Irish Catholics armed for war and with no orders for them to set sail for the British mainland, MacDonnell's forces spread out across the rural Irish countryside. They attacked and ruthlessly murdered Protestant residents living on isolated farms. News of the rising quickly spread throughout Britain, and a force of Scottish Protestants was put together and sent to Ulster. Not only did they protect their kinsmen by putting down the rising in Ulster, they established the Army Presbytery on June 10, 1642, making it the first permanent Presbyterian Church body in the English-speaking world.

The king's initial involvement in the Catholic rising only made matters worse for him among his English and Scottish subjects and certainly contributed to the looming civil war. But when faced with tough situations, the Stuarts were willing even to accept help from Catholics, despite the majority of their subjects' concerns about the Catholic religion. In the end, though, the Plantation of Ulster was an economic venture, and Roman Catholic Gaels were deprived of their holdings and subjected to humiliating circumstances, including the need to ask for menial jobs on the lands they once owned.[63] Lands that were allocated to Catholics of good merit were typically in remote upland areas that required intensive timber harvesting before crops could be planted.[64]

Pressed between 1642 and the Restoration in 1660 were the staunchly Puritan years of Cromwell's Protectorate. Irish Presbyterians suffered little under Cromwell, but his Protectorate made it certain that Ulster was not to be a sanctuary for their Scottish Catholic counterparts, Catholic landownership in Ulster was eradicated, and Catholics were treated with a widespread assault. Cromwell viewed his army's assault on Irish Catholics as the manifestation of divine retribution for the slaughter of English victims during the 1641 rising. A statistician of the period, Sir William Petty, calculated that of the estimated 1,448,000 inhabitants of Ireland, 616,000 died from the acts of war, famine, and plague. Of that number, Petty estimated that 504,000 were native Irish.[65] After the restoration, Charles II tried to give relief to the Irish who had been deprived of their lands. He sympathetically called them the "innocent Irish." The Earl of Antrim, after spending time in the Tower of London for his part in supporting Charles I, was restored. By 1688, however, only four percent of the land in Ulster was owned by the native Irish.[66] In all of Ireland, according to Ford, two-thirds of the land was owned by natives prior to Cromwell's Protectorate, and the reverse was true after the restoration.[67]

Besides religion, the plantation initiative intended to replace the Gaelic language with a standard form of communication. The Lowland Scots' English differed from the king's preferred dialects spoken in the south of England. The prevailing tongue in the Lowlands was Scots, a dialect that evolved from the Northumbrian variety of English after the Norman Conquest in 1066.[68] It seems that their tongue made little difference to the king, though, because out of the seventy-seven Scots who made application, fifty-nine were granted land, which by 1611, amounted to a total of eighty-one thousand acres. English planters were granted a total of 81,500 acres. Of the Scots, five of the fifty-nine were nobleman, all of them were Lowlanders, and at least eighteen were lairds from the southwestern counties of Scotland.[69] Most of the great houses of the southwest took part, including Sir Patrick Vans of Barnbarroch, Robert McClellan (Laird Bomby, who later became Lord Kirkcudbright), Sir Thomas Boyd, the Cunninghams and Crawfords of south Ayrshire, John Murray of Broughton, Dunbar of Mochrum (a Stuart of Garlies), and Sir Patrick M'Kie.[70]

Of those who took part as planters, many expressed Presbyterian orientations, and certainly most were doctrinal Calvinists.[71] For the time, their beliefs coincided with those of the English Puritans who settled near them. As the Calvinist theologian J. I. Packer writes, theological discourse in Great Britain was an intriguing subject, for "in the seventeenth century it was every gentleman's hobby."[72] In other words, social pressure was on economic and political elites to demonstrate knowledge about God, regardless of their commitment to personal piety. The ease and eloquence with which a person spoke of doctrinal points, especially from a Calvinist perspective, was a mark of an educated person, and with seventeenth-century Scotland boasting more universities than its larger neighbor to the south, religious discourse was made a common feature of social, economic, and political life among the country's leaders. This was especially true in the southwest where religious discourse with political overtones was intense.

As a result of living on confiscated lands and amongst a people bitter toward the English monarch for its war against them, the antipathy expressed by the Irish toward the Scots Protestants caused Lord Deputy Chichester to write, "They [the Irish] hate the Scottyshe deadly."[73] The Scots who settled in Ulster had, as a result of the feelings demonstrated by the native Irish, a strong incentive to maintain ties with familiar institutions, family, and friends in their old communities.[74] The western sea routes connecting Southwestern Scotland and Ulster made the maintenance of those social and institutional linkages possible.

Reverse Migration to Scotland

The monarchy was thus a critical player in the evolution of Protestant Ulster and its culture of religious segregation that featured an ingrouping process reinforcing social and institutional ties with the southwest of Scotland. Until the ascension of Archbishop William Laud and Lord Deputy Thomas Wentworth in 1633, Irish bishops and ministers made allowances for diversity in religious practice, so polity issues amongst Protestants during the formative years of the plantation were of minimal importance.[75] With Laud and Wentworth to help him, Charles I stubbornly continued his father's attempts to create ecclesiastical uniformity throughout his realm. Charles insisted on the deposition of Ulster ministers who opposed his model of episcopacy, breaking the short-lived tradition of toleration in Protestant polity.

A Presbyterian element within the Kirk launched its successful protests against Laud's Liturgy, which precipitated the National Covenant in 1638.[76] At least seven of the ministers who led the revival—Robert Blair, John Livingstone, George Dunbar, Henry Colwart, James Hamilton, Robert Cunningham, and John Ridge[77]—in the Six Mile Water Valley in eastern Ulster relocated to Scotland to fill pulpits in the southwest (see map 2). Two more ministers were deposed, but Josias Welsh died in 1634 and Edward Brice died before their depositions could be carried out. Robert Blair accepted a ministry at Ayr in July 1638. Under the direction of the General Assembly, he relocated to St. Andrews in October 1639. Also, Blair became an active member of the Scottish General Assembly.[78]

Upon arriving in Scotland, the seven leading ministers from Ireland joined the charismatic, staunchly Presbyterian and Puritan divines in the region. David Dickson of Irvine and Samuel Rutherford at Anwoth were not only among the southwest's most charismatic and inspirational spokesmen for their Puritan, antiprelatic cause, they were also articulate, educated, and well-connected members of the Melvillian network.[79] In addition to those returning ministers, many of their loyal followers relocated with them as well. As Livingstone writes in his autobiography, "Many of the religious people in the North of Ireland had left it in the year 1637, when the deposed ministers were forced out of it."[80] Many parishioners who did not relocate often made the trip across the North Channel to take communion from their ousted ministers. Still others made the trip to have their babies baptized.[81] David Dickson and his congregation welcomed ousted preachers and visiting Ulster laity into their church at Irvine. According to Robert Blair, on "the 26th of March that year, 1637, the communion was celebrated at Irvine, where Messrs Blair and Livingstone were employed. Many resorted to this communion from Ireland, out of the parishes Bangor and Killinchie; their wives and some of the eldest . . . children came over."[82] Before their depositions, Blair had served as minister at Bangor, and Livingstone had likewise served at Killinchy.

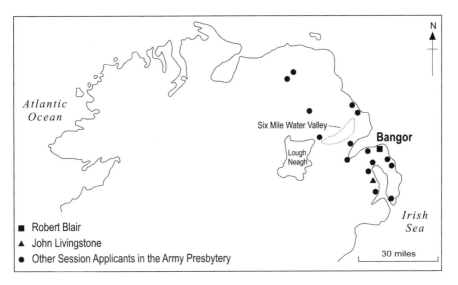

MAP 2: *Key Irish Locations of Scottish Presbyterianism*

The relocation of the ousted Ulster clergy and members of their respective congregations on the eastern shores of the Irish Sea had an impact on the Scottish religious and political landscapes. "A shipload of Ulster-Scots," writes G. W. Sprott, "returned to the West of Scotland in 1638 and introduced their Irish novations into their Mother Church. Such was the origin of the party which degraded our worship and in the end, allied itself with Cromwell and secretaries, and ruined the Covenanting Movement."[83] In this instance, Sprott is speaking of the National Covenant (1638) and the Solemn League and Covenant (1643; a mutual defense of Reformed religion, signed by both the Scottish and English parliaments). An important distinction to make here is that he was not referring to the militant Covenanter movement in the southwest that surfaced after the Stuart restoration.

In discussing Sprott's observation, W. D. Baillie points out that the Ulster-Scots brought practices with them to the southwest of Scotland that they had learned in Ireland through commingling with English Puritans, such as John Ridge and Henry Colwart, who also relocated to the southwest of Scotland after their depositions.[84] With an emphasis on teaching reading skills and a belief in the "priesthood of the individual," these clergy and their Scottish colleagues had empowered laymembers of the congregations in Ulster to assume leadership roles in informal worship services. Those skills allowed the laity to continue their religious practices during the extended absence of their ministers. Robert Blair's exhausting teaching duties were not limited to Sunday sermons. In Ireland, Blair taught and ministered to twelve hundred adult parishioners and their children. He felt they needed more instruction in the catechism, so he conducted four public services per week and then spent one or two days a week providing instruction to families in the community.[85] Regardless of the reason for the absence of a minister, the education provided by Blair and other ministers enabled lay people to hold private meetings and prayer conferences without the immediate oversight of clergy.

Through the Ulster experience, Baillie explains, "The Ulster-Scots soon began to fall into the form and spirit of Congregationalism, or Brownism as it was called. Brownism was renowned for its opposition to all set forms in public worship, including the use of the Lord's Prayer; to private devotions in church by the minister; to the singing of the Gloria at the end of the Psalms; and to the use of the Creed at Baptism, and was indifferent to all rules of ceremonial, however simple."[86] When ousted Irish ministers, such as Ridge, Blair, and Colwart, relocated to Scotland, they brought those novations with them. Their opposition to the Kirk's Episcopal polity after the restoration and the government's lack of tolerance for their dissenting practices encouraged them to meet in conventicles, which were private, outdoor meetings of the kind they had held in Ireland.[87] Theologically literate congregations on the shores of southwestern Scotland and of Ulster no doubt increased expectations of many to participate in polity matters.

Diversity among Ulster Protestants

Many of the clergy and settlers who went to Ulster during the reign of James I, such as Edward Brice and John Livingstone, wanted a Presbyterian polity, but a number of Scottish settlers and prelates were not so inclined. Between 1603 and 1625, at least sixty-five Scottish ministers served in Ireland, and twelve more Scots served as bishops, including seven who were installed in Ulster.[88] Bishop Andrew Knox of Raphoe and Bishop Robert Echlin of Down were Scots who advocated episcopacy. These bishops, however, were not averse to recruiting Presbyterians, for with respect to recruiting ministers to fill Irish pulpits they were faced with the restrictive law of supply and demand. Before Charles I began his policy in 1632 of deposing Ireland's Presbyterian-minded ministers, the Church of Ireland in Ulster tolerated a hybrid polity. Marilyn Westerkamp argues that Robert Blair's willingness to serve in the Church of Ireland shows his "ability to fit into an Episcopal communion, provided that certain key rituals and beliefs could be retained within individual parishes."[89] On the other hand, Mullan counters that to be a seventeenth-century Presbyterian minister meant harboring a deep hostility to episcopacy, and Robert Blair certainly was a Presbyterian.[90]

Although scholars may never agree on Robert Blair's true thoughts on episcopacy as it manifested itself in Ireland, a system to which he clearly submitted, one of his Scottish colleagues in Ulster showed less commitment to any form of polity. In 1625, James Glenndinning, a graduate of St. Andrews University, ignited revivalism (characterized by emotionally charged services) in the Six Mile Water Valley in County Antrim, but his support for Presbyterianism was questionable at certain times in his career. For example, he left Ulster in 1630 ostensibly to tour the Seven Churches of Asia, but in 1648 he was back in Scotland where he signed the Solemn League and Covenant. In 1662, he withdrew his objections to episcopacy.[91] Like Glenndinning, most Scots in the southwest of Scotland and in Ulster after 1638 were supporters of the National Covenant, and unlike him, many after the Stuart Restoration were Covenanters.[92]

Charles II, for a brief time, treated Presbyterians with disregard. The Irish Parliament passed the Act of Uniformity (1662) to enforce the king's plan to revise Episcopacy. The Ulster-Scots, unlike their counterparts in Scotland, had a friend in one of the king's trusted lieutenants in Ireland, Sir Arthur Forbes.[93] Before settling in County Longford, the powerful friend, himself a Scot, had fought with the Marquis of Montrose on the king's behalf. Through the efforts of Forbes, the king changed his tactics in dealing with the dissenting Presbyterians. Thanks in large measure to the persistence of Forbes in 1672, Charles II initiated the regium donum, an annual payment to Presbyterian ministers.[94] In 1690 King William renewed the practice of what amounted to a block grant, at which time it amounted to £1,200, a handsome sum of money then.[95]

The mixing of Scottish and English settlers and their clergy in Ulster during the first few decades of the Plantation created a hybridized Puritan ethos that became in the minds of many southwestern Scots and Ulster folk inextricably linked to the Presbyterian polity that empowered the congregation relative to ministers and government officials.[96] Whether that ethos was a factor in decisions to fight or to make flight among the Scots and their counterparts in Ulster depended in large measure on how they were viewed by the governments in England, Scotland, and Ireland at any given time.[97]

In spite of everything, the flow of English Puritans eventually shifted away from Ulster to New England during the 1630s and to Virginia after 1650, but the impact of Congregationalism introduced into Ulster by the dissenting nature of their freestanding, voluntary polity strengthened the session and the congregation's positions relative to ministers, presbyteries, synods, and general assemblies.[98] As English Congregationalists redirected their migration flows to New England, French Huguenots, who were mostly Calvinist merchants persecuted on their native soil, began arriving in Ulster after the revocation of the Edict of Nantes in 1685. Their skills and business acumen in the linen industry help to further diversify the Protestant-controlled economy in Ireland. The steady increase in the population of dissenting Protestant groups in Ulster made officials in the established church nervous about their own situations. By the time of Queen Anne's reign (1702 to 1714), they had sufficient anxiety to go to Parliament with a case against the dissenters. It took little effort by Parliament to redirect the Erastian impulses of the monarch toward all dissenting groups.

Polarizing and Dividing the Protestants

The remaining years of the plantation movement (1685 to 1715) were times in which politics began to divide even the Protestants. In addition to Scottish, English, and French settlers, smaller numbers of Welsh and German dissenters were by now living in Ulster. The growth in the number of dissenting Protestants raised a number of concerns among officials in the established church. Political persecution was slowly directed toward them. Faced with adverse circumstances at home, members of nonestablished Protestant communities were receptive to the recruitment campaign of agents from the Pennsylvania colony in America. By 1718 this assemblage of dissenting Protestants initiated an emigration stream from Ulster to North America that lasted until 1775, diffusing political and religious idealism to places like the uplands and valleys of the southern colonies.[99] America presented them with the opportunity to live in a Puritan gemeinschaft.

The three-year reign of James VII and II (1685 to 1688), the converted Roman Catholic brother of Charles II, was an abysmal time for Ulster Presbyterians. His policies, like those of his father but unlike his brother, caused a temporary dampening of the flow of Scots to Ulster.[100] James II had served his brother as viceroy in Scotland during Charles's attempts to deal with the petulant leaders of the Covenanters. He, like his brother, had a low opinion of ardent, Presbyterian-minded Scots. As king, he unleashed on the Scots John Graham of Claverhouse, whose fearsome reputation traveled with eighteenth-century Ulster folk to the American backcountry of southern Appalachia.[101] In Ulster, James II made Richard Talbot the Earl of Tyrconnel (1685). A dedicated Catholic, Tyrconnel was given command of the Catholic forces in Ireland, causing serious concerns among Protestants in Ireland and Great Britain.[102] Making political matters worse for himself, James also purged Protestants from the army and replaced them with Catholics. It was rumored among Ulster-Scots that Tyrconnel planned to eradicate Protestantism from Ireland in a manner similar to the efforts of the king's dragoons against Covenanters in the southwest of Scotland. It was amidst those rumors that hundreds of families left Ireland, presumably back to Scotland.[103]

Protestants in England and Scotland began a rebellious dialogue with Prince William of Orange and Mary, his wife, the daughter of James II, about an overthrow of the monarch. When William and Mary's forces landed in England, James summoned his forces to his defense. Despite advice to stand and fight, James fled the country. The English Parliament drafted the Bill of Rights of 1689 in which the grounds for assumption of power by the new monarch, William, were also written. James, whom no one ever accused of being of brilliant mind, received some aid from France and with an army landed in Ireland where he hoped fellow Catholics would support his cause.

Despite having help from French and Irish Catholics, James failed to take Londonderry after a 105-day siege. He then lost on the battlefield at the Battle of the Boyne in the summer of 1690. William's victory over his father-in-law set the stage for the emergence of the Ulster Protestants' premier political hero. Unionists still have high regard for William, and that devotion is displayed widely with the color orange as a symbol of triumph over their Catholic neighbors. It is likewise displayed in the west of Scotland and in certain parts of the southern United States. Although institutional histories may not recognize a connection to Ireland, a good number of universities, intriguingly, built along the migration route of Ulster Protestants in the United States claim orange as a school color. Among them are the University of Virginia, Virginia Tech University, the University of Tennessee, Clemson University, Oklahoma State University, and the University of Texas.[104]

Nonetheless, in the wake of the Battle of the Boyne, it seemed that all Protestants composed a unified political force in Ulster, but that illusion was short-lived. Just as the acts of indulgences authorized by Charles II to reinstate repentant Presbyterian ministers in Scotland weakened the solidarity of the Presbyterian community in the southwest, Protestant unity in Ulster seems to have suffered as a result of the suspension of the regium donum under Queen Anne. The annual payment was finally ended by her successor; George I. Leyburn argues that the immigration of Ulster folk to America was partly caused by the suspension of the donum.[105] That was not the only political action taken against dissenting Protestants. Presbyterian marriages were made illegal, and members of the Presbyterian Church lost jobs through the passage and enforcement of the Test Act of 1703, which required marriages and funerals to be in accordance with the rituals of the established churches of Scotland, England, and Ireland.

> The Presbyterian Synod at first determined to stand by the defendants who resisted the Act, but they were soon dissuaded—and by financial arguments. The *Regium Donum* . . . was suspended. Presbyterian businessmen, fearful of a revival of animosities in Ulster if too great an issue were made of the Act, threatened to withhold their contributions to the Church. It seemed wise, therefore, to make the necessary submission and hope for lenient administration of the Act, despite its indignities.[106]

There was and continues to be disagreement over the impact of the Test Act on dissenting Protestants. As Bishop William King wrote to Jonathon Swift in April 1708, "I do not know any officer that has on account of the Test parted with his command and I do not believe there will."[107] In the words of Primate Hugh Boulter, "I have been assured that if the test were taken off there are not twenty persons amongst them qualified for substance to be justices of the peace."[108] In his sermon in 1943 to commemorate the three hundredth anniversary of the founding of the first Irish Presbytery, the Reverend R. L. Marshall remarked that in his home church (First Derry), a simple plaque on the wall recognizes twenty-four local Presbyterians who lost their positions of employment in the city's corporation because of their refusal to "prejudice their consciences by obedience to the iniquitous Test Act of 1703. It is only one that might have been erected."[109] However, twenty-four acts of indemnity between 1719 and 1778 allowed Presbyterians the opportunity to hold public office and serve in the militia. According to Bardon, the Test Act remained in the statute book, but it was never enforced after the great migrations to America began in 1718. On the other hand, S. J. Connolly adds some perspective on the impact of the Test Act by noting that the indemnities did not give continuous exemption, adding that they did not extend to positions within municipal corporations.[110]

In 1719 the passage of the Toleration Act gave Irish Presbyterians official recognition.[111] Presbyterians throughout the rest of the eighteenth century could vote while Catholics were still denied that right.[112] The policies of the government, including trade restrictions against the lucrative Ulster linen industry, combined with rising rents for renewed leaseholders, famine, and disease afflicting livestock initiated the migration of Ulster-Scots to America, effectively ending the plantation movement begun 110 years earlier by James I.[113]

Although Protestants of English and Scottish descent intermingled and even intermarried, communities in seventeenth-century Ulster were often segregated into Catholic, Anglican, and Presbyterian areas with each consisting of Irish, English, and Scottish residents, respectively. Because of the opportunity to settle among others from their home communities—less culture shock—English and Scottish migration to Ireland was more appealing than moving to other parts of Great Britain.[114] However, the harmony between the English settlers who adhered to Anglicanism and the Scottish Presbyterians apparently did not last long. By the 1690s Bishops William King of Derry and Tobias Pullein of Dromore, acting on behalf of the established Church, waged a "paper war" against dissenting divines Joseph Boyse and John McBride over issues of liturgy and the validity of Presbyterian orders. The established Church's case was carried on by the vindictive writings of the vicar of Belfast, William Tisdall. Beyond those participants, even level-headed high churchmen were alarmed at the gains of the Scots and Irish Presbyterians. Their concern was greatest in Ulster, where their Church of Ireland congregations were sparse and their resources stretched thin.[115] Today those Protestant areas, not to mention Roman Catholic communities, have distinctive identities and speech ways that reveal which colonial group was dominant.[116]

Those resilient spatial patterns with ethnic overtones are products of the Plantation of Ulster, and that initiative was a policy of the Stuart Dynasty and the Cromwellian Protectorate. As a political, social, and demographic phenomenon, the policy took on a life of its own, and subsequent governments have played substantive roles in abusing and massaging ethnic relations. This does not dismiss the need to evaluate the effectiveness of the plantation as a policy because scholars frequently declare that the Ulster Plantation was a success.[117] The Jacobean Plantation was designed to create religious and social confrontation. The schemers, however, probably did not envision a scenario in which that conflict would become institutionalized.

With respect to the formation of a trans–Irish Sea Presbyterian community, the ethnoreligious policies of the government certainly reinforced the strength of social and institutional ties between Irish and Scottish Presbyterian communities. Those ties were also maintained through the well-established western sea routes. Social networks of Puritan Presbyterian divines stretched across the Irish Sea.

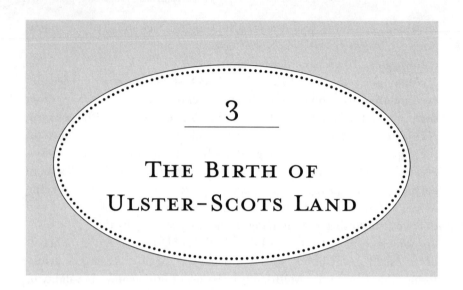

3

THE BIRTH OF
ULSTER-SCOTS LAND

To some observers, the Irish Sea in the 1600s was the major factor sepa-
rating Ireland and Scotland, but throughout the seventeenth century, the
real point of division was their distinct parliaments. Although they had
the same monarch after 1603, each country, with varying degrees of success, maintained its own unique laws, courts, and methods of enforcement. The shores washed by the Irish Sea and their adjoining lands
witnessed numerous waves of immigrants coming and going across the
North Channel. When environmental or political pressures from Irish or
Scottish authorities were applied on either shore, it caused a movement
of people across the North Channel in the opposite direction. Because of
this situation, the North Channel served more as a highway to freedom
for dissenting Presbyterians than as an intervening obstacle. The settlement of Scots in Ireland during the plantation era was simply a new
episode in a centuries-old process that tied Ulster with the highlands and
the west of Scotland in a seemingly continuous network of human in-
termingling that began in the early sixth century.[1] It was the first time,
however, that the geoapocalyptic[2] and geoeschatological elements of a
dissenting Protestant religion became an important factor in shaping the
identity and character of an Ulster-Scots community and its belief system.[3] Through reverse migration and newly created social and commer-
cial networks, lands on both shores of the North Channel became a
dissenting culture area, Ulster-Scots Land.

Although some theologians, especially in North America, may disagree
with James B. Torrance's interpretation of some of the changes in Scottish theology, he argues that the community's belief system was affected

by a shift among seventeenth-century Scottish ministers away from the sixteenth-century notion of the covenant of grace, effectively a unilateral, if conditional, promise of salvation that lay at the heart of Luther's theology and the Scots Confession (1560), to a more contractual covenant of works that placed greater emphasis on righteous behavior.[4] Although piety is arguably an obligatory response to grace, many Scottish and English Puritans stressed the works component of the plan of salvation to such an extent that it made the social meaning of eternal redemption dependent on true piety and works, which were in their minds discernible in the visible church.[5] This meant that piety and good works would be displayed in the spaces containing networks of religious life and would not be limited to the confines of a physical church structure. Piety and visible examples of internal salvation, which the Puritans believed were reflected in their works as the "fruits of faith," also had an impact on the community's perception of lands and public behaviors in Scotland, Ireland, and America. The parallels between English and Scottish Puritanism in the seventeenth century are striking and are not the result of coincidence.

The Birth of Scottish Puritanism

The pedagogical pedigree of Robert Rollock (c. 1555 to 1599) is full of first-order Puritan Presbyterians. He served as an important link between Scottish theologians and other ministers in England and on the continent. Rollock was mentored by James Melville (1556 to 1614) and James's uncle Andrew Melville (1545 to 1622), the founder of Presbyterianism.[6] Rollock was also instructed by Thomas Buchanan, the nephew of George Buchanan (the tutor of James VI) who was instructed at St. Andrews by John Major (1470 to 1550), an early promoter of Anglo-Scottish friendship, democracy, the separation of church and state, and an advocate of Catholic Church reform.[7]

Rollock was doctrinally important in the imagined community of English and Scottish divines because through his efforts the concept of the covenant of works, as part of the federal theology of the English Puritans, was introduced into Scotland in 1596, a move that neither John Calvin nor James Knox would have supported.[8] This innovation "soon became the absolute criterion of orthodoxy and was equated with Calvinism."[9] In effect, this change in doctrine diminished the meaning of grace, central in Luther's understanding of salvation, and therefore Christ's role in bringing salvation to humanity. In the place of grace, Rollock and his colleagues, both English and Scottish, inserted works as evidences of internal election, which in effect made salvation conditioned upon the works of the individual.[10] Legalism (or moralism) stressed Christian responsibility to such an extent that obedience became a "requirement," a "demand," and a constitutive element of justifying faith. Such legalism undermined Christian assurance and joy, leading to an unevangelical self-centered piety that was markedly introspective and generated anxiety about one's "qualifying" righteousness. The adoption of this interpretation of the relationship between God and humans among Scottish ministers was a significant change in the belief system of the Presbyterian community.

With its emphasis on appropriate behaviors as evidences of the assurance of salvation, the notion of a bilateral contract between the individual and God had social and political ramifications. For instance, the community embraced the Calvinistic orthodoxy of the Westminster Confession of Faith (1643–1648) that was adopted by the Scottish Kirk, although ministers from the southwest, most notably David Dickson (1585 to 1662) and Samuel Rutherford, regarded even its Calvinism as too light.[11] In *The Sum of Saving Knowledge*, Dickson and his regional compatriot James Durham described their notion of the covenant of works. Their understanding of the plan of redemption (salvation) was rather moralistic and was indeed, according to Torrance, semi-pelagian, as it seemed to grant scope to qualifying human merit in salvation.[12] However, on the basis that semi-pelagianism, as qualified by the belief that an individual's faith in God can be born without grace, little evidence supports Torrance's view that classifies Dickson and Durham as semi-pelagian. Nevertheless the bilateral nature of seventeenth-century Scottish theology, with its dual emphasis on pious behavior and realized sanctification among the elect, ushered in an era in which rigidity in theology made disruptive actions with political repercussions likely.[13]

The forces behind the change in the belief system are debatable. For instance, Buchan and Smith argue that this shift was caused more by the Scottish reformers themselves, including Knox, through their adherence to Old Testament legalism (righteous behavior) and less through contacts with English Puritans.[14] Certainly the characteristically Reformed emphasis on the unity of the Old and New Testaments, with a corresponding diminution of the contrast between law and the Gospel, made the transition to covenantal moralism easier. Consequently, in the process of salvation, the way shifted from the free grace of God to human compliance. In contrast the explanation involving Scottish ministers' altering their views because of interaction with English Puritans is posited by J. B. Torrance and David George Mullan.[15] Whichever was the impetus, the shift in the belief system did occur, and Andrew Melville and his pupil

Robert Rollock nurtured a community of divines who embraced it. Through print and travel to the Continent as well as England, Scottish ministers formed extensive social networks, admitting into their community of Puritan-Presbyterians both real and imagined members.

The intellectual training of the core of the Scottish Presbyterians (detailed later) seems to have centered in Glasgow and to a lesser extent Edinburgh and St. Andrews universities. Upon graduating and receiving ordination, the ministers took their Puritan belief system to the hinterlands of the southwest and to the north of Ireland where their fiery messages on damnation—a theology of deterrence—were mitigated by reassuring sermons offering guidance on how to receive the cooling waters of redemption.[16] Under the unevenly applied Erastian and old, moderate Calvinist policies of the monarchy, many members of the community of Puritan-Presbyterians were pushed back and forth across the Irish Sea, reinforcing the transchannel nature of Ulster-Scots Land, the geopious, dissenting culture area.[17]

Puritan and Presbyterian Community of Imagination

The Scottish Puritans who constructed communities of imagination were highly literate people led by divines who regarded themselves spiritually as also part of the true catholic, or universal, Church, the invisible body of Christ. Puritans, whether Scottish or English, were instrumental in shaping the thoughts of each other as well as the members of their respective congregations. The community-of-imagination construct is appropriate here because Puritans considered themselves to be part of a larger community that included noninteracting English, Irish, colonial American, and European Calvinists.

Together with the letters of key regional ministers, particularly those of Samuel Rutherford, two Scottish divines left their autobiographies that detailed accounts of church life, including statements describing the construction of their real and imagined communities during the first thirty-five or so years of Ulster settlement. Both were educated at the University of Glasgow by professors whose mentors were socially and intellectually traceable to Andrew Melville, the chief architect of Scottish Presbyterianism and the facilitator of a cadre of Scottish divines whom Donaldson called an ecclesiastical intelligentsia.[18] The two divines are Robert Blair (1593 to 1666) and John Livingstone (1600 to 1672).[19]

Blair's Presbyterian pedigree is quite impressive. Robert Boyd (1578 to 1627), a son of James Boyd the Archbishop of Glasgow, was Blair's mentor, and he was instructed by Robert Rollock, who was one of Andrew

Melville's graduates at St. Andrews. Robert Boyd, a professor and a friend and ministerial colleague of the staunch Presbyterian Robert Bruce (c. 1559 to 1631), was also a blood relative of John Livingstone. His family was related to the Earl of Arran, and he was made principal of Glasgow University in 1615, a year after Blair finished his formal studies.[20]

In addition to Livingstone, Blair mentored at least 150 others in philosophy as they pursued studies in theology at the university.[21] In recounting his days with Blair at Glasgow, Livingstone wrote that he "was then under the oversight of the precious Mr. Robert Blair, who, for two years, was my Regent in that college."[22] Livingstone's sentiments about his former mentor and colleague reflect David Mullan's perspective on the function of the close-knit, Puritan-minded, transchannel community headed by Scottish ministers:

> The fraternity of Scottish divinity embraced a group of men bound by numerous ties of blood, doctrine, and emotion. They were often related to others of the circle, and married from within it; they studied together; they influenced each other's thinking and fashioned themselves after shining lights in their midst; they suffered together; they wrote letters to one another, describing their joys and especially their sorrows, and generally tended to each other's emotional and spiritual needs, not least of all on their death beds. Laymen and women were not excluded from this select group, but the clerical aspect warrants a special view since its members were those who defined the religious community and its terms of membership.[23]

As Mullan indicates, Melville's intelligentsia had significant emotive influence over its younger members. For example, Robert Blair, while serving in Ulster, wrote a note to Robert Boyd, his mentor and colleague, who had remained in Scotland: "I perceive more and more what great difference there is between evil grounded fitts of civil friendship and that other whilk is in the Lord which cannot be interrupted either by space of time or distance of place."[24] Ulster's John Livingstone also had great respect for Robert Boyd and his close colleague Robert Bruce. Livingstone's assessment of Bruce was: "In my opinion never a man spake with greater power since the apostles' days."[25]

Trans–Irish Sea Presbyterian divines also held English Puritans in high regard and considered themselves to be their spiritual brothers and sisters. Although English ministers were serving in both the Church of Ireland and Irish Presbyterian churches,[26] their geographic residential areas were segregated from each other. It seems likely that the Scots' sentiments toward their English Puritan counterparts were most likely the products of their imagined communities developed through reading materials. Although those people from disparate locations may not have physically met, their ideas certainly diffused into each other's space.

A number of English ministers with Puritan beliefs who labored in Ireland were educated at Cambridge University. Like most of its educational counterparts in Scotland, Cambridge University in the sixteenth and seventeenth centuries was a center of low-church Puritanism, and the writings of its professors were read by a number of Scottish divines. Cambridge was also the principal institution from which many bishops and ministers in the Church of Ireland were drawn: "It is historically accurate to say that English Puritanism during the reign of Elizabeth was a movement inside the Church of England which sought to re-establish that Church on a Presbyterian basis."[27] However, as Ian Hazlett states, there were Episcopalian Puritans as well.[28] With many Puritans leading Irish Protestantism before the appointments of Lord Deputy Wentworth and Archbishop Laud in 1632, it is not too difficult to understand why bishops such as Robert Echlin, Henry Leslie, and Andrew Knox in the Church of Ireland employed Puritan Scots with Presbyterian convictions.

James I employed Arthur Chichester as Lord Deputy of Ireland. Chichester was arguably a Puritan and was tutored by Cambridge professor of divinity Thomas Cartwright, a leading Presbyterian protagonist in England.[29] Before his Cambridge appointment, Cartwright served as a chaplain in Ireland, where he developed many of his opinions on reformed worship.[30] At Cambridge, he influenced a number of ministers who later made their careers in Ireland, including in Ulster where English Puritans were modestly represented among the Church of Ireland's Presbyterian-oriented parish ministers. John Ridge, a Cambridge graduate, and Henry Colwart (Calvert) worked alongside Blair, George Dunbar, and Josias Welsh in Antrim during the Six Mile Water Revival, which took place in the 1620s and early 1630s.[31] John Livingstone described the origins and collegiality that characterized the ministerial leadership of the Antrim meetings: "Among all these ministers, there was never any jar nor jealousy, nor among the professors, the greater part of them Scots, and a good number of gracious English, all whose contention was to prefer others to themselves. . . . I do not think there were any more lively, experienced Christians than were these at the time, yea, and of persons of good outward condition in the world."[32]

Blair and other Scots ministers such as David Dickson were influenced by the literary works of English Puritanism. Through his brother William who served as minister at Dumbarton, Blair came under the influence of the English minister Ezekiel Culverwell, the resolutely Puritan author of *Treatise of Faith*.[33] Culverwell, whose sisters married Cambridge Puritan divines William Whitaker and Laurence Chaderton, had a covenanted relationship with fellow English Puritan Richard Rogers, the author of an important work entitled *Seven Treatises*, which by 1630 had gone through eight editions.[34] In his book, Rogers stressed the importance of godly fellowship in Christian living. He and Culverwell practiced this notion in their personal lives, and they invited others from Wethersfield to join their body of believers whom they called a "covenanted society."[35] Blair reflected on Thomas Culverwell's writings: "I was thereby much satisfied and confirmed by his uptaking of the nature and notion of faith."[36] In terms of communities of imagination, David Dickson was quick to acknowledge the work of others, "especiallie from His (God's) Church in England."[37]

Scottish nonclerical social thinkers were also affected by the thoughts of English Puritans. Archibald Johnston of Wariston, who along with Alexander Henderson of Leuchars coauthored the National Covenant of 1638, left a record of his reading list. An attorney and somewhat of a social philosopher, Johnston was frequently in contact with leaders of the Covenanting Party. He was a member of the Westminster Assembly in England and served as Lord Advocate of the Covenanting administration. During the Protectorate he served under Cromwell as Lord Clerk Register.[38] His diary identifies a number of works of English piety. Among the English Puritan authors he listed are the martyrs Henry Burton and William Prynne.[39]

The geographic nexus for continental, English, Irish, and Scottish Puritanism was not confined to Ulster, Dublin, Edinburgh, or Cambridge. The nexus originated in Geneva, where Andrew Melville met and developed a friendship with Thomas Cartwright: "Cartwright and Melville were as eager for 'conformity' between the realms as their opponents, but conformity on their basis, the Presbyterian-Puritan basis."[40] That community was deliberately nurtured by earnest divines "who worked hard to build a Christian community among their members, and they clearly had some degree of success."[41] From a trans–Irish Sea perspective, the tangible social networks of the Scots were the most important components of the community of Puritans who diffused westward their version of the Christian faith. The structure of the Scottish ecclesiastical intelligentsia who made up a significant part of the tangible community of Scottish and English Puritan divines is explained next.

The Scottish Ecclesiastical Intelligentsia

The inspirational founder of the network of Scottish theologians that transcended both time and space, including the Irish Sea and the English border, was Andrew Melville, a gifted social-organization builder who held tremendous sway in the education of Scottish divines. Melville was born near Montrose at Baldovy. Although he was orphaned, his older brother Richard provided for his education. Though a considerable scholar and linguist, he was not a prolific writer, and he had never served as a parish minister, although he was, technically at least, minister of Govan at Glasgow. As Donaldson writes, "His remarkable influence . . . was exercised by personal contacts and through his work as a university teacher and organizer, which made him the dominant figure in the education of Scottish divines."[42] Melville was well traveled and spent several years in France and Geneva where he came under the influence of Theodore Beza, Calvin's successor and principal of the Geneva Academy. He was loved and respected by many of his colleagues and most of his students, although a few of the original reformers were unimpressed with his overt Presbyterianism.[43]

Andrew Melville wholeheartedly believed in and espoused the concept of two kingdoms, which, when one considers its political implications, meant theocracy. The most important kingdom, which is sovereign over all things, is headed by Christ. The other kingdom is led by the magistrate and is subservient to Christ's kingdom. Because Melville believed that the monarchy should listen and respond to the wise council of the Kirk, of which Melville was the head, he behaved with an air of disrespect when in the presence of James. While visiting the court at Falkland Palace, Melville grasped the king by his sleeve and lectured him, calling him "but God's sillie vassal." He sternly admonished the king to understand his role in God's universe: "Sir, as divers times before, so now again I must tell you, there are two kings and two kingdoms in Scotland: there is King James, the head of this commonwealth, and there is Christ Jesus and His kingdom the Kirk, whose subject King James the Sixth is, and of whose kingdom not a king, not head, nor lord but a member."[44] His attitude toward the king and his overt disrespect for Anglican surplices, which he regarded as Romish rags, led James to banish him from Scotland. After imprisonment in London for some years, he lived his remaining years in exile from 1611 to 1622 as a professor at Sedan.[45] Regardless of his political shortcomings with the king, Melville's people and organization skills initiated the formation of a Puritan brotherhood centered on his pupils and colleagues, who in turn, nurtured the continuation of that sense of community among their congregations and with each other.

Robert Blair, like Andrew Melville, was a superlative social networker and community builder. He was born and raised on the shores of the firth of Clyde in the burgh of Irvine. His father died when Robert was young. His mother and he were impressed with the ministry of Irvine's David Dickson, but the first man to catch his attention was a deposed English minister who was staying and preaching in Irvine as he waited for transportation to cross over to Ireland.[46] From his reflections in his autobiography, it is easy to see that young Robert Blair was impressionable and that people of strong conviction served as his role models. Most, if not all, of the men who inspired him were deeply immersed in dissenting, antiprelatic activities that seemed to have characterized religious discourse in the southwest of Scotland. His views and his conduct throughout his life suggest that he was a sincere adherent to the region's belief system as articulated by its spiritual and intellectual leaders. In like manner, he was a dedicated mentor to others such as James Hamilton, whom he recruited into the Ulster ministry. He also seems to have recruited Robert Cunningham, his Scottish brother-in-law who received ordination at Holywood and served in Ulster.[47]

Blair's involvement with certain ministers who resisted the Erastian implications of episcopacy caused him some political problems. His whirlwind visits in 1622 to see Robert Boyd, Robert Bruce, and David Dickson, all opponents of the king's prelatic policies, caused John Cameron, his (pro-Crown and revisionist of Calvinism) supervisor and Robert Boyd's replacement as principal of Glasgow University, to view him with suspicion, which in turn contributed to Blair's decision to resign his post as regent, making himself available to relocate to Bangor.[48]

Robert Blair's daughter by his first wife, Beatrix Hamilton, married William Row, the son of the historian John Row.[49] His son-in-law wrote an important historical supplement to Blair's unfinished autobiography. Aside from his autobiography, however, little of what Blair wrote has survived. Although Blair was neither a great writer nor apparently an original thinker, he was a member of a group of elites who were everything he was not. The archetypical covenanter Samuel Rutherford held him in very high esteem as a divine of the right persuasion.[50] Blair's social and intellectual networks thus have quite a Presbyterian and Puritan pedigree.

Robert Rollock was the instructor of John Row, a son of one of the leading Scottish reformers.[51] Row's father was a colleague of John Knox and was one of the six men named John who composed the Scots Confession of 1560. Row was likewise a social networker and freely interacted at communions with ardent Presbyterian divines such as Robert Bruce. He was a noted minister, and he invited Irish ministers to his services after they were deposed by Laud and Wentworth.[52]

Another of Robert Rollock's students was Charles Ferme (or Fairholme, d. 1617). Ferme taught John Adamson, who became the principal of the University of Edinburgh (1630 to 1647). Ferme was also an instructor of Edward Bryce or Brice (1569 to 1636), who was one of the first, if not the first, Presbyterian-minded Scottish ministers to make Antrim his home in 1613.[53] Brice, who was deposed from the ministry at Drymen in Stirlingshire for his opposition to the appointment of Spotiswood (Archbishop of Glasgow) as the permanent moderator of the Synod of Clydesdale, was recruited to Broadisland (Ballycarry) by William Edmonston, a former parishioner who had become a planter in Ireland.[54]

Ferme instructed David Calderwood (1575 to 1650), who was exiled for a time to Holland because of his views against episcopacy. While in exile, he wrote an important defense of Presbyterianism, *Altare Damascenum.* Calderwood also wrote *History of the Kirk,* an extensive, eight-volume history of the Church of Scotland. In addition to his influential writing, he helped shape the earliest views of another dissenting preacher and writer who was a friend to many Presbyterian Ulster divines. Calderwood ministered to a young Samuel Rutherford (1600 to 1661), who became a leading proponent of Presbyterianism and the National Covenant, served as a delegate to the Westminster Assembly of Divines, and authored many extant sermons and letters as well as a number of books.[55]

Samuel Rutherford was born in Roxburghshire and spent most of his ministerial career in the Galloway village of Anwoth, which is about twelve miles from Kirkcudbright where John Welsh, the son-in-law of John Knox and father of Ulster's Josias Welsh, had successfully served as parish minister before moving on to Ayr. Rutherford had a great deal of respect for John Welsh, calling him a "heavenly Prophetical and Apostolick Man of God."[56] In a letter written during his exile in Aberdeen,[57] Rutherford told James Lindsay about his respect for some of his colleagues who were serving the people in the southwest of Scotland: "I say, first, there are with you more worthy and learned than I am, Messrs. Dickson, Blair, and Hamilton, who can more fully satisfy you."[58] The Hamilton in this instance refers to James Hamilton, who was Blair's ministerial recruit and had served for a time in Ireland.[59]

Rutherford also served as regent at the University of Edinburgh, his alma mater, and later as professor at St. Andrews. He served as a delegate on behalf of the Kirk to the Westminster Assembly and preached before the English Parliament in 1643 and 1645. In 1644 he published *The Due Right of Presbytery,* and in his *Lex Rex,* he argued for the people's right to depose their king. When the Engagers split from the Covenanter Party,[60] Rutherford aligned himself with the more extreme element.[61] Like Blair, Rutherford was also influenced by Robert Boyd and Robert Bruce.[62] He was also a friend and an admirer of David Dickson.[63]

David Dickson was highly influential in the theological development of the young Robert Blair. Dickson was Blair's childhood minister in Irvine, and they maintained a collegial and supportive relationship throughout their professional lives. Like Samuel Rutherford, Dickson admired John Welsh, who ministered at nearby Ayr.[64] Dickson entertained Livingstone and other Ulster divines at Irvine and administered communion to them. After the National Covenant, Dickson became professor of divinity at Glasgow University and later in Edinburgh.

Dickson was an evangelical preacher who, as a member of a trans–Irish Sea community of Scottish divines, mirrored his Irish counterparts' passion for revival. It is important to note that concurrent with the highly emotional revival meetings in the Six Mile Water Valley of Antrim were the revivals springing up across the rural landscape of Ayrshire. According to James Kirkton, who was an apologist for an Episcopalian polity in Scotland, David Dickson instigated the meetings.[65]

Social ties between Robert Blair and Dickson are well documented, but Dickson was also highly respected by John Livingstone. While preaching in Wigtonshire at the request of the Earl and Countess of Wigton, Livingstone interacted with Dickson as part of a formidable group of Scottish divines led by Robert Bruce, William Scot, Alexander Henderson, and John Row. Livingstone was impressed with the writings of Dickson as well as with those of Bruce, Rollock, and Welsh.[66] As a confidant, Dickson also played an important role in Livingstone's career path. Early on, Livingstone battled his own conflicting sense of pride and despair as they related to his ability to preach sermons. Dickson was instrumental in helping him come to grips with those debilitating emotions, which Livingstone attributed to the work of Satan:

> Preaching in Irvine, I was so deserted, that the points I had meditated and written, and had them fully in my memory, I was not for my heart able to get them pronounced. So it pleased the Lord to counterbalance his dealings, and hide pride from man. This so discouraged me, that I was upon resolution for some time not to preach, at least not in Irvine; but Mr. David Dickson would not suffer me to go from thence till I preached the next Sabbath—to get

(as he expressed it) amends of the devil; and so I stayed and preached with some tolerable freedom.[67]

In the wake of the National Covenant (1638), which gave increased power to Presbyterians, Livingstone was presented with a choice in selecting a charge in Scotland. Like Melville and Blair, Livingstone was also a good social networker and formed an informal committee of six divines to help him make a decision on which parish to choose: his father, Dickson, Blair, Rutherford, Andrew Cant, and Henderson. He chose Stranraer and stayed there until 1648.[68]

In addition to Blair, Livingstone, and Hamilton, many Ulster ministers in the seventeenth century had a familial or strong social link to the founding Presbyterian divines, leading Covenanters, and covenanting martyrs. Scottish-born and moderate Episcopalian bishop Andrew Knox of Raphoe, nephew of John Knox, ordained his kinsman Josias Welsh, who was a Presbyterian, and installed him as minister at Templepatrick.[69] Josias Welsh, John Knox's grandson through his daughter Elizabeth, was an important friend and colleague of Blair and Livingstone.[70] Welsh's father, John, was an eminent minister of Ayr, and Josias and his father disliked the Perth Articles (1618).[71] Michael Bruce, who succeeded John Livingstone as minister at Killinchy (1657 to 1689), was the great-grandson of the Reverend Robert Bruce. Several sermons and a book, *Mystery of the Lord's Supper,* by Robert Bruce are extant. Bruce was recommended for the Killinchy charge in 1657 by John Livingstone, who wrote a letter on his behalf to Captain James Moore of Ballybregagh.[72] Bruce, upon finishing his studies in Edinburgh in 1654, brought a number of young men with him to Ulster. Among those he introduced into the ministry in Ireland was Andrew MacCormick, who "was bred a tailor in the country."[73] MacCormick was deposed for nonconformity from his charge at Magherally in 1661 and fled to Scotland. He was a participant in the Covenanters' march on Edinburgh and was killed November 28, 1666, at the Battle of Rullion Green, Pentland Hills.[74]

Several reasons and methods took the members of the Scottish ecclesiastical intelligentsia to Ireland. Their settlement in Ulster strengthened institutional, intellectual, and social ties with Scotland generally and the southwest specifically. Through those contacts and reverse migrations as at least sixty-two ministers resettled in Scotland, including Andrew Mac-Cormick and a number of other divines who had served in the Church of Ireland with Presbyterian sympathies, the religious landscape of the southwest of Scotland by the late seventeenth century resembled Ulster more than it did the Lothians and Fife.

Scottish Ecclesiastical Intelligentsia Expands to Ireland

Unmindful of the social networks and theological complexities of life among the southwest's rural lairds and peasants who thirstily drank of the milk of Puritan dogma, James VI and I believed he had a good understanding of the social dynamics in "his ancient kingdom Scotland," for he thought that the physically closest gentry to Ireland would help recruit the right settlers.[75] Despite the king's intentions to convert backward Gaeldom through socialization with a planted people loyal to the Crown, however, both shores of the North Channel of the Irish Sea became a hotbed of Covenanter protest throughout much of the later half of the seventeenth century. Its residents would be viewed by both the Irish and Scottish governments as more troublesome than the Catholic natives.[76] His son Charles I knew even less about the country of his birth, and his lack of knowledge of Scottish culture and society was seemingly matched by his lack of concern for the people's religion. He and Archbishop Laud believed, as they blindly marched toward imposing episcopacy on a people who were at best split on the issue that they were building upon the Five Articles of Perth. The articles were a bane to the leaders of the Scottish ecclesiastical intelligentsia. If Charles I cared to know the depth to which Calvinism and Presbyterianism were embraced, he would have spent time in the southwest, especially in Irvine on Monday for market day. There he would have heard "the full trumpet blast of preachers like Robert Bair and David Dickson thundering against the iniquitous destruction of the godly Church by such as Archbishop Laud and his corrupt and tyrannical lackeys, the bishops."[77]

Early in the plantation, two lairds from Ayrshire introduced members of this Scottish social structure into Ireland.[78] In 1603 Hugh Montgomery learned that Con O'Neil, an Irish chieftain with large landholdings in counties Down and Antrim, was in prison. Montgomery conspired with O'Neil for his escape. The covert arrangement called for the transference of O'Neil's estate to the Ayrshire laird in exchange for Montgomery's help in securing his early, illegal release. King James, however, would not ratify the reassignment of lands. Undaunted, Montgomery called upon the help of an Ayrshire neighbor James Hamilton, who had great influence with the king. Hamilton was successful in securing lands for both him and Montgomery, although each received only a third of O'Neil's lands, who, incidentally, was knighted by the king as compensation for his loss.[79] Montgomery and Hamilton actively recruited ministers to their lands in Ireland. Once these recruits were settled in their ministerial duties, financial support was provided to them by the lairds. According to the *Hamilton Manuscripts*, Lord Clandeboye (another James

Hamilton, who was also a sir), educated at St. Andrews as many members of the Scottish ecclesiastical intelligentsia were under the principalship of Andrew Melville, made a personal effort "to bring very learned and pious ministers out of Scotland, and planted all of the parishes of his estate with such."[80] Lord Clandeboye recruited Robert Blair[81] to Bangor through the personal efforts of his Scottish kinsman John Hamilton of Kirktonholm.[82] In a similar manner, Sir Hugh Clotworthy brought several ministers over to Ireland.[83]

The king also had thoughts about the proximity of the southwest of Scotland to Ulster in regard to recruiting ministers to Ireland. In a letter to Sir Arthur Chichester, the Lord Deputy of Ireland, James nominated Bishop Andrew Knox (educated at Melvillian Glasgow University) for the see of Raphoe in Ireland to commence August 12, 1610. According to the king's letter, his nomination of Knox was based on the fact that he hailed from a nearby place (the Scottish Isles) with a close relationship with Ulster. Knox was bishop of the Isles and former minister at Paisley. By 1622 the Renfrewshire-born Bishop of Raphoe had recruited several ministers, at least seven of whom moved across the Irish Sea with him.[84] The bishop of Raphoe was arguably guilty of nepotism with family members who shared his heritage to John Knox, for he supervised three ministers named Knox. Because of the early date of his arrival in Raphoe, it leaves little room to speculate about who was responsible for their recruitment.[85]

The recruitment of ministers from the southwest of Scotland, where the adoption of the covenant of works was most intense, brought hyperbolic, emotion-charged sermonizers to Ulster. Evidence shows that at least certain elements within the Lowland Scots population were captivated by the Puritan message preached in Ulster. The Six Mile Water Revival, which ran from 1625 to the early 1630s, demonstrated that Scottish migration to Ulster was, after the death of James I, sometimes accomplished through the intricacies of the cross-channel religious community and its geopious orientations. As a place of sometimes buoyant and evangelical Christianity, Ulster, at times, pulled some migrants without any other significant push factor. In addition to the belief that the Scottish nation was God's second chosen people, the fervor of their faith, as it found outlet in the Ulster wilderness,[86] seems to have contributed to some immigrants' desire for membership in the religious community life flourishing there. As reported in an Irish Presbyterian Church document,

> Several of the ministers of the Church of Scotland who accompanied these emigrants to Ireland were pre-eminently distinguished for piety and devotedness. As the result of their Apostolic labors for years, a

remarkable revival of religion took place. The Valley of the Sixmile-water was the centre of the movement, but its influence extended over the surrounding counties. The prominent characteristic was an insatiable thirst for the preaching of the Gospel. As the preacher proceeded multitudes were powerfully moved, and audibly appealed for forgiveness. Whole nights were spent in prayer by great congregations, the circles affected widened and widened, the showers of blessings fell more copiously; numbers from day to day professed to have been turned to the Lord in penitence and faith, and it has been estimated that seldom has the Christian Church in any land obtained so large an addition to her membership in so short a time. Attracted by the reports of the abundant outpouring of the Holy Spirit on the Church in Ulster and the consequent high tone of spiritual life in her congregations, many came from Scotland that they might unite in her religious services.[87]

Michael Perceval-Maxwell acknowledges the revival and its ability to draw congregations of seven hundred and fifteen hundred people to a single service, but he restricts the geographic radius from which the participants were drawn to a mere twenty miles.[88] He effectively discusses the Calvinism of the Scottish settlers, but the context of migration, community, ideas, and beliefs, which are potent driving forces in directing singular and collective human behavior, is absent from his analysis. With respect to push-and-pull factors, or migration dynamics, Perceval-Maxwell does not stray too far from assigning economic interests as principal reasons for moving to Ireland, including in his discussions about the migrations of bishops and ministers.

His view is not supported by Robert Blair, who writes in his autobiography that these monthly meetings, sometimes called the Antrim Lectures, also attracted Separatist ministers from as far away as London, who, "hearing tell that there was a people zealous for the Lord in the North of Ireland, came to Antrim, where our monthly meetings were, and there set up their dwelling, thinking to fish in these waters."[89] Blair regarded their unsuccessful attempt to attract followers away from the Antrim meetings as one of several signs that God had established a protective fence around their work. The towns of Antrim, Templepatrick, Ballynure, Ballyclare, and Doagh were the most affected by the revival in the Ulster portion of the Irish Sea culture area while the Scottish parishes of Shotts and Stewarton witnessed similar revivals.[90]

Blair acknowledged in his autobiography, "At this time the Lord was pleased to protect our ministry, by raising up friends to us, and giving us favour in the eyes of all the people about us. Yea, the Bishop of Down himself used to glory of the ministry in his dioceses of Down and Connor."[91] Unfortunately for Blair, Dunbar, Livingston, and Welsh, they could not stop the efforts of Lord Deputy Thomas Wentworth from deposing them when it seemed that their meetings produced unorthodox manifestations, which Blair denounced and regarded as coming from Satan. Nevertheless congregations were empowered with knowledge gained through their ministers' lessons, and their meetings continued, guided by lay leaders, albeit covertly for nearly a half dozen years until the establishment of the first Presbytery in 1642.

Even after the inception of a legal Presbytery, revival meetings continued in Ulster, and within seventy years, attendance at Presbyterian revival meetings doubled as did the distance traveled by some who worshipped in them.[92] A recurrent theme stressed by ministers in those meetings was that their church extended beyond the single parish. The parish was part of a wider Presbyterian body, including congregations in Scotland and North America.[93] Modern scholars regard this psychological construct as a community of the imagination.[94] The growth in the community as well as the cohesiveness of its members, whose beliefs in the sovereignty of God pushed the sacred above the profane and pushed divines over secular leaders of the state, had political undercurrents that threatened the existing order in both Scotland and Ireland.[95]

The Church of Ireland, under the Erastian policies of Lord Deputy Thomas Wentworth acting on behalf of Charles I, deposed several of the Ulster divines who led the Six Mile Water. Many of them returned to Scotland—among them, John Livingstone, Robert Blair, James Hamilton of Ballywalter (the nephew of the first Lord Clandeboye), Sir Robert Adair, and a teacher-turned-minister John McLelland of Newtonards—where they became participants in the movement that led to the National Covenant in February 1638. That year in November and December, they attended the General Assembly,[96] which was noticed by Charles I and Wentworth. As support for the National Covenant grew in Ulster, the lord deputy was induced to take stock of the situation. He and the king were running out of options: "At Charles' instigation there was framed what was to become known as the Black Oath. Under the measure all Scots in Ulster over sixteen years, male and female, were required to renounce the National Covenant."[97]

While the ousted ministers took refuge in Scotland, their former congregations in Ireland lived relatively unaffected, although the passage of the Black Oath temporarily drove their meetings into private quarters.

The work of the ministers had created a self-directing religious community. The Six Mile Water Revival had featured monthly meetings of ministers and concerned members: "This is where the importance of the Antrim Lecture Meeting comes to light. It helped to create a studious and self-sufficient people, who, when their leaders were finally silenced by the prelatic authorities, were able to meet in private homes [private, microspaces] for study groups and maintain their Presbyterian principles until a better day should dawn."[98] When the first Irish Presbytery was formed on June 10, 1642, congregations from the eastern part of Ulster inundated its officials with applications for membership. Requests to join with the Presbytery were received from Antrim, Ballymena, Ballywalter, Bangor, Belfast, Cairncastle, Carrickfergus, Comber, Dervock, Donaghadee, Holywood, Killyleagh, Larne, Newtownards, Portaferry, and Templepatrick.[99] During the inaugural services at Carrickfergus, which ran from June to July 1642, long-time Ulster Presbyterians were able to hear John Livingstone once more, for upon his return to Ireland, he organized the congregation and session at Carrickfergus.[100]

The newly formed Presbytery did not have enough ministers to meet the demand from its congregations, so a committee was put together and sent to the General Assembly meeting of the Kirk in St. Andrews during July 1642 to ask for help in filling pulpits. John Gordon and Hugh Campbell, two laymembers who had hosted Antrim Lectures in their homes during the early days of the Six Mile Water Revival, went to St. Andrews to attend the meeting and to deliver their Presbytery's pleas for help.[101] That those two men who had been worshipers in Ireland for seventeen years is evidence of the strength of community among the Irish Presbyterians, especially when it is recalled that they and their fellow laymembers went without a minister for over five years. The first two Scots to answer the call for help were former Ulster ministers Robert Blair and his recruit James Hamilton.[102] Blair remained in Antrim until December, during which time he preached against the teachings of two Baptist ministers who had settled in the county.[103] John Livingstone also answered the call and stayed for six weeks at Carrickfergus.[104]

In 1644, the Kirk sent four ministers to assist the Irish Presbytery with its shortage of ministers while they presented the people of Ireland with the Solemn League and Covenant. At Carrickfergus on April 4, 1644, John Weir, one of the four, preached to a crowd of over two thousand. Weir's comment was delivered to the Kirk's General Assembly: "Two thousand in all, including the army and the people about, were entered into the Covenant, which took place here on the 4th of April and several days following."[105] The remaining members of the group of four who accompanied Weir on that mission trip were from the southwest of Scotland and included James Hamilton of Dumfries, Hugh Henderson of Dalry, and William Adair of Ayr.[106] Like Livingstone, the ministers who volunteered to serve in Ulster were allowed by the Scottish Kirk to stay on a temporary basis because they concurrently held charges in Scotland.

Like John Major, Scottish preachers such as Blair, George Dunbar, Gillespie, James Hamilton, Alexander Henderson, Livingstone, Rutherford, Welsh, and others of less renown such as John Nisbet, James Nisbet, and Perthshire's William Reid believed that civil rule emanates from the people and that a system of church councils (that is, Kirk sessions, presbyteries, and synods) is its ecclesiastical equal. It is highly likely that the Covenanter strife existing in the southwest after the Stuart Restoration was in part a function of that aspect of their belief system.[107] In addition to the above-mentioned ministers, at least twenty-four Scots ministers who served in the Irish Presbytery made at least one migration back to Scotland during their careers, and another twenty-five returned to Scotland as a result of overt political forces resulting from their depositions for refusing to renounce the Covenant or conform to episcopacy.[108] Among those divines were ministers Andrew MacCormick, John Law,[109] and Thomas Whylie,[110] who took an active part in Scottish Covenanter strife. It seems that this trans–Irish Sea culture of nonconformity was encouraged by the uneven application of monarchical power and facilitated by western sea routes.

In Ulster, and eventually through reverse diffusion to southwestern Scotland, many would come to the conviction that power and influence in the church should greatly diminish beyond that of the Kirk Session, making their Irish polity very close to English Congregationalism, or Brownism as it was called then.[111] This inclination in polity was diametrically opposed to the Erastian views of the monarchy and the religious culture of much of the rest of Scotland. On the surface, it seems to be in conflict with James B. Torrance's notion that the Westminster Confession was viewed as too mild by leading ministers in the region, most notably Dickson and Rutherford. In Torrance's view, the Westminster Confession calls for a modified Erastian system based on a state church with a Presbyterian polity, which is close to what developed after 1690 in the Scottish Kirk. The real issue for Rutherford and Dickson and a number of other ministers in the southwest of Scotland and Ulster, though, was indeed the mildness of the confession's Calvinist doctrines in regard to church-state relations. It is difficult to read Rutherford's *Lex Rex* and believe he would support any form of Erastianism, although his support of theocracy is another matter.[112] Rutherford and Dickson likely saw the Westminster Confession as a means to set a moral agenda for the magistrate.[113]

The contrast amongst the regions of Scotland was no more pronounced than between the areas in and around Aberdeen, which was the Episcopal center of the nation, and the southwest of the country. The contrast was equally great between Ulster and Aberdeenshire. The country and institutions of origin reveal a regional culture influence on the ministers who served in Irish Presbyterian churches between 1642 and 1690.

Origins of Ministers 1642 to 1690

Few attempts have been made to quantify the impact of Scots and particular institutions with their regional flavor on the establishment of Irish Presbyterianism. The discussion of such an evaluation must begin with national ties before the establishment of the Synod of Ulster (1690), for despite the existence of an imagined community of English and Scottish Puritan divines, social networks and real geographies in Ulster were heavily influenced by the national origins of the ministers. As the existence of dialect regions in Ulster delineate English and Scottish cultural influences in the north of Ireland, it is clear that the migrants from both nations were likewise attracted to areas offering known cultures as well as institutional and social ties.[114]

During the reign of James I, Scottish ministers and perhaps some bishops in Ulster were for the most part tolerant of Presbyterians. This was encouraged by the willingness of the Church of Ireland to employ them, provided the recruits were not too reticent about compromising their convictions by accepting ordination from bishops in the Church of Ireland, who generously provided them with modified ordination rituals so as not to offend their notions of polity.[115] Many of the English bishops in the established Church of Ireland were Puritans, so they shared the low-church style and Calvinist theology held by their Scots colleagues while tolerating, if not secretly enjoying, their polity practices. However, comparatively few English bishops in Ireland actually recruited or at least were successful in recruiting Scots ministers. Of the sixty-five ministers of Scottish birth who served in Ulster during the reign of James I, 76 percent served under Scottish bishops.[116] This high percentage perhaps shows Scottish social and community links as well as a sense of Scottish nationalism. Only a few English Puritans served as ministers under Scottish bishops; thus there were restricted opportunities for the diffusion of

English Puritan ideas into the community of Ulster-Scots through inter-personal contact. It would seem, then, that most of the intellectual inter-mingling of English and Scottish Puritans in Ulster occurred in the context of imagined communities created by theological writings or distant social contacts of their respective mentors.

Although two notable Englishmen with Presbyterian leanings, John Ridge and Henry Colwart, served in Ulster under the auspices of the Church of Ireland prior to the creation of the Irish Presbyterian Church, only six among the Irish Presbyterian divines between 1642 and 1690 can be identified as English-born and/or English-educated.[117] The numbers of Scots ministers who served between the years 1642 to 1690 show their country's dominance in the church structure, which provided part of the social infrastructure for intensifying chain migration between 1690 and the close of the plantation era around 1715.[118] Of the 188 ministers who served in Irish Presbyterian churches between the years 1642 and 1690, 125 (67 percent) can be positively connected to Scottish birthplaces. Another thirty (16 percent) were born in Ireland, and six (3 percent) were born in England. Of the 27 (14 percent) ministers whose birthplaces cannot be confirmed, sixteen (9 percent) were educated in Scottish universities. Because a number of Irish-born ministers were educated in Scotland, the total number of ministers who served in Irish Presbyterian churches with confirmed Scottish connections (birth and/or educations) is 162 (86 percent).[119] It is not possible to make a conclusive link with respect to education or place of birth for only ten (5 percent) ministers. However, according to the data on family names made available by George Black, most of the surnames (25 out of 27, or 93 percent) of ministers who held charges during this time frame and whose birthplaces are not known belong to paternal families that were represented in Scotland before or during the seventeenth century.[120]

These data suggest a strong relationship between Scottish universities and Irish Presbyterian ministers with over two-thirds of them coming from Glasgow and Edinburgh universities. Specifically the University of Glasgow trained seventy-nine (42 percent) of the ministers, and Edinburgh educated forty-seven (25 percent) of those who served in Ireland as Presbyterians. Nine ministers (5 percent) were from the University of Aberdeen, and seven (3 percent) graduated from St. Andrews. Three other ministers were educated in Scotland, but it is not known at which university they earned their credentials. These data show that at least 145 (77 percent) of the ministers were educated in Scottish universities.[121]

If a transchannel Presbyterian community existed in the seventeenth century, it is logical that a reverse flow of ministers to Scotland would be measurable. As it turns out, such movements were common. Data extracted from the *Fasti* for the Irish Presbyterian Church make it possible to determine subsequent migrations or the lack thereof for the denomination's first 188 ministers. Seventy-three (38 percent) of the ministers were internationally mobile after filling a charge in Ireland. Of the seventy-three who migrated, sixty-two (85 percent) moved to Scotland, six (8 percent) to America, four (6 percent) to England, and one (1 percent) to Holland. It is also possible to determine if the ministers returned to Ireland. In this case, twenty-four ministers, including at least three known circuit-riding conventiclers, returned to Ireland.[122] Of the twenty-four ministers who made migrations to Scotland and back to Ireland, making at least one full circuit, political factors were involved in fifteen (63 percent) cases. Obvious political push-and-pull factors were involved in the one-time move to Scotland for another twenty-four ministers, making political push-and-pull factors the most important determinant in thirty-nine cases of migrations in which Scotland was either a point of destination or temporary sojourn, or a hold-over.

These data indicate that in sixty-three percent of the migrations involving Scotland, at least one major political force precipitated the movements. Of the thirty-nine political migrations, the fears, hopes, or goals of the Glorious Revolution of 1689 caused the most movement with fourteen cases; failure to take the Republican Engagement (1649 and 1650)[123] produced nine migrants. Although a much larger percentage of the divines were deposed for nonconformity, migrations were precipitated in only nine of those cases. Implications concerning personal involvement in Blood's Plot of 1663 pushed another three to move.[124] Ministers who left to take an active part in the Scottish Protester movement (1650 and 1651) accounted for two relocations,[125] and the remaining two ministers were pulled by the Scottish Covenanter movement (1682 to 1686).[126]

The movement of Presbyterian ministers to Scotland in 1689 could have occurred because they saw an opportunity to live on sacred earth (a topic taken up in more detail later) and work under the auspices of a Presbyterian Kirk, as provided by William's Glorious Revolution, or on the other hand, they were terrified by the prospect of being subjected to Roman Catholic rule under James VII and II. Based on known sources, it is difficult to determine the motives and perceptions that influenced those migrants. Those who fled because of their failure to take the Republican Engagement as well as swear the abjuration oath in 1661 and 1662, both of which would have forced them to renounce the Solemn League and Covenant, perhaps did so because they regarded their oaths as sacred and unbreakable.[127] Of the twenty-three nonpolitical relocations, calls to other ministries were involved in twelve moves, and retirements caused another eight.[128] At least three (former Irish Presbyterian ministers, in addition to Robert Blair) served in the Kirk's General Assembly.

These numbers suggest that the Scottish ecclesiastical intelligentsia influenced the creation of the trans–Irish Sea Presbyterian community. Political push-or-pull factors stemming from dissenting religious positions were more often the cause of migrations than all the other reasons combined. This relationship suggests that the beliefs of the Scottish ecclesiastical intelligentsia, which facilitated schismatic behaviors when set against real and imagined Erastian religious forces, contributed much to the fluid movement of ministers between Scotland and Ulster.[129] It is also likely that as leaders of large flocks of parishioners, the divines had a similar impact on the greater Presbyterian community.

English ministers, like their Scottish counterparts, sometimes returned to the country of their birth. Edward Veal, an Oxford graduate (B.A.), resettled in England. After serving in Dublin, he returned to England as a result of a call from Sir William Waller of Middlesex for whom he served as chaplain.[130] Thomas Harrison was born in England in 1619, but he grew up in New England. He labored intermittently as the chaplain to the governor of Virginia, served as a minister in East London, and later held a charge as a minister in Dublin. He was deposed for nonconformity in 1665, like many of his Scottish counterparts, and left for England where he officiated at Chester for a time. He returned to Dublin in 1670 and organized a new congregation on Wine Tavern Street.[131] One English divine served in Connaught and another in Westmeath. Of the six English Presbyterian ministers who served in the Irish Presbyterian churches, only two worked in Ulster. William Keyes worked in Belfast, and Thomas Cobham served in Holywood.[132]

The Scots and Ulster-born Scots who served as Presbyterian divines in Ireland during the years 1642 to 1690 held a virtual monopoly on ministries.[133] Further, it seems that the relocation leaders who set in motion their chain migration were social and doctrinally linked to Andrew Melville and his Scottish ecclesiastical intelligentsia. With only two English ministers in Ulster between the years 1642 to 1690, which is only 1 percent of the total, their presence in statistical terms is insignificant when assuming that 5 percent or more could have been English-born simply by random chance. In other words, at 5 percent, this percentage of English ministers indicates that their absence from the ranks of the

Presbyterian divines would not have happened if the distribution were simply controlled by random factors. It shows the strength of the Scottish ecclesiastical community in Irish Presbyterianism.

Although it is beyond the time frame of this study, which ends at 1690, the issue of Presbyterian migration from Scotland in the 1690s is worth probing briefly. As the transchannel region's ethos abhorred the Anglican episcopalian polity and sought a theocratic world controlled by the strictures of strong Calvinism emanating from a devout people, it is likely that the moderate Erastianism of the Kirk after the Presbyterian settlement of 1690 offered them little solace. The community of Scots divines and their congregations were convinced that they were the descendants of the children of Israel. As such, they saw themselves as playing a significant part in the creation of sacred history. In the minds of many, Scotland and its people were chosen to be God's elect.[134]

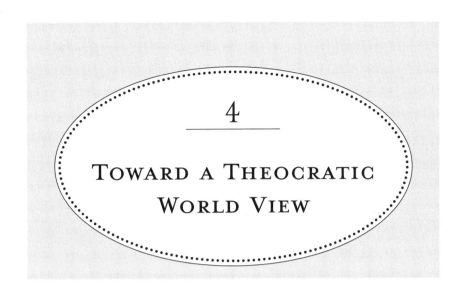

4

TOWARD A THEOCRATIC WORLD VIEW

The National Covenant of 1638 was as much a political manifesto as it was a statement of faith.[1] Although it references "true religion" as articulated in earlier confessions, in reality it offered little to define it anew. Instead it provided a litany of complaints that were generally anti-popish. The catalyst for the movement, or the "traditional" cause that ignited the powder keg of ill will against the obstinate king, occurred when Charles I instituted a new prayer book known as Laud's Liturgy, named after the Archbishop of Canterbury William Laud. When it was introduced to the congregation at St. Giles Kirk in Edinburgh on July 23, 1637, Jenny Geddes and her cohorts, who were most likely part of a concerted and well-timed resistance effort, erupted into a seemingly spontaneous and venomous protest.[2] To help his embattled sovereign, the archbishop claimed he authored the prayer book. That was a claim that Charles bravely but foolishly denied.[3]

What the National Covenant presented theologically borrowed from the Negative Confession or King's Confession that James VI had signed in January 1581. The Negative Confession drew on the theological sinew of the Scottish Reformation and the Scots Confession of 1560.[4] As the National Covenant shows, seventeenth-century Scottish divines and their colleagues who settled in Ulster fed increasingly on the strict interpretation of doctrines while accepting rigid bilateral covenants—between the nation and God—that were, as political circumstances changed, easily broken to the dismay of those who held them to be sacred and binding. It is worth demonstrating this point as it relates to the political consequences of ecclesiastical dissent (for example, the deposition of ministers): the

Irish Sea culture area was, when compared to other regions of Scotland, uniquely schismatic, a thesis informed by an analysis of Scottish and English confessions of the Reformed faith, as well as of other thinking expressed by seventeenth-century divines. With respect to relationships between schismatic actions and how those actions and beliefs influenced the formation of the trans–Irish Sea Presbyterian community, it is argued that it was their beliefs and steadfastness to their oaths that created situations in which political and social conflict, as well as theological schisms, could occur, with spatial relocation for many being the consequence.[5]

The Geography of the Scottish Reformation

The ecclesiastical dissensions that marked the later half of the seventeenth century were certainly not unique in the history of Reformation Scotland. While some participants arguably saw the Reformation and its lingering effects as positive change, others were no doubt disappointed by the persistence of social and political tensions inherent in any event designed to reform traditions and the distribution of power in social relationships. The Scottish Reformation was a schismatic action against the "auld alliance with France" and the pope. In comparing the Scottish Reformation to those of other countries, including England, David Stevenson writes, "Among the latter was the Reformed Church of Scotland, born not by royal decree but through armed rebellion [though no shots were fired] against [catholic] royal authority."[6] It was ignited by the return to Scotland of John Knox, the former understudy of the martyred George Wishart. After serving time in French confinement for his part in the seizing the home of Cardinal Beaton of St. Andrews, who was murdered by Protestant usurpers, Knox spent time as a minister in England but was forced into exile at Frankfurt and Geneva as a result of the ascendancy of the staunch Roman Catholic Mary Tudor. Knox spent much of his time in exile absorbing the teachings of John Calvin and his colleagues who were establishing the Genevan Academy that would later become the University of Geneva.[7]

Armed with Old Testament, covenantal legalism, and the Calvinist expression of Protestantism, Knox came home on May 2, 1559. Nine days later, during a sermon at St. John's Kirk in Perth, his fiery oratory against idolatry and the evils of popery set off a riot that led to the overthrow of the Roman Catholic Church in Scotland. Though the reformation of the Kirk had begun, it was not complete. The settlement of polity issues that plagued the Kirk throughout much of the plantation era was not finally made until 1690 when Presbyterianism became the official form of church governance in Scotland. However, its establishment did not stop thousands of Scots families from migrating to Ulster. Nor did the Presbyterian settlement stop dissension within the Kirk. Over the next century and a half, schism upon schism struck the Church of Scotland. The Kirk's offspring in Ulster and its Irish American child likewise split time and time again. In this section, the doctrinal roots of those schisms are examined because they produced a unique spatial pattern of ecclesiastical dissension that clearly matches the culture area from which Ulster-Scots were drawn to America.

As discussed previously, a Presbyterian Kirk, as was conceived by the members of the Scottish ecclesiastical establishment, was Christ's manifested body in the sanctified lands occupied by Scots, and the Scots themselves were destined to play a clear geotheological part in sacred history. Such an ambitious, lofty objective required an equally soaring statement of faith to guide the Scots, who would in turn guide the kirks of other nations into a closer and abiding relationship with their creator and redeemer. After pondering the fabric of the true religion, John Knox and five other men named John took only four days to write and edit the Scots Confession. It was approved in 1560 by the Scottish Parliament as containing "doctrine grounded upon the infallible word of God."[8] Knox was keen to identify Scotland with the true visible church as exemplified by Calvin's Geneva, which Knox referred to as "the most perfect school of life that was ever on earth since the days of the apostles."[9]

The Scots Confession was the Kirk's statement of faith until it was replaced by the Westminster Confession of Faith in 1647. The Scottish Parliament, acting alone in the absence of a godly prince as it did during the monarchical crisis of 1560, approved the Westminster document. The Scots Confession had nonetheless served as the basis for doctrines for nearly ninety years, laying the foundation for a national, antityrannical religious ethos that established deep, pervasive roots in the Lowland culture. Its doctrines provided the theological anchor for the National Covenant. It had survived the polity strife that characterized the relationship between Andrew Melville and James VI, and it was used by John Craig as the statement of faith on which he based the drafting of the King's Confession (Negative Confession) that was signed by James VI in 1581.[10]

The Scots Confession embraced the concept of unilateral covenants (*diatheke*), whereas its replacement, the Westminster Confession, was based more on the quid pro quo (*suntheke*) premise of English contract law, which James B. Torrance calls federal Calvinism. In terms of polity, it reflected a compromise between the various orientations of those who attended the assembly. Included in the assembly were ministers with

Erastian views such as Dr. John Lightfoot, divines from the Melvillian Presbyterian (two kingdoms) camp, and separatists (Congregationalists). The perspectives on polity among these divines could well be plotted on continuums from theocratic to Erastian and autocratic to democratic. Moreover, the Westminster Confession was a statement of faith based on moderate Calvinism, yet the bilateral or *suntheke* aspects of its doctrinal points, along with its clear position on predestination, still made it a stronger Calvinist statement of faith than the Scots Confession.

Torrance argues that the polity articulated in the Westminster document is a modified Erastian model with a state church based on a Presbyterian structure.[11] However, as demonstrated later, the part of the confession discussing the civil magistrate and religion shows the framers of the document to have been less Erastian in mind and more guided by a subtle distinction that requires the true Christian to be obedient to a sinful magistrate.[12] Furthermore it is evident that Scottish divines such as Samuel Rutherford and David Calderwood were certainly not inclined to Erastianism. To draw that kind of power structure from the Westminster Confession is hence an error. The Scots Confession and the Westminster Confession both suggest a two-kingdom, Melvillian relationship between church and state. Torrance is correct, on the other hand, in his discussion of the predestinarian Doctrine of Decrees that characterizes the Westminster catechisms.[13] The two-kingdoms, Melvillian notion of polity is, upon close examination, a call for theocracy wherein the magistrate is working on behalf of Christ's kingdom, the Kirk. As such, the magistrate is subordinate to the church in all spiritual and ecclesiastical affairs. This important distinction frames a very different vision of social order to that which was held by the Stuarts, who saw the church as a tool for creating social stability and political uniformity but saw the office of the crown as being divinely appointed with a kind of Caesar-papist authority over all secular and ecclesiastical matters. The role and authority of the crown were consistent with the kings of Israel and Judah. Confrontation of a political nature was bound to occur, and that conflict resulted in spatial separation for many of those who held visions of the Knoxian notion of Scotland as a "perfect school of Christ."

The Doctrine of Decrees placed pressure on the individual to demonstrate obedience to God's commandments in social and public settings as a visible sign of internal election and sanctification. In federal Calvinism, according to Torrance, the "practical concern means that the emphasis moves away from what God has done for us and for mankind in Christ to what we are to do to know we are among the elect and in the covenant with Christ."[14] In effect this doctrine stressed the man-law-sin-repentance-grace model of salvation that characterizes the Old Testament plan of redemption.[15] Although both statements of faith show the futility of a life without Christ and also the destructive force embodied in sin, the Westminster Confession has a softer emotional tone. Unlike the comparatively strong theological statements in the Westminster Confession, the Scots Confession employs terms and expressions that only suggest the doctrine of limited atonement such as "God's chosen ones" and "This Kirk invisible, known only to God, who alone knows whom he has chosen," yet it also promises that God will give "power to as many as believe in him to be the sons of God."[16] The Scots Confession comes much closer to the Lutheran concept of unmerited salvation by grace through faith than does the Westminster Confession.

Modern Scottish theologians sometimes deemphasize the doctrine of predestination suggested in the Scots Confession. For instance, Torrance argues that the origin of the doctrine of limited atonement rests with Theodore Beza. In discussing the weakness of the Doctrine of Decrees, used in the Westminster Confession, Torrance writes, "It leads logically to the Bezan and post-Reformation doctrine of limited atonement."[17] Torrance's assigning the origins of the doctrine of limited atonement and double predestination to Beza is not supported by Calvin's own pen, for he described it as a decree in *The Institutes:*

> Predestination we call the eternal decree of God by which He determined in himself what would have to become of every individual of mankind, for they are not all created with a similar destiny, but eternal life is foreordained for some and eternal damnation for others. Every person, therefore, being created for one or the other of these two ends, we say is predestined to life or to death.[18]

Calvin's use of the decree is stressed by James D. Tracy:

> In 1550 Calvin debated before the city council of Geneva an ex-friar who maintained that while God does indeed predestine for salvation all who are saved, He offers his grace to all men. . . . Calvin responded that it made no sense to say that God decrees the salvation of those who are saved but not the damnation of those who are damned. God offers his grace only to those whom he chooses, and if man has no free will to participate in his own salvation, neither has he the free will to turn aside from God's decree. God displays his infinite mercy by saving those sinners He chooses to save and His

infinite justice by condemning to Hell those sinners He chooses
to condemn.[19]

Calvin clearly described a doctrine of limited atonement and double predestination, but he did not originate it, for it was espoused earlier in the
fourteenth century by Gregory of Rimini, father general of the Augustin-
ian Friars and a leading theologian of his time.[20] This is an important
realization because it would seem that Knox and his fellow reformers who
admired Calvin were familiar with the doctrines of limited atonement and
double predestination, but, for unknown reasons, they softened them in
the Scots Confession. However, predestination is implied in the Scottish
statement of faith.

In addition to the issue of doctrines, the two distinct cultures and histories of English and Scots Protestantism, with the former being born by
royal decree and the latter emerging from a popular movement, meant a
compromise on polity would need to be made at the assembly at Westminster. Just as the Second Helvetic Confession, which in 1566 replaced
the Heidelberg Confession, healed sacramental conflict between Luther-
ans and the Swiss-German Reformed Church, the Westminster Confession of Faith was written with the Solemn League and Covenant (1643)
in mind. It was intended to bring the polity of the Anglican Church in line
with that of the Kirk in exchange for Scottish support against Charles I.[21]
However, Cromwell's Protectorate, guided by the Lord Protector's vision
of an independent, congregational polity, along with a limited role for
both the parliament and monarch, dismissed the divines in 1649. England, which had convened and dominated the Assembly of Divines,
never used the Westminster Standards in the Anglican Church.[22] Nonetheless the soft Calvinist doctrines espoused in the old Scottish statement
were stiffened in the Westminster Confession.

In addition to varying levels of adherence to Calvinist doctrines in
the two statements of faith, however, the symbolic verbiage is used with
respect to the magistrate in the Scots Confession. This sets it apart
from its contemporary Reformed counterparts and its successors (the
Heidelberg, the Second Helvetic Confession, and the Westminster
Confession of Faith).[23] The Scots Confession uses many polarizing
words and phrases in reference to the Kirk's beliefs and those of people
holding other views or expressing contrary behaviors. For example, such
phrases include the "Kirk militant," "reprobate" and "unfaithful," "lost in
oblivion," "fear and torment,"[24] "horrible harlot," "condemnation,"[25] and
"doctrine of devils."[26] By using symbolic expressions such as these, perhaps the authors of the Scots Confession assumed they could encourage

a corrective response to a sense of guilt.[27] On the other hand, the West-minster Confession simply told the people of Scotland that God's laws were to be followed and in specific ways. Failure to do so placed one in opposition to the true Church of Christ, and those sins would have consequences that would be used by God to draw his children closer to him. As written by the Westminster divines,

> The most wise, righteous, and gracious God, doth often-times leave for a season His own children to manifold temptations and the corruption of their own hearts, to chastise them for their former sins, or to discover unto them the hidden strength of corruption and deceitfulness of their hearts, that they be humble; and to raise them to a more close and constant dependence for their support upon himself, and to make them more watchful against all future occasions of sin and for sundry other just and holy ends.[28]

This innovation mimicked the structure of English contract law ("if then, what then" scenarios). The Westminster document on faith clearly laid the theological groundwork for both puritanical behaviors (based on biblical legalism, efficacious righteousness, and realized sanctification) and schisms over interpretations of the true faith.[29]

The Puritan influence is evident in its emphasis on the manifestations of God's grace in the lives of the regenerate. It shows the futility of good works without God's grace, as if grace is an object or power to be given when grace is an act of giving freely.

> Works done by unregenerate men, although, for the matter of them, they may bee things which God commands, and of good use both to themselves and others; yet, because they proceed not from a heart purified by faith; nor are done in the right manner . . . they are therefore sinfull, and cannot please God . . . yet, their neglect is more sinfull, and displeasing to God.[30]

As Gordon Marshall points out, such beliefs imposed psychological pressure on the individual to be assured of his/her state of salvation.[31] David Dickson and the Presbyterian divine James Durham (1622 to 1658) provided guidance to the Scottish parishioner of ways to be assured of election. The divines insisted that diligence to works reveals evidence of internal election and justification: "The way to be sure both of our effectual calling, and election, is to make sure work of our faith in new obedience constantly: *for 'if ye do these things,* (saith he), *ye shall never fall,'* understanding by these things, what he had said of sound faith, and what he said of the bringing out of the fruits of faith."[32]

The Westminster Confession was drafted with little official input from Scottish divines, although they were involved in the informal discussions on doctrines and the need for a Presbyterian polity. The primary theologians who represented the Kirk at Westminster also led in the creation of the movement that brought about the Covenanting cause associated with the National Covenant. They were also inspirational leaders of the divines associated with the southwest of Scotland. They were younger men steeped in the Melvillian, Presbyterian tradition.[33] Samuel Rutherford (1600 to 1661), who had served as minister at Anwoth by the Solway since 1627, was accompanied by George Gillespie (1613 to 1648), the author of *Dispute Concerning the English Popish Ceremonies Obtruded upon the Church of Scotland.* They were joined by the statesman-like minister of Leuchars, Alexander Henderson (1583 to 1646), who had coauthored the National Covenant a few years earlier.[34] Henderson was the only nonwesterner in the group. The Scottish ambassadors to the Westminster Assembly were also joined by Robert Baillie, professor of divinity at the University of Glasgow. Their positions on polity and theology were clear, although Baillie became a moderate Resolutioner and supporter of Charles II. For his loyalty, he was made principal at Glasgow after the Restoration and served in that capacity until his death in 1662.[35]

Rutherford in *Divine Right of Church Government and Excommunication* wrote, "That there is nothing so small in either doctrinals or policy, so as man may alter, omit, or leave off these smallest positive things that God hath commanded."[36] Gillespie had already vehemently condemned episcopacy in favor of Presbyterianism and warned of God's wrath against Scotland as a result of that "corruption" in the Kirk.

> The Church of Scotland was blessed with more glorious and perfect reformation than any of our neighbor churches. The doctrine, discipline, regiment, and policy established here by ecclesiastical and civil laws, and sworn and subscribed unto by the king's majesty. . . . But now, alas! Even this church, which was once so great a praise in the earth, is deeply corrupted, and has "turned aside quickly out of the way" (Ex. 32:8). So that this is the Lord's controversy against Scotland: "I had planted thee a noble vine, wholly a right seed; how then art thou turned into the degenerate plant of a strange vine unto me" (Jer. 2:21).[37]

Rutherford, Gillespie, and Henderson endorsed the adoption of the Westminster Confession of Faith, and it was approved by the Scottish Parliament in 1647. Its importance in Scottish religious thought and application to practice in pastoral theology increased over the next decades and was becoming widely accepted when the Presbyterian settlement was made in 1690. Its statements, especially on polity, led to many confrontations with Cromwell and with the House of Stuart after the Restoration in 1660, for "religion was too powerful a force for religious autonomy to be acceptable to the state."[38] This was especially true when the Westminster Confession seemed to support the commonly held notion amongst Presbyterians that "it was the state's duty to help the church when asked, and it was the church's duty to show civil powers (including kings) how to perform their duties in godly ways."[39] This doctrine, which depended upon the sword of the magistrate to ensure proper social conduct in public spaces as well as defense against external foes, descended directly from the Scots Confession, which in turn, was brought from Geneva to Scotland by Knox where he learned it from Calvin, who wrote, "For the Church has not the right of the sword to punish or restrain, has no power to coerce, no prison, nor other punishment which the magistrate is wont to inflict."[40] The Scottish divines who supported Presbyterianism also embraced the Westminster Confession. They, like their reforming predecessors in Scotland, believed that the magistrate was supposed to support the Kirk.

The political and social implications of the Westminster Confession were in strong opposition to the Erastian impulses of the Stuarts, who wanted an episcopal polity. As would be expected when two opposing visions of social and political power meet in a small country experiencing tremendous change, including demographic transition, conflict was frequent, especially in the southwest where those pressures were intensely felt. Indeed, despite the triumph of Presbyterianism in 1690, many ministers and congregations in the region were unhappy with the lack of national will to achieve the vision of Scotland as a sacred place, "a perfect school of Christ."[41]

Like the southwest or the eastern part of Ulster-Scots Land, the Border country was a region of Presbyterian activism. The western Border country was also a region where Puritan and Presbyterian ministers such as David Calderwood stirred antiprelatic dogma that inspired Rutherford, who as a child sat transfixed in his Roxburghshire pew absorbing the words and ideas of the fiery preacher.[42] David Stevenson points out that with respect to the National Covenanting movement of 1638 to 1639, the Border country was among the most zealous regions in Scotland, which also included parts of Lanarkshire, Argyllshire, the Lothians, Fife, and the rest of the Lowlands.[43]

The parishes where Dickson, Livingstone, and Rutherford preached were located to the west of the Border country along the Irish Sea at

Irvine, Stranraer, and Anwoth, respectively. Parishioners in this region also listened to the impassioned sermons of Robert Blair, Richard Cameron, James Hamilton, James Nisbet, James Renwick, and John Welsh, to name a few, as they espoused the virtues of doctrinaire Puritan-Presbyterianism while denouncing the evils of papacy and the threat of Erastianism through episcopal orders.[44] Pastor "George Gillespie condemned Arminianism for its relationship to Erastianism, which promoted magisterial sovereignty over the church and the exercise of religion."[45]

The Scottish ecclesiastical intelligentsia and its members in the Irish Sea culture area were not only imbued with preferences for a Presbyterian polity, they were convinced of Scotland's geotheological importance. Returning to Scotland for some Ulster-Scots ministers serving in the Synod of Ulster was regarded as an opportunity provided to them by an omniscient, graceful God. The Reverend John Anderson, for instance, consented to preach in Antrim in 1671 provided he would be released "to return to Scotland 'when it pleased God to open a door.'"[46] In February 1688, he was "called to his former people" and served in the General Assembly after the 1690 Presbyterian settlement.[47] Blair was convinced that God enabled him and his colleagues to return to Scotland to fulfill an important role in sacred history.[48] Informed by a geopious world view and committed to a participatory polity, a Puritan-Presbyterian minister serving in the Irish Sea culture area was prone to react schismatically to opposing world views. The next sections explore the doctrines and spatial patterns of ministers who were deposed at the Restoration. These analyses provide empirical evidence for the argument that institutional and social ties along with regional sea and land features encouraged the development of a unique dissenting Irish Sea culture area.

Schisms Forming in the Dissenting Irish Sea Culture Area

Unhappiness among trans–Irish Sea Presbyterians in the late seventeenth century is perhaps best explained by Thomas Hobbes, who wrote that Presbyterianism because of its rigidity "was liable to hive into sects."[49] As a region away from the political power center of Scotland, the rugged lands of the southwest with its seaward orientation were ideally prone to hold religious views that ran contrary to a monarchy bent on Erastianism through episcopacy. Even when established as the official polity of the Kirk in 1690, there were dissenting voices in the region. The first schism occurred in the southwest of Scotland among some of the followers (Cameronians) of the martyrs Richard Cameron (1648 to 1680) and Donald Cargill (1619 to 1681). John Macmillan (1670 to 1753), a conventicler and a leader among the Cameronians, led the way in organizing the region's societies, the conventicles, into a presbytery that in 1743 grew into the Reformed Presbyterian Church in Scotland. Ebenezer Erskine wrote, "There is a difference to be made between the established Church of Scotland and the Church of Christ in Scotland."[50] The Reformed Presbyterian Church diffused into the western part of the Irish Sea culture area, and with the help of Scottish divines who made regular trips to Ulster, the Reformed Presbytery was formed in Ireland in 1763. The Irish church body grew into a synod by 1811. Nowhere in Scotland was anti-Erastian sentiment felt with as much passion as in the Irish Sea culture area. In speaking of the Ulster Presbyterians, John Dunlop, an Ulster Presbyterian minister and author, said that it is important to recognize that Presbyterians have a strong tendency to split over breaches in principle. He hints of the inevitable geography of schism.

> The Presbyterian people who live in Ireland have connections with the Presbyterianism of Scotland and the rest of the world. There is a well-established tendency to divide rather than to accommodate conflicting diversity when a perceived betrayal of principle is involved. Anyone who thinks that these people from this tradition are going to be domesticated and turned into easy-going people who will agree to anything, does not appreciate that the traditions which inform their lives have been with them for some hundreds of years.[51]

Historical events seem to confirm the thoughts of Michael Fry: "It is a peculiar trait of presbytery that, when established, no religion could be more regular and loyal; but, disestablished or dissenting, it may turn radical to the point of sedition."[53] But it is likely that the real issue that created rigidness and thus schism was Puritanism, not the polity. Old Testament legalism was the basis of Puritanism, and it was feared that God's wrath would be visited upon nations that were visibly sinful. Dissension occurred when one person or perhaps a group of people thought that one (or several) of their members' actions violated God's strict laws. It was somewhat like the biblical mandate to pluck out the offending eye.

In a retrospective examination of its affairs as it reunited with the Free Church of Scotland, the Kirk in 1929 accepted three general reasons for the schisms that rocked its solidarity, including the Disruption of 1843.[53] These reasons are relevant to the plantation movement because they are intertwined with the mindset that spread throughout the Irish Sea culture area. First, Ninian Winzet, a Catholic apologist, in his conflict with Knox, believed he showed how the reformers wedded together biblical passages to validate their creed instead of pulling a creed from the scriptures. The range of interpretations that could be drawn from the Bible, therefore, represents a primary reason for schisms. George Gillespie expressed his belief that true Christian liberty would lead to a unified Church and that true Christian liberty would be assured by God if his written word was the foundation of church doctrine. Gillespie pleaded with his colleagues:

> Hath not God promised to give us one heart and one way . . . ? Hath not the mediator prayed that all his may be one? Brethren, it is not impossible, pray for it, [and] press hard toward the mark of accommodation. How much better it that you be one with the other Reformed churches, though somewhat strained and bound up, [than] be divided through at full liberty and elbowroom?[54]

Gillespie's plea, which was primarily directed at Baptists and Separatists, centered on his belief that divisions and contentions hinder the preaching and learning of Christ that come from his Word. Moreover, so he believed, the body of Christ, the Church, cannot be divided unless it divided Christ. James Durham believed that schismatic beliefs and behaviors were a great evil, and as he neared his death, his concern over schisms was great. In dealing with his anguish over tensions within the Kirk, he wrote *The Dying Man's Testament to the Church of Scotland; or, A Treatise Concerning Scandal.* "Sure there is no evil doth more suddenly and inevitably overturn the church than this," he stated, that it "makes her fight against herself, and eat her own flesh, and tear her own bowels: for, that a kingdom divided against itself cannot stand."[55] Because Christ is the sovereign ruler of the world, it is impossible truly to divide him. Like most of the Divines at Westminster, Gillespie wanted to advance God's kingdom on earth, and any dissension from their interpretation of scripture and polity was counterproductive. The potential for conflict within Protestantism was necessarily great, especially when it is recognized that the Baptists and Separatists tended to be microtheocrats, that is, small, insulated communities of believers, Episcopalians leaned toward Erastianism, and Gillespie and his Presbyterian compatriots were arguably macro- or universal theocrats. There are possible geographic implications for these orientations. The belief that Christ could not truly be divided meant that congregations, including those that were autonomous and Baptist, must follow the true religion in order to bring God's favor upon the state, the land, and people. The goal of the theocrats (both micro and macro) was to promote a Christ-centered society wherein the magistrate would follow the guidance of church officials, who, through the scriptures, were in a better position to know God's sovereign will. In opposition to Congregationalists, Gillespie believed that an overarching (macro) church structure would best ensure that congregations followed the true religion. In his way of thinking, which was shared by Robert Blair, diverse communities among Baptists were developing abhorrent expressions of the faith. Moreover, the state's and the nation's land would be blessed by God through his rewarding their good works in both public (visible) and private spaces. A sinful magistrate in charge of Erastian episcopacy could not, in the minds of Gillespie and his colleagues, know God's will without guidance from the Kirk. God's blessings would not flow upon the land under such a polity.

This led to a situation in which disagreements with one's obstinate neighbor could lead to charges of heresy. It is a short distance from this view to the idea that if a person's neighbor is operating outside the will of God, then God is not his/her master. And, the only other alternative is that if God is not his/her master, than Satan is. The belief that God would only allow one true interpretation of the scriptures was at the root of Christian liberty during the seventeenth century. What this meant in practical terms is that the civil magistrate could not dictate doctrine to the Church, but the Church also could not allow for diversity in scriptural interpretation.[56]

A second closely related reason for schisms rested with the conception of the church as universal. This idea was carried over from the medieval church. The major difference, however, was that the post-Reformation church was to be based on Calvinism.[57] The Scots Confession states, "This Kirk is catholic, that is, universal, because it contains the chosen of all ages, of all realms, nations, and tongues, be they of the Jews or be they of the Gentiles, who have communion and society with God the Father, and with his Son, Christ Jesus, through the sanctification of his Holy Spirit."[58] The Scots Confession also stressed the responsibility of the civil magistrate to ensure the viability of the universal Kirk.[59] This doctrine was not lost in the National Covenant, which clearly reminded the magistrate of both the acts of parliament and the king's signature that approved it:

> Likeas many Acts of Parliament are conceived for maintenance of God's true and Christian religion, and the purity thereof, in doctrine and sacraments of the true church of God, the liberty and freedom thereof, in her national, synodal assemblies, presbyteries, sessions, policy, discipline, and jurisdiction thereof; as that purity of religion, and liberty of the church was used, professed, exercised, preached, and confessed, according to the reformation of religion in this realm: As for instance, the 99th Act, Parl.7; Act 25, Parl. 11; Act 114, Parl. 12; Act 160, Parl. 13 of King James VI. ratified by the 4th Act of

King Charles. So that the 6th Act, Parl. 1, and 68th Act, Parl. 6 of King James VI.[60]

This doctrine was not displaced by their English counterparts who met in the Westminster Assembly. Those divines, with the advice of the Kirk's Rutherford and Gillespie, added it to the Westminster Confession of Faith. The Westminster Confession admonished the magistrate to protect the purity of the Church without assuming any role in the administration of the rights of the clergy:

> The Civill Magistrate may not assume to himself the administration of the Word and Sacraments, or the power of the keyes of the Kingdome of Heaven: yet, he hath authortie, and it is his dutie, to take order, that Unitie and Peace be preserved in the Church, that the Truth of God be kept pure and intire, that all Blasphemies and Heresies be suppressed, all corruptions and abuses in Worship and Discipline prevented, or reformed; and all the Ordinance of God duely settled, administered, and observed. For the better effecting whereof, he hath power to call synods, to be present at them, and to provide that whatsoever is transacted in them, be according to the mind of God.[61]

This doctrine was applied in most Scottish parishes, but because of the doctrine of the universal church, its use resulted in at least two major problems for the Kirk. It required a prohibition against variety in religion, and it made manifest the need for coercion. Knox and his successors, believing the Kirk to be the embodiment of divine will, saw themselves as the protectors of the true religion. As the frequency of reported witch trials seem to indicate, the adoption of the Westminster Confession, which reflected the ethos of the times, reinforced the use of coercion throughout England, Ireland, and Scotland.[62] The task of making people abide by the divine will as interpreted by the Kirk was daunting. To be effective, it was necessary to use the powers of the civil magistrate to enforce discipline on the masses.[63] The power of the magistrate to compel all to comply with divine law was enhanced by the fear that God's displeasure over the lack of lawful conduct from the elect would cause God to dispense his wrath on the community or even the nation.[64] The doctrine also applied to Roman Catholicism and any other forms of ecclesiastical diversity, including with respect to sects and those Arminian doctrines that Rutherford strongly opposed.[65]

Coercion in the Church was not a novelty. In speaking to the schismatic fourth-century Donatists of North Africa, Augustine advocated coercion as a means to "compel them to come in."[66] In the minds of the leaders of the Kirk, ecclesiastical diversity was no better than moral apathy. The result of this opinion, whether held by Episcopalians or Presbyterians, was a pervasive desire to make the visible church resemble the invisible church, which they believed was known only to God. As a result, the most secular aspects of life received supervision from the Kirk session, clearly blurring the boundaries between the "two kingdoms." This oversight was insisted upon by those who sought evidence of election and sanctification in the lives of both themselves and others because of their belief that such a favored condition by God would manifest tangible signs.[67]

The collusion of church and state was a third reason for schism and separation. The ethos of the Scottish ecclesiastical intelligentsia insisted upon coercive control of both the elect and the unregenerate (they audaciously assumed that they would know who was of the invisible church), thereby obscuring the relationship between the Kirk and the state. This notion has its roots in how the Emperor Constantine had used his power to call councils to control heresies in the Church. The earliest reformers, however, had accepted the *Corpus Juris* of Justinian, which defined the respective rights of church and state. That principle collapsed as the Old Testament increasingly guided their thoughts toward a paradigm in which political power was seen as a gift from God. Knox conceived the Kirk as having unlimited power, subject of course to scripture, which meant that conflict with the crown was bound to occur. The basis for this situation in the Kirk perhaps rested with Knox's emphasis on the supremacy of scripture and his belief in Scotland's geotheological significance: "Though Knox adhered to the basic principles of the Reformed tradition, he was a man of the Old Testament. . . . He strove for a corporate return of Scottish religion to the ideal of spiritual Israel."[68] Drawing from Deuteronomy 12:32, Knox insisted that every aspect of worship should be taken from scripture; further, he believed it was the responsibility of the civil authority to abolish any forms of religion that were contrary to the true faith.[69] According to the Scots Confession,

> We state that the preservation and purification of religion is particularly the duty of kings, princes, rulers, and magistrates. They are not only appointed for civil government (by divine order) but also to maintain the true religion and to suppress all idolatry and superstition. . . . We further state that so long as princes and rulers vigilantly fulfil their office, anyone who denies them aid, counsel, or service, denies it to God, who by his lieutenant craves it of them.[70]

The *Westminster Standards,* as already discussed, continued this line of thought. However, it states that, unlike the Scots Confession, the magistrate's infidelity and indifference in religion do not relieve the true Christian citizen from being subject to the magistrate's authority.[71] According to the Scots Confession, those civil leaders who did not act vigilantly (as determined by the ecclesiastical authorities) invited social dissent. The authors of the Scots Confession said that Christ is the head of his Kirk, the just lawgiver: "To which honours and offices, if man or angels presume to intrude themselves, we utterly detest and abhor them, as blasphemous to our sovereign and supreme Governor, Christ Jesus."[72] Depending on which document two people chose to consult, one person could come away with a different opinion than the other on issues of political dissension. At any rate, the Kirk reformers in the sixteenth century provided their colleagues and parishioners with a doctrinal precedence for civil disobedience in the name of conscience and purity; but through collusion with the state as articulated in the Westminster Standards, the Kirk in the later half of the seventeenth century could bring the weight of the state down upon all citizens except the monarch.[73]

This subtle difference in the two statements of faith supports Torrance's thesis that the Westminster Confession called for a modified Erastianism exercised through an established Presbyterian Kirk, a distinction that perhaps Rutherford and Gillespie missed. Perchance they believed the Kirk would greatly influence the adoption and enforcement of laws designed to regulate sinful behavior and that the institution of government, as opposed to the individual magistrate who would likely fall into one of Satan's snares, would dispassionately abide by the bilateral conditions of the Westminster Confession, which clearly stipulates that the government is to work to ensure purity and unity in religion and to provide the Kirk with assistance in bringing about social order.[74]

When Knox's successor Andrew Melville declared to King James VI in October 1596 that Scotland had two kings and two kingdoms, it seemed a reasonable statement about spiritual independence.[75] However, Melville also informed the king that the earthly monarch was only a member of the Kirk, which is the embodiment of Christ's kingdom on earth.[76] Melville's points were intended to validate the right of the Kirk to interfere in secular policy, a practice that Knox had taken quite seriously and harshly in trying to guide the policies of Mary, Queen of Scots.[77] To Melville and his followers Rutherford, Blair, Bruce, Livingstone, Gillespie, and Henderson, all was well when the magistrate followed their views on civil policy. As the hierarchical order of church-state relationships rested on varying interpretations of the Westminster Confession, this made it relatively easy for schisms to develop. The subtle differences in interpretation when applied to society and social order meant completely different visions of control based on the potentially capricious nature of Erastian morality or the increasingly hard-line goals of theocrats.

However, a fourth reason escaped the attention of the Kirk in 1929, and because it was related to the psychological and social response (evidence of sanctification revealed in public spaces) to the doctrine of justification by faith, it centered on the practical everyday social understanding and application of that doctrine. Inherent in this point was the shift in the structure of local social power that was mentioned in the discussion about the collusion between church and state to ensure proper behavior in public spaces. James B. Torrance describes the Lutheran view of salvation as being based upon the doctrine of a unilateral covenant between God and the believer.[78] The Westminster divines, as discussed earlier, saw a need for external or behavioral evidence of internal grace and election because of their concern for the "if then, what then" legalism scenarios that developed in their statement of faith. When examining this shift, Torrance contends that the salvation doctrine also shifted from the "covenant and grace" basis espoused by Luther to the "contract and merit" premise that characterized Old Testament beliefs about redemption. Among the masses of people, this shift made godly conduct a social and personal premium because sinful behavior was subject to punishment by the local session acting through the civil magistrate. The Reverend Robert Rollock, whom Torrance regards as the first Scottish minister to embrace the bilateral covenant of English law and thus the salvation doctrine of contract and merit, said,

> Good workes are not causes of our justification, of life: they are but the fruites of justification. A man doeth not good workes to be justified; but is justified to bring out good workes: they have their own use: they are only comfortable to them who worke them, and to confirm their calling, justification, and life: but also those who stand by, and looke to them . . . they are edified by their onlooking.[79]

Whereas in the Scots Confession, grace and salvation are provided to the elect on a unilateral, Lutheran basis with the expectation that there would be a response, Scottish theologians in the seventeenth century saw it necessary to demonstrate godly behaviors as a reflection of internal election, giving rise to the need to demonstrate evidence of salvation in public places, which David George Mullan quite accurately labels Puritanism.[80] As the church was the gatekeeper of heaven, it was incumbent upon the elders in a parish to provide guidance and direction on appropriate behaviors.

Through this theological shift and its implications on policing social behavior, the power in the southwest, as elsewhere, was altered. Rutherford and Dickson were regional leaders. They only mildly supported the Westminster Confession because they felt the document was theologically too weak and perhaps too strong on Erastianism, but they certainly felt that the church had a role to play in providing direction on appropriate conduct.[81] Through their strong sermons and writings made during the ascendancy of Presbyterian rule in the wake of the National Covenant of 1638, their views were widely accepted in the southwest. It followed that Kirk-sessions and presbyteries, which were composed of men who in many instances held positions of civil authority, took on a leading police role.[82] By their positions of secular authority as well as through the apparatus of the Presbytery, communication among parishes effectively enforced a code of conduct that aided the visible church's efforts to personify the invisible body of Christ.[83] Some members of the nobility were not immune from sanctions emanating from Kirk sessions.[84] Arguably this situation placed much of the everyday enforcement of morality on the conscience of the local magistrate, who was often an elder in the established church and a member of the gentry. However, the Engager movement of 1648, which was led by the gentry, instigated a popular protest in the west as thousands of mostly humble folk gathered in defiance to decry the Engagers as betrayers of the Covenants.[85] As discussed earlier, the power structure in the southwest of Scotland was significantly changed by the Restoration because of the feuing of farm land, which with respect to lowly farmers broke the traditional basis of their loyalty to local elites. The deposition of charismatic ministers committed to the Covenants also provided fodder for dissension because of their unhappiness with the status quo.

Theocratic Expectations, Repression, and Exile

From the time of the Scottish Reformation, Puritan-Presbyterian divines, along with many Episcopalians, took note of their presumed high place in sacred history. In doing so, Scotland took on geoteleological significance, a topic covered later, as a leader in the universal Reformed Kirk. The clear beliefs of the Scottish ecclesiastical intelligentsia set the stage for political actions and monarchical repression that led to their great disappointment, followed by a rationalization that there was indeed biblical precedence for taking refuge outside of Scotland.[86] The founders of the Reformation in Scotland had themselves sought refuge in religious sanctuaries, most notably in Emden, Geneva, Frankfurt, Copenhagen, and England. They believed that sojourns of this nature were a part of the unfolding drama of providence and that they themselves were connected to biblical icons as leaders in the true church. Refuge such as the wilderness (for example, Egypt or the nearly destroyed lands of Ulster) allowed the true followers of Christ to avoid a wrong-headed monarch's staff and rod as they were let loose to control their nation. The Scots Confession gave the justification.

> For he called Abraham from his father's country, instructed him, and multiplied his seed; he marvelously preserved him, and more marvelously delivered his seed from the bondage and tyranny of Pharaoh; to them he gave his laws, constitutions, and ceremonies; to them he gave the land of Canaan; after he had given them judges, and afterward saw, he gave David to be king, to whom he gave his promise that of the fruit of his loins should one sit forever upon his royal throne. To this same people from time to time he sent prophets, to recall them to the right way of their God, from which sometimes they sometimes strayed by adultery. . . . For righteousness he was compelled to give them into the hands of their enemies, as had previously been threatened by the mouth of Moses, so that the holy city was destroyed, the temple burned with fire, and the whole land desolate for seventy years, yet in mercy he restored them again to Jerusalem, where the city and temple were rebuilt, and they endured against all temptations and assaults of Satan till the messiah came according the promise.[87]

In helping to overturn Laud's Liturgy, the returning Scots ministers from Ireland were empowered by the unfolding political events. Their empowerment strengthened their visions of fulfilling sacred history. The Scottish ecclesiastical intelligentsia acting through the Presbyterian Party nearly achieved a theocracy in Scotland in the wake of the signing of the National Covenant in 1638. Their expectations were high but were short lived because their theocratic rigidity manifested itself in harsh ways. Ministers were among the leaders of the forces against royalists who astounded moderate observers when they cried, "Jesus and no quarter." Their defeats at Dunbar (1650) and subsequent disaster at Worcester (1651) forced Charles II, the would-be-puppet monarch of the Covenanters and their leaders, the Campbells of Argyll, into a depressing nine-year exile. The Presbyterian Party was pushed from the fore of Scottish political power. With the fleeing, young monarch went memories of his bad experiences, specifically at the hands of the Marquis of Argyll and his compatriots. Among his tortuous memories were the many lectures he was forced to hear denouncing his family.[88]

To the astonishment of the Marquis of Argyle and those of his party who worked with Cromwell and his commander in chief, General George Monk, the Protectorate ended within ten years. They were also shocked when they discovered that General Monk was a key activist in facilitating the Restoration of the House of Stuart in 1660. Charles II returned to Britain with pomp and ceremony, and the Marquis of Argyle, once leader of the Covenanters, found his offer of fealty to the returning king ignored. Charles broke what unity remained among his former masters by appointing James Sharp from their ranks as Archbishop of St. Andrews. Also that same year, he executed Argyle for his earlier "treasonous conduct." To Charles II, the word *Covenanter* had a sinister meaning. He tried unsuccessfully to eradicate completely the institutionalization of its anti-Erastian sentiments, but the spirit of the National Covenant remained, though by now a lost cause, especially among the Presbyterians in the southwestern Lowlands.[89] For Presbyterian-minded Scots, the years from 1638 to 1690 were times of great expectations followed by depths of sorrow and bitter disappointment over the passing away of their dreams for a Scottish theocracy.[90]

Charles II tried with limited success to dispense indulgences to dissenting preachers, as he hoped such offers to those ministers willing to renounce the Covenants would bring about peaceful unity in his northern kingdom. He also paid the regium donum to dissenting Protestants in Ireland. Despite his efforts, the last three years of his reign (1682 to 1685) were the most troublesome, and the 1680s have even been called the "killing times."[91] According to Leyburn, the killing times after 1679, which was the year that the Covenanters suffered a major defeat at Bothwell Brig, produced massive migrations of dejected Lowland Scots to Ulster.

Dogmatic and impassioned sermons that emphasized apostolic and apocalyptic visions—laced with nationalistic sentiments that sacralized Scotland, its people, and their institutions—affected their perceptions of reality. Regardless of the historicity of the fates of so-called Presbyterian martyrs, those men and women, in the folk memory of the trans–Irish Sea Presbyterian community, were gallant heroes, who sometimes made the ultimate sacrifice in the name of what they believed to be religious freedom for themselves, although it did not mean freedom for others of differing beliefs. Those sentiments were certainly used as propaganda tools by community and religious leaders, who were breaking free of the time-honored model of community power that was being wrested from the hands of the nobility: "If the reformed church . . . did anything to break down the old social ties which had dominated Scotland in the past, it was done in this period (1660 to 1700), and not either at the Reformation or at the time of the National Covenant. The leadership of the nobility was displaced to some extent by the leadership of ministers, but mainly perhaps by the leadership of the area."[92] Local leaders typically served on legal parish sessions, in illegal conventicles, or perhaps, in the cases of some, in both simultaneously.[93]

With an ethnocentric interpretation of the Christian religion and a geopious regard for the home of the Scottish nation, the world of the Scot lay anywhere that the hand of the omnipresent God, through his earthly vassals, led. Just as Abraham led his people from Ur in Mesopotamia in search of the gemeinschaft of Canaan, "the land flowing with milk and honey," or as Moses who led his people from Egypt, so the Scots could suffer a time in Ireland. The overt confidence or national conceit, as it is called by Donaldson, held that Scotland was a blessed kingdom, but such a view was shaken by the political events of the second half of the seventeenth century, causing a rippling diffusion of those geopious sentiments across the Irish Sea.

During times of unusual persecution or adverse environmental conditions brought on by overpopulation and crop failures, apostolic messages from the region's pulpits reassured worried people of their place in God's Providence. Such messages must have been eagerly received, prompting some to seek refuge in Ireland or perhaps to return to Scotland when Providence, as it was believed by Blair and Livingstone, made the opportunity available. The clergy of seventeenth-century Scotland made use of apocalyptic sermons.

> The prevalence of this . . . helps also to explain the motives that lay behind those half-forgotten efforts to bring about a truly reformed ecumene. . . . The blessed truth of the Evangel was not given to every people but only to those with a special mission and charged with leading the way toward Christ's universal kingdom which would be founded upon his universal church. As a result, the loyalties of religious rebels were sometimes directed toward a foreign power, unless and until such time as the religion of the state coincided with their own.[94]

With the nobility and its conservative orientation to preserving the status quo challenged in the southwestern Lowlands, religious leaders of the masses of poor farmers and laborers depended on the use of symbols and imagery (centripetal forces) gleaned from apostolic and prophetic messages to propagate and maintain their positions of power. However, in greater Scotland what served as a unifying symbol for some in the southwest was seen by others outside the region as disuniting, centrifugal forces.

Schismatic Regionalization in Scotland and Ireland

The Irish Sea culture area was heavily influenced by the beliefs of the Puritan Presbyterian followers of Andrew Melville. Even before the Restoration in 1660, the west of Scotland was highly volatile with respect to religion and politics. In 1648, while many in the east and north of Scotland were quite willing to engage with Charles I, the west remained committed to the principles of the Covenants. Several thousand westerners, mostly people of low birth and without the leadership of the nobility, gathered in defiance of the Engagers but were dispersed after a skirmish at Mauchline Moor.[95] In 1666 a rising of Galloway Covenanters culminated in a march on Edinburgh, and like their effort in 1648, it was attempted without the help of the nobility. It ended with their dismal defeat on November 26 at Rullion Green.[96] Charles II alternated between the use of the military to suppress the dissenting groups and more lenient, conciliatory efforts such as indulgences to deposed ministers.

Alexander Peden was born in Ayrshire, educated at the University of Glasgow, and served as minister at New Luce in Galloway from 1658 until his deposition in 1660.[97] He was among the most influential and schismatic ministers deposed during the Restoration. Peden made numerous relocations across the North Channel of the Irish Sea. The Covenanter James Nisbet certainly regarded him as one who was sent to Scotland by the sovereign will of God.[98] Peden, although concerned about moral conduct among the elect, believed that Scotland and Ireland would soon see blood flowing over Scotland's covenanted land for its apostasy.[99] Peden eventually settled into life as a recluse in a cave near the place of his birth, and he died there in 1686. Shortly afterward in 1690, Presbyterianism was made the official polity of the Church of Scotland. While dissenting groups of Covenant supporters such as the Society People remained somewhat active and tolerated in the southwest of Scotland, their appeal was greatly diminished amongst a people tired of religious conflict.[100]

Nonetheless the deposition of ministers at the Restoration can be viewed as empirical evidence that Puritan Presbyterianism made an indelible mark in southwestern Scotland and Northern Ireland and in doing so created a dissenting Irish Sea culture area. It is perhaps logical to assume that when the restored monarchy deposed dissenting ministers throughout Scotland, England, Ireland, and Wales in 1660, regional patterns would reveal a similar rate of deposition for Ireland and the southwest of Scotland. Gordon Donaldson's analysis of dissenting, nonconforming ministers in Scotland can be used as a partial basis for reconstructing the Scottish and Irish religious landscape with respect to dissention in 1660 and 1661. Because of his focus, Donaldson failed to look eastward or attempt an explanation of regional peculiarities in Scotland (compare table 1 below). Instead he compared Scotland's aggregate ministerial nonconformity to that of England, which, he states, was two thousand or "about a fifth of the total number of ministers in that country."[101] On the other hand, the monarchy, Donaldson reports, deposed 270 or 25 percent of Scotland's ministers.

His analysis apparently only considers the difference of five percent (a fifth minus a quarter) between the nonconformity rates for England and Scotland because he concludes that Scotland was not unique in the way it dealt with ecclesiastical nonconformity. Although he admits that the desire for a unified church was sufficiently strong in Scotland to curb ecclesiastical secession among those who held Presbyterian sentiments, Donaldson concludes, "Arithmetic hardly supports the assumption that there was a peculiarly strong antipathy to episcopacy in Scotland."[102] His conclusion that Scotland harbored no noticeably strong antipathy to episcopacy nonetheless begs a deeper, regional analysis that includes data from Ireland and the Presbytery of Ulster.

A regional rank order for the percentages of deposed ministers during the Stuart Restoration shows a closer relationship between Galloway and Ireland than it does between Galloway and Scotland north of the Tay River. A comparison of data from the southwest of Scotland and Ireland with England, which itself may have had regionally variable nonconformity rates, shows that Donaldson's conclusion, although it may be correct in a national comparison between England and Scotland, is insufficient in showing the true spatial pattern that depositions formed across the landscape.

TABLE I. Ranking of regions for deposed ministers in 1660 Scotland

Region	Total number of ministers in region	Number of ministers deposed	Percentage of ministers deposed*
Presbytery of Ulster	72	64	89
Galloway	37	32	86
Glasgow and Ayr	121	75	62
Dumfries	—	—	50–55

TABLE I (*continued*)

Region	Total number of ministers in region	Number of ministers deposed	Percentage of ministers deposed*
Fife	—	—	33
Lothians and the Borders	—	—	<33
North of Tay	—	—	<10

SOURCES: G. Donaldson, *Scotland: James V–James VII,* 365–66; Ulster data, McConnell, *Fasti.*

NOTES: After a review of the data on Scottish depositions in Hew Scott, *Fasti Ecclesiae Scoticanae,* the author concurs with the numbers used by Donaldson. See also the appendix, tables A1 and A2.

*Galloway, Glasgow, and Ayr account for 107— or 40 percent (107/270)— of the ministers deposed in Scotland.

Table 1 shows that regions away from the southwest of Scotland were less likely to have ministers demonstrably inclined to Presbyterianism. In other words, ministers in southwestern Scotland and Ulster were much more likely to be deposed for nonconformity than their colleagues in the eastern and northern areas of the country.

Based on Donaldson's logic, which assumed that England provided a benchmark (rate of deposition stated as "a fifth") and that Scotland showed no strong antipathy toward episcopacy, regions in Scotland would have had the same proportion of deposed ministers. By applying this logic to the data, Scotland should have had only 216 (a fifth) of the country's ministerial staff deposed. The actual number of deposed ministers in Scotland, however, was 270 (fifty-four more ministers or 25 percent more). The same analysis when applied to Ireland produces an expected deposition of only fourteen ministers, but the actual number of sixty-four is over four times greater. Glasgow and Ayr would have deposed only twenty-four divines, and Galloway only seven. Like the Presbytery of Ulster, Galloway deposed more than four times as many, and Glasgow and Ayr deposed over three times as many divines as Donaldson's logic would predict. Stating the differences in terms of regional categorizations makes Donaldson's conclusion seem weak and incomplete.[103]

These analyses demonstrate that the southwest of Scotland and Ulster shared a unique religious characteristic. This pattern provides strong support for the contention that Puritan-Presbyterian mobility in and along the Irish Sea in the seventeenth century created a unique cross-channel community of dissenting Protestants, or Ulster-Scots Land (see map 3).

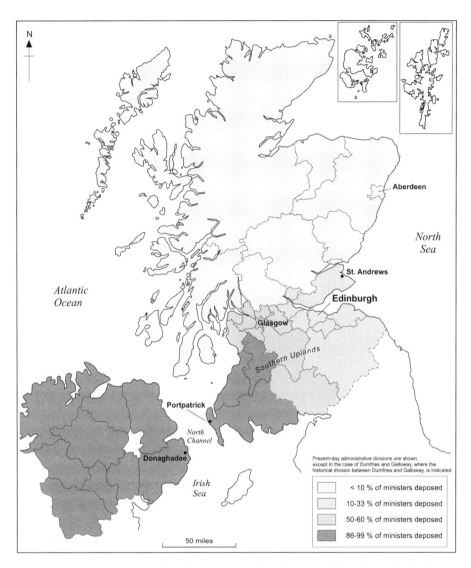

Map 3: *Deposition of Presbyterians in Scotland and Northern Ireland*

The Melvillian Scottish ecclesiastical intelligentsia strongly supported doctrines that placed its members at odds with the Erastian policies of the monarch. Through strict adherence to Old Testament paradigms and the adoption of the "if then, what then" basis of English contract law, the Puritan-Presbyterian element in the Scottish population, heavily concentrated as it was in the southwest of Scotland and in Ulster, became a rigid group, at least until 1690. Their rigidity and uncompromising adherence to the National Covenant and the Solemn League and Covenant throughout most of the later half of the seventeenth century made them vulnerable to government sanctions, which they regarded as religious persecution. Because their geotheological beliefs were tied to the children of Israel, migration or seeking refuge in other lands was a palatable option for many of them. Others, for perhaps a variety of reasons, stayed behind, and a number of the latter took part in illegal conventicles or field meetings that Leyburn contends were brought to the American South. Nonetheless, through the social interchange made possible by the routes traversing the Irish Sea, the culture area took on many of the community's theological and polity orientations. That notion is clearly supported in the pattern of depositions that came to characterize the Irish Sea culture area during the early years of the Stuart Restoration.

*Situated in the densely populated central-belt region,
Stirling, Scotland, is the ancient gateway to the Highlands.*

Scotland's Southern Uplands are a barrier to inland travel.

Ulster's Newcastle is pressed between the high hills of Northern Ireland and the Irish Sea.

*Land-use patterns in Northern Ireland's County Down
have changed little in four hundred years.*

*Located on Scotland's east coast in Fife, St. Andrews is the home of
golf and the site of the country's first university, established in 1411.*

A storm is brewing over the Irish Sea.
Conditions such as these made Robert Blair seasick.

*The Highlands are barely visible on the misty horizon
to the north of County Perth.*

*Like similar land in southern Appalachia, this farm country in the
Scottish Lowlands is devoted primarily to grazing.*

This Protestant farm country is located in County Down in Northern Ireland.

The set for the Passion play in Eureka Springs, Arkansas, is perhaps a cultural link to the outdoor worship services conducted by Presbyterian ministers in Ulster-Scots Land during the seventeenth century.

The Cumberland Gap, the pass across the Cumberland Mountains, was the chief passageway through the central Appalachians during the westward expansion.

These highlands are located in Washington County, Arkansas, about thirty miles from the Oklahoma state line.

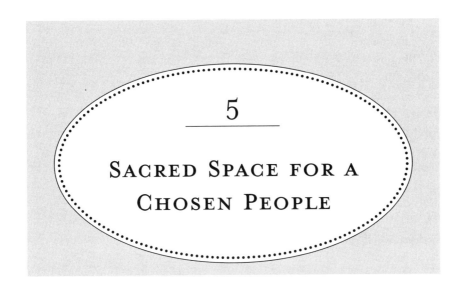

5

SACRED SPACE FOR A CHOSEN PEOPLE

Geographers such as John K Wright and E. G. Bowen pay particular attention to space, including people's attitudes and feelings toward it. When communities and nations regard space as sacred, they do so because these areas are inextricably linked to their worship of the divine, a concept that Wright captures in his term *geotheology*.[1] David George Mullan quite effectively refers to its manifestations in Scotland as national divinity.[2] The spaces that contain networks of worship, for example, people scattered across land or sea, could likewise be imbued with sacred qualities. It is difficult to read the Scots Confession, the National Covenant, or any number of letters or autobiographies of seventeenth-century Scottish ministers and not see the depth to which they regarded their nation and land as uniquely chosen by God for his Providence. The rigidness of Puritanism gave its English and Scottish adherents added incentive to develop such notions about their nations and homelands. When they felt oppressed or excluded from political power, they were also prone to desacralize them. When they experienced feelings such as these, relocating or going into exile was to them a justifiable response to unpleasant secular situations.[3]

Scottish Puritanism took on national importance between 1590 and 1638, and, Mullan also points out, Scottish Puritans encouraged, if not directed, the drafting and signing of the National Covenant. The rise of Puritanism was in part a reaction to monarchical efforts to remake the Kirk in the image of the Church of England, for these years roughly correspond to the period of the first episcopacy (1610 to 1638) when its theology was firmly Calvinist.[4]

The National Covenant was certainly a pledge seething with geotheo-logical attributes, and its impact was felt all across Britain and Ireland.[5] Fuelling intense loyalty to the National Covenant was a "national conceit with a theological foundation."[6] Along with migrating ministers who were recruited to Ulster by Scottish planters, such as William Edmonston, James Hamilton (Lord Claneboy), and Hugh Montgomery, as well as Church of Ireland bishops such as Andrew Knox of Raphoe, their belief system, including ideas about sacred people and lands, diffused to Ireland more than a decade before the formation of the Army Presbytery in 1642. This was accomplished through no less than the ministerial efforts of Robert Blair, Edward Brice, Henry Colwart, Robert Cunningham, George Dunbar, James Glenndinning, James Hamilton, John Livingstone, John Ridge, and Josias Welsh.[7] Through institutional and social networks, at least 125 other highly literate divines from Scotland followed them and served in Irish Presbyterian congregations between 1642 and 1690.[8] These sentiments also spread to America and took deep root in the South. At any rate, while in Ulster, the earliest ministers cut their teeth on what they perceived was political oppression, reinforcing their sense of being persecuted for the sake of righteousness.[9] When the Church of Ireland deposed Blair, Dunbar, Hamilton, and Livingstone, the men relocated to Scotland in 1638 where widespread resistance (though not in the north and northeast) to the Erastian policies of Charles I provided them with public forums from which to speak.[10] From a number of pulpits, includ-ing some in Edinburgh, the ministers fed their parishioners a steady diet of sermons that some felt were "foolish and seditious."[11] Their protesta-tions no doubt added fuel to the movement that led to the signing of the National Covenant.[12]

Scottish geotheology helped form Ulster-Scots Land, the new dissent-ing culture area that stretched across the Irish Sea. From 1632 to 1690 at least seventy Presbyterian ministers in Ireland relocated to Scotland.[13] All but two divines—Colwart and Ridge—were born and/or educated in Scotland. Other Scottish ministers also served in Ireland on a temporary basis, which was especially true during the 1640s when a number of Scottish ministers provided short-term service in the fledgling Army Pres-bytery, renamed the Presbytery of Ulster in 1646.[14] John Livingstone, despite being fully employed as a minister at Stranraer and Ancrum (Wig-tonshire and Roxburghshire, respectively), returned to Ireland to conduct services in 1643, 1645, 1646, 1648, 1654, and 1656.[15]

To appreciate fully the influence of Scottish Presbyterians in this new Irish Sea culture area, it is important to examine their geotheological beliefs and doctrinal positions that set them and their theocratic world view involving church autonomy at odds with the increasingly Erastian policies of the Stuarts. Those conflicting paradigms of authority encouraged disruptive behaviors that brought political forces down on a number of their most charismatic and influential leaders. Others of less renown, like Andrew MacCormick, returned to Scotland after ministering in Ulster. He took part in the Covenanter march on Edinburgh in 1666 and was killed en route at the Battle of Rullion Green.[16] Nevertheless, for some ministers whose appointment in Ulster was intended to be lengthy, if not permanent, an opportunity to return to Scotland was seen as a situation prescribed to them by a sovereign God, even if the catalyst for their return was facilitated by a political policy and its implementation.

Scottish Geotheology

Images of Scotland's geotheological place in sacred history reinforced a sense of nationhood among most Scots, including those who adhered to beliefs associated with Puritan-Presbyterianism.[17] There was a psychological reason for the people living in such a small country on the periphery of Europe to sacralize themselves and their land: "Scotland might be a small and poor nation but, mysteriously, she had been specially favoured by God to provide a model for others."[18] Piotr Wandycz makes a similar observation with respect to small, peripheral nations: to compensate for a sense of weakness, these nations look for ways to glorify their national history and promote a sense of national uniqueness.[19] Mullan responds to Wandycz, "For Scotland, this sense was exacerbated by its northerly setting. Antiquity portrayed the north as a dangerous, unruly, even satanic place."[20] Being in the north of Europe and on the northwest coast of Great Britain, residents of the Irish Sea coastal area arguably had an intense psychological need for adopting exalted national ideas.

With respect to geotheology and its spread throughout the dissenting Irish Sea culture area, coastal settlements have historically served as the last bastions of culture and "function both as places of refuge and as stepping-stones of coastal diffusion."[21] Along with migrating ministers, Scottish geotheology spread across the North Channel and into Ulster and later into America.

Ministers' sermons greatly expanded their congregations' appreciation of their nation's role in prophetic and apostolic events in the creation of sacred history. Literature expanded the intellectual and spiritual reference points and hence the communities of imagination of Blair and his colleagues. Through instruction and community visits, they could likewise expand the world of the lowly member in the private space of home. The ideas and social role models, such as biblical figures, presented to the

parishioner were served on a platter garnished with Reformed and Covenant theology and seasoned with participatory polity ideals. James Leyburn describes the theological imagination of the seventeenth-century
Scot who saw Scotland as part of Palestine's biblical community:

> Like most Europeans, he believed that God had created the world
> only a few thousand years before, with each species of creature
> suddenly and uniquely formed and fixed, as the book of Genesis
> affirmed. The hand of God could be seen in personal and national
> calamities, for God intervened in history now, as always, to punish
> sin. Heaven and hell were tangible realities, whose details could be
> known from scripture and whose glories or torments had been made
> even more vivid as the creative imagination developed them in thou-
> sands of sermons. . . . The Hebrews of the Old Testament had been
> much like the Scots in their constant warfare, their pride, their pre-
> carious life in a poor country with dangerous neighbors, their strug-
> gle against idolatry (for Baal read popery). The very images of
> scriptures applied as much to Scotland as to Palestine: the shep-
> herds, flowers of the field, mighty fortresses, the woman who had
> lost a coin. Scots were no more seafarers than the Hebrews; yet they
> fished, as did the men of Galilee, and they knew the danger of sud-
> den squalls blowing down on their lochs.[22]

For many Lowland Scots, February 28, 1638, was "the glorious marriage day of the Kingdom with God."[23] That day marked the beginning
of the signing of the Scottish National Covenant. Members of the Scottish ecclesiastical intelligentsia, in which returning Ulster ministers who
had been deposed by Lord Deputy Thomas Wentworth certainly belonged, had high expectations and standards for the Scottish nation. The
National Covenant was sacred to them. It signified God's sovereignty and
election of Scotland as "the original godly nation—even before England
and Rome."[24] It also signified Scotland's geoteleological place, a perception among seventeenth-century divines of the nation's relationship to
Providential end-times scenarios in fulfillment of sacred history.[25] As
Archibald Johnston and Alexander Henderson wrote in the National
Covenant of 1638, Scotland and its Kirk would lead all kirks in defending the true faith:

> Each one of us under-written, protest, That, after long and due
> examination of our own consciences in matters of true and false reli-
> gion, we are now thoroughly resolved in the truth by the word and
> Spirit of God: and therefore we believe with our hearts, confess with

our mouths, subscribe with our hands, and constantly affirm, before God and the whole world, that this only is the true Christian faith and religion, pleasing God, and bringing salvation to man, which now is, by the mercy of God, revealed to the world by the preaching of the blessed evangel; and is received, believed, and defended by many and sundry notable kirks and realms, but chiefly by the Kirk of Scotland, the King's Majesty, and three estates of this realm, as God's eternal truth, and only ground of our salvation; as more particularly is expressed in the Confession of our Faith, established and publickly confirmed by sundry acts of Parliaments, and now of a long time hath been openly professed by the King's Majesty, and whole body of this realm both in burgh and land.[26]

The Confession of faith that is referenced in this passage from the National Covenant is the King's Confession, or the Negative Confession, that was subscribed by James VI in 1581. The Negative Confession draws its theological sinew from the Scots Confession of 1560.[27]

The authors of the Scots Confession claimed for their Kirk a special place in the history of the true church of Christ, and they believed that future generations would look back to the example of the Scottish Kirk in the same manner that they would behold the first-generation churches established by the Apostle Paul. Backed by the belief of the continuity with Old Testament Israel, the reformers believed "the temple here is not tied to place or to the institutions of history. It is the blessed society, which was wondrously joined to Jesus Christ. It is the Church as community which takes the place of the Old Testament people."[28] Their logic, to which Thomas F. Torrance points, reflects a peculiar understanding of the concept of institutionalized sacred history. It suggests that fifteen hundred years of church history meant little to Scotland's reforming Kirk leaders. The Scottish Reformers saw themselves as directly connected to the people of the Old Testament as if sacred history was suspended after the resurrection of Christ until their time. From what John Knox and his colleagues delineated in the Scots Confession, it is clear that they believed the characters and events of the New Testament, especially the ministry of the Apostle Paul, served to connect the Old Testament people to the Scots reformers, who would in turn pass on the Gospel for future generations to achieve the fulfillment of God's Providence:

> Then wherever these notes are seen and continue for any time, be the number complete or not, there, beyond any doubt, is the true Kirk of Christ, who, according to his promise, is in its midst. This is

not that universal Kirk of which we have spoken before but particular, such as was in Corinth, Ephesus, Galatia, and other places where the ministry was planted by Paul and which he himself called Kirks of God. Such Kirks, we the inhabitants of the realm of Scotland confessing Christ Jesus, do claim to have in our cities, towns, and reformed districts because of the doctrine taught in our Kirks, contained in the written Word of God, that is, the Old and New Testaments, in those books which were originally reckoned canonical.[29]

Like the National Covenant, the Scots Confession, which was the founding Reformed document in the kingdom and written seventy-eight years earlier, provides a vivid illustration of the ministers' sense of their place in sacred history. Furthermore, because of the widespread support for the National Covenant, the divines who made up the Scottish ecclesiastical intelligentsia and their parishes in the southwest of the Lowlands swore oaths of loyalty to documents that stressed Scotland's role in the continuity of sacred history. As a participant in the unfolding drama of sacred history, that is, salvation history, the land holding the Scottish people and their Kirk also became sacred, although Knox arguably saw Reformed Scotland as a pathetic place—a form of desacralization consistent with some of the later remarks by Samuel Rutherford.[30]

The National Covenant, stressing geoteleological and geopious feelings, also marks a clear change in the tone of sentiments among ministers in Scotland and their perception of the nation's place in sacred history. It struck a resounding chord among the Presbyterian leaders of the Scottish ecclesiastical intelligentsia. A good number of committed Episcopalians who had similar feelings toward their land, especially those in the northeast, did not sign the Covenant. In 1628, William Struther, a minister with Presbyterian sympathies, wrote that the Scots made up a "sinfull nation," and as a result, God had a great controversy with Scotland.[31] Just before the summer, 1637, Church revolt at St. Giles Cathedral in Edinburgh against Laud's Liturgy, which protesters believed to be the start of a return to papacy and which led to the signing in 1638 of the National Covenant, Rutherford referred to the Scottish Kirk as his "harlot church mother."[32] Also in 1637, the staunch Presbyterian George Gillespie expressed his dismay with his Kirk and nation.

> The Church of Scotland was blessed with more glorious and perfect reformation than any of our neighbour churches. The doctrine, discipline, regiment, and policy are established here by ecclesiastical and civil laws, and sworn and subscribed unto by the king's majesty. . . . But now, alas! Even this church, which was once so great a praise in

the earth, is deeply corrupted, and has "turned aside quickly out of the way." (Exod. 32:8) So that this is the Lord's controversy against Scotland: "I had planted thee a noble vine, wholly a right seed; how then art thou turned into the degenerate plant of a strange vine unto me."[33] (Jer. 2:21)

From a geotheological perspective, these Scottish divines, like their English Puritan counterparts, were capable of desacralizing the land of their birth, making it easier to emigrate.[34] They were also keen to resacralize it, which provided the justification to return. Rutherford remarked in 1633, which were more optimistic times, "Scotland whom the Lord took off the dunghill and out of hell and made a fair bride to Himself. . . . He will embrace both [of] us, the little young sister, and the elder sister, the Church of the Jews."[35]

The National Covenant movement provided fodder for geotheological sentiments that reinforced the Scottish national conceit. After the National Covenant was signed, Rutherford aired this thought to his country and nation, "Now, O Scotland, God be thanked thy name is in the Bible."[36] Archibald Johnston, in his diary, was jubilant: "The desire of true knowledge wrought by it [the National Covenant] in the hearts of the people may approve it bee a speciall meane appointed by God for reclaiming this Nation to himself. . . . Thou haist confirmed to thyselth the people of Scotland to be a people unto thee for ever (according to thy servands Wischart, Knoxs, praedictions) and thou, Lord, art becom thair God."[37] In expressing a degree of amazement yet tempered by a touch of national humility at his country's lofty place in salvation history, Alexander Henderson wondered how and why God would choose wicked Scotland as his dwelling place over some mighty nation.[38] Scotland's favored position in Providence, however, was based on merit earned in satisfying the nation's bilateral covenant with God. Rutherford feared that God would leave Scotland for "an inn where He will be better entertained."

The National Covenant supported the polity that underlies the Melvillian idea of two kingdoms and supported the theology expressed in the Scots Confession of 1560.[39] As made clear in the National Covenant by Henderson and Johnston and by the many people who supported it, their sentiments ran against the bishopric as a control office of episcopacy. It is clear that the body that made final decisions or "determinations" with respect to ecclesiastical matters was the General Assembly and not the king's bishops:

> The article of this covenant, which was at the first subscription referred to the determination of the General Assembly, being now

determined; and thereby the five articles of Perth, the government of the kirk by bishops, and the civil places and power of kirkmen, upon the reasons and grounds contained in the Acts of the General Assembly, declared to be unlawful within this kirk, we subscribe according to the determination aforesaid.[40]

The followers of Andrew Melville were deeply committed to the National Covenant and the vision that Scotland was a critical and important component in God's plan for universal yet limited redemption.[41] In discussing the Kirk and its place in sacred history, Johnston of Wariston observed that there was a "verrie near parallel betwixt Izrael and this churche, the only two suorne nations to the Lord."[42]

Even the English Puritan Thomas Brightman was convinced that the Scottish Kirk had geoteleological significance. In connecting historical churches with the sixth church of Revelation, Philadelphia, the church on which God will write "New Jerusalem," Brightman included "the Church of Helvetia, Suevia, Geneve, France, Scotland."[43] Johnston of Wariston declared, "Scotland, like Israel, was God's chosen land, and its people, like the Israelites, were God's chosen people."[44] The anti-Erastian, geopious, and geoteleological beliefs of Melville's followers are important to consider because "this is what the likes of Blair, Dickson, and Rutherford and countless other ministers [in the southwest] preached, and this is what their flock fervently believed."[45] Rutherford's vacillating appraisal of the Kirk's ability to fulfill its role in Providence also shows a readiness to desacralize the institutions of the land of his birth in the same manner as English Puritans.

During the later decades of the seventeenth century, those Covenanters who remained in Scotland were described as "fanatics."[46] Although the Covenant cause certainly was a lost one and the actions of the "fanatical Covenanters" may seem impractical, even foolish, those who believed in the oaths of sacred covenants held their words to be indissoluble and perpetual.[47] The National Covenant made provisions for perpetual obligations to its stipulations.

Being convinced in our minds, and confessing with our mouths, that the present and succeeding generations in this land are bound to keep the foresaid national oath and subscription inviolable. . . . That with our whole heart we agree, and resolve all the days of our life constantly to adhere unto and to defend the foresaid true religion, and (forbearing the practice of all innovations already introduced in the matters of the worship of God, or approbation of the corruptions of the publick government of the kirk, or civil places and power of kirkmen, till they be tried and allowed in free Assemblies and in Parliament) to labour, by all means lawful, to recover the purity and liberty of the Gospel, as it was established and professed before the foresaid novations.[48]

In the spirit of bilateral covenants, the National Covenant made references to oaths and to the consequences of failing to abide by them. The framers and supporters of the document believed in the sovereignty of God, his use of human conscience in understanding truth, and his final judgment of human actions and Christian works.

> We therefore, willing to take away all suspicion of hypocrisy, and of such double dealing with God, and his kirk, protest, and call the Searcher of all hearts for witness, that our minds and hearts do fully agree with this our Confession, promise, oath, and subscription: so that we are not moved with any worldly respect, but are persuaded only in our conscience, through the knowledge and love of God's true religion imprinted in our hearts by the Holy Spirit, as we shall answer to him in the day when the secrets of all hearts shall be disclosed.[49]

The National Covenant, which mostly points out what is not acceptable to the "true religion" as articulated in the Scots Confession and the King's Confession, was backed up by strong, militant oaths that invited martyrdom or political exile for some who fully supported the document.

> And therefore, from the knowledge and conscience of our duty to God, to our King and country, without any worldly respect or inducement, so far as human infirmity will suffer, wishing a further measure of the grace of God for this effect; we promise and swear, by the GREAT NAME OF THE LORD OUR GOD, to continue in the profession and obedience of the foresaid religion; and that we shall defend the same, and resist all these contrary errors and corruptions, according to our vocation, and to the uttermost of that power that God hath put in our hands, all the days of our life.[50]

Theologians in the Scottish ecclesiastical intelligentsia believed it was of the utmost importance to keep covenants with God, especially as the country was seeking restoration from being a "sinfull nation."[51] Many ministers previous to the signing of National Covenant believed that Scotland had experienced decay in piety and religion.[52] Robert Rollock feared that if Scotland fell from grace, God would not give her a second chance.[53] It was imperative to keep and defend the true religion as defined in the National Covenant and its supporting documents, for, as Rutherford admonished, "The breaking of the staff is the breaking of the covenant: the staff itself is the word of God and covenant."[54] Struther warned the people of Scotland that their sense of "securitie" was "odious to God" and that they must not assume that he would "dwell with obstinate and impenitent sinners, whom his soule abhorreth: & to keepe his covenant with them who proudlie breake it."[55]

In the midst of the political turmoil of the 1630s that led to the signing of the National Covenant, the emerging Puritan ethos added a Providential, geoteleological flavor to all events and gave validity to the belief that the Scots and their land would be used by God in his Providence. Although the events leading to the signing of the National Covenant as well as the consequences of that event were mostly of a political nature, the ministers working in the trans–Irish Sea community of Puritan-Presbyterians saw them as the unfolding of God's plan. Those forces and their interpretation increased the numbers of the community's impassioned leaders and potential martyrs as well as its absorption of Ulster into the sacred space occupied by Presbyterian Scots.

In the Trans–Irish Sea Culture Area

Through social contacts and relocation, beliefs about the sacredness of the Scottish nation diffused to the north of Ireland with manifestations of geopious and even geoteleological attributes. Robert Blair believed that Providence was at work in bringing ministers and members of congregations alike to Ireland, and that, in addition to himself and a few other godly people, "The Lord was also pleased to bring over from Scotland, Mr. Josias Welsh. . . . I meeting with him in Scotland and perceiving of how weak a body and of how zealous a spirit he was, exhorted him to haste over to Ireland, where he would find work enough, and, I hoped, success enough."[56] Blair also felt the same way about George Dunbar's situation, which was clearly precipitated by political events.

> Also, the Lord brought over to Lern (Larne) the ancient servant of Christ, Mr. George Dunbar, who was deposed from the ministry of Ayr by the High Commission of Scotland, and by the Council was banished to Ireland. So careful was the Lord, and bountiful towards that Plantation of his in the north of Ireland, that whoever wanted, they might not want.[57]

Dunbar's arrival in Ireland, incidentally, was the only reliable example of a Scottish minister resettling on the island because he was banished to it.[58]

Nevertheless, as far as Puritan-Presbyterians were concerned, the north of Ireland, like Scotland, took on geotheological significance.

Once in Ulster and seeing the land and their roles on it as part of the Divine plan, Scottish ministers were quick to recruit others into their ranks of Erastian-opposing Presbyterian leaders whose geographic region transcended both shores of the Irish Sea. Although John Livingstone was offered a charge at Killinchy, which was under the supervision of the bishop of Down, Lord Claneboy (James Hamilton) sent him to Bishop Andrew Knox of Raphoe for ordination.[59] The bishop of Raphoe, wrote Livingstone, "told me he knew my errand, that I came to him because I had scruples against Episcopacy and ceremonies, according as Mr. Josias Welsh and some others had done before; and that he thought his old age was prolonged for little other purpose but to do such offices."[60] Lord Claneboy's nephew James Hamilton, who served his uncle as chamberlain, was another recruit. As Blair described Hamilton's recruitment, "Mr. Cunningham and I put him to private essays of his gift, and being satisfied therewith, invited him to preach publicly at Bangor in his uncle's hearing, he knowing nothing until he saw him in the pulpit. . . . But having heard him publicly, he put great respects upon him that day."[61] Like Blair, the nephew Hamilton later moved to Scotland and became involved in the adoption of the National Covenant. Also like Blair, Hamilton was among the Scots who returned to Ireland to help establish the Army Presbytery.[62]

As a cultural area with common geotheological beliefs, political dissension was bound to happen because the monarchy held an opposing view of ecclesiastical and social power. Many of the divines and common folk in this community agreed with Andrew Melville's assertion that the king was "but a member"[63] in the Lord's kingdom. This view was incorporated into the polity stressed in the National Covenant, and it certainly went against the will of Charles I, who, like his more astute father, wanted to keep the power of the church under his control. Even though James had been seemingly less obstinate than Charles, he was adamant about his place in ecclesiastical affairs: "A Scottish Presbytery as well fitteth with the monarchy as God and the Devil."[64] The king also cried, "No bishop, no King!"[65] Because of the political ineptness of Charles I and his deputies in Ireland, they created a reverse migration flow of deposed, politically oppressed divines who reinforced and strengthened their commonly held views of oppression for righteousness sake. This process of diffusion added fuel to the Covenanter strife in Scotland generally and the southwest specifically,[66] and "on the eve of the National Covenant such radical ideas as would emerge shortly resided only in the minds of a few. However, the pulpit soon overcame its reticence in 1638, influenced by those who had cut their teeth on the oppression they had experienced in Ireland."[67] However, the majority of the ministers in Ulster during Wentworth's purges of dissenting divines from the Church of Ireland actually conformed.

Those returning ministers certainly reinforced the established beliefs in the sovereignty of God. For instance, when Livingstone and Blair returned to Scotland in 1637, they were asked by David Dickson to preach from his pulpit at Irvine. However, Livingstone learned that a local man had warned Dickson not to allow the Ulster divines to preach in his pulpit for fear that the bishops would put him out of his ministry. He told Dickson that they did not want to cause him trouble. Dickson declared, according to Livingstone, "I dare not follow their opinion so far to dis-countenance you in your sufferings, as not to employ you as in former times, but would think rather so doing would provoke the Lord, that I might be on another account deposed, and not have so good a con-science."[68] Dickson and Livingstone feared God's sovereign rule more than that of the magistrate.

Livingstone's return to Scotland followed a chain of events that con-vinced him and other Ulster Presbyterians of their role in God's plan for their nation. In February 1634, John Livingstone and William Wallace, Livingstone's boyhood teacher who had relocated to Ireland, were selected by Irish friends to visit New England to determine the suitability of resettling there.[69] The two men planned to set sail from Ireland for London with the intention of making an Atlantic crossing from the south of England in the spring. Wallace was two days late in joining Living-stone, during which time the weather was fair. However, upon arrival at their point of departure, Livingstone and Wallace were then delayed for a fortnight because of contrary winds. When they arrived in England, all but three ships had left for America. Again, contrary winds arose and delayed their departure for nearly two weeks. Wallace fell ill and was advised by doctors not to go to sea. Friends also advised Livingstone not to go alone, so they returned to Ireland. "When we were coming back," Livingstone wrote, "I told him I apprehended that we would get our lib-erty in Ireland: and accordingly when we came, we found that we four who had been deposed were restored by the Deputy's letter in May 1634."[70] Despite their reinstatement lasting for only six months, Living-stone happily believed that his initial attempt to reach America was redi-rected by God: "Therein I perceived, howbeit I trust the Lord did accept and approve our intentions, yet wonderfully he stopped our designs."[71]

In 1636, Blair and Robert Hamilton, like Livingstone, had little prospect of being reinstated in their Ulster charges. They convinced each
other to attempt another Ulster-Scots resettlement in the New World.[72]
The ill-fated crossing nearly cost them their lives. The raging seas that
caused the failure of the party, which included 140 of their Ulster followers, to reach New England on board a ship called the *Eaglewing* was
interpreted by them as a sign of God's desire for them to work to achieve
a Christian society in Ireland that would eventually affect Scotland as
political circumstances allowed. By so naming their ship, the leaders of
the group hoped to claim God's promise that is referred to in Exodus
19:1–8.[73] The adoption of the name *Eaglewing* for the ship that would
have carried them into the wilderness of North America was consistent
with the English Puritan use of the words *wings* and *wilderness* in reference to seeking exile during times of oppression.[74]

To Robert Blair, William Row, and John Livingstone, the potentially
calamitous consequences awaiting them if they had continued their
Atlantic crossing made returning to Ireland seem theologically clear. To
the members of their community, God ordained the storms that caused
them to turn back on the high seas. Being similarly convinced of God's
plan for their earthly work, many English Puritans undertook passage
into the wilderness of North America. Unlike their English counterparts
who had successfully desacralized England, making it easier to leave the
land of their birth, the geotheological importance of Scotland and to a
lesser extent of Ulster arguably kept deposed Presbyterian divines near
their sacred land and people. Their perception of the returning *Eaglewing* and its passengers as they came in sight of the Irish coast is described by Blair's son-in-law William Row.

> When they came near to Ireland, they began to consult what to
> do for the future. The major part inclined to set to sea again the
> next spring, beseeming themselves that they set to sea, the winter
> approaching; but Mr. Blair said, that though he was the last man
> that was induced to return, yet they having made a fair offer, not
> only of their service, but of themselves to God, to spread and propa-
> gate the gospel in America, and the Lord had accepted their offer,
> yea, and of themselves, he thought they had done enough to testify
> their willing mind to glorify God; and for himself, he for the present
> resolved never to make a new attempt, seeing the Lord, by such
> speaking providences and dispensations, had made it evident to them
> that it was not his will they should glorify him in America, he having
> work for them at home. All the company of passengers hearing Mr.

> Blair thus express himself, both ministers and others were of his
> mind.[75]

Like Livingstone and Row, Blair was convinced of God's Providential plans
for Ireland, England, and Scotland.

> As the Lord has given us a wonderful proof of his omnipotence and
> kindness to us in stilling the noise of the seas and the noise of their
> waves, so shall the Lord as evidently give us proof of his sovereignty
> and dominion over the unruly spirits and tempers of wicked people,
> in stilling and calming the tumults of the wicked people to whom
> we are going, and among whom we are to live a space.[76]

Row expressed the view that God made a way for their work to continue in Scotland. Row's reflection shows their belief that political events
were caused by God in accordance with his plan.

> The Lord fulfilled the word of his servant that not only the wicked;
> yea, the prelates and their followers were much dismayed and feared
> at their return. But neither the prelates and conformists, nor they
> themselves, knew that within a year [by the end of 1638] the Lord
> would not only root out the prelates in Scotland, and after that out
> of England and Ireland, but make some of them, especially Messrs
> Blair, Livingstone, and Maclellan, &c., to be very instrumental in the
> work of the reformation.[77]

Livingstone assessed his return to Scotland: "It pleased the Lord to bring
he and his family safely to Lochryan and Stranraer."[78] To Livingstone, this
experience, coming on the heels of all the other portentous events that he
and his colleagues had experienced, was solid confirmation of Scotland's
place in salvation history, for on a trip to London three years earlier,
Alexander Leighton, an English Puritan, had prophesied to him: "He was
confident of the downfall of the bishops in Scotland; which came to passe
within three years."[79]

Despite relocating to Scotland where he and his colleagues contributed to the National Covenant movement, which Row called "the
work of the reformation," Livingstone remained committed to ministering to Scots living on both shores of the North Channel of the Irish Sea.
In 1638, he was presented with several employment opportunities in
Scotland. Faced with a choice in selecting a pulpit, he consulted with six
divines whom he felt understood true religion. Although he was first
inclined to move to Straiton, Livingstone wrote, "They all [his advisers]
having heard both parties, advised me to hearken to the call of Stranraer,

being a thoroughfare way within four miles of Portpatrick, and so nearer for the advantage of our people in Ireland."[80] His advisers were David Dickson, Samuel Rutherford, Robert Blair, William Livingstone (his father), Alexander Henderson, and Andrew Cant.[81] Livingstone's mentioning of "our people" indicates that a fair portion of Scotland's leading Presbyterian divines recognized the existence of a Scots-Irish community of Presbyterians. Indeed, Livingstone regarded the Scots who lived on both shores of the North Channel or in Atlantic-facing areas such as Derry and Donegal as residents of one community and believed that he was called by God to minister to both southwestern and Scots-Irish portions of it. In the summer of 1656, he visited Killinchy and made a number of trips to Dublin. A church session in Dublin offered him a stipend of two hundred pounds sterling per year to entice him to stay on as its minister. Livingstone recalled, "I was not loosed from Ancrum, and if I had been, I was resolved rather to settle at Killinchy, among the Scots in the north [Ulster], than anywhere else."[82] Livingstone clearly regarded the people who lived on both shores of the North Channel as residents of one community and that he was called by God to minister to them.

Although reinstated in Scotland, he was deposed in 1662 by Charles II, went into exile, and died in Rotterdam, The Netherlands, in 1672.[83] His death in exile made a martyr out of him. As such, in the eyes of the southwest's post-Restoration Covenanters, his example encouraged their notion of trans–Irish Sea migration for the sake of religious expression, if not theocratic impulses with political consequences.

Like Livingstone, Rutherford was convinced of God's Providence in the personal lives of people as well as their communities and realms. To Rutherford, the southwest of Scotland was especially geoteleological. In a June 16, 1637, letter to William Dalgleish, Rutherford expressed a belief that the Lord was using Galloway to "make a new kirk unto himself."[84] Rutherford also believed that Scotland's role in Providence would be shaped by punishment, so less than a month after writing to Dalgleish, he presented a letter to his parishioners at Anwoth in Galloway warning them that "heavy, sad and sore is that stroke of the Lord's wrath that is coming upon Scotland. Woe, woe, woe to this harlot-land."[85] With the parishioners in Galloway fed a diet of geoteleological expositions on their place in sacred history, it is easy to understand how the later Covenanter movement found fertile soil on the eastern shores of the Irish Sea culture area.

With the encouragement of numerous offers of indulgences to deposed ministers, a number of the region's divines were ready to give up forcing their beliefs upon a nation that was relatively content with compromises over polity issues, for governance structure probably made little difference to the average parishioner. The merciless campaigns of the Covenanters during the Civil War, together with their threats to those social classes who traditionally held power, contributed much to the Covenanters' inability to capture a wide appeal in Scotland.[86] Nonetheless, the southwest of Scotland remained a schismatic region. The geoteleological aspects of Scottish national conceit were carried no higher than when a Covenanter during this time remarked, "Scotland is the betrothed Virgin: We are espoused to Jesus Christ, and joined to Him, by a marriage covenant, never to be forgotten."[87] With the Sanquhar Declaration on June 22, 1680 in which the Covenanting element of the population in the southwest declared itself to be the true representatives of the Presbyterian church and the covenanted country, the government, following its Erastian impulses, had little choice but to suppress the movement with more ruthlessness than was shown in prior efforts that featured numerous offers of indulgences to nonconforming divines.[88] Still, the pervasive belief that God had a special plan for Scotland was maintained. In 1683, at the height of the "killing times,"[89] James Renwick, the young and highly controversial leader of the southwest's Covenanters, wrote these geopious thoughts about both his country and God's orientation toward it.

> The Lord is wonderfully to be seen in every thing and assists in what he calls unto; for, in coming through the country, we had two field meetings, which made me think, that if the Lord could be tied to any place, it is to the mosses and moors of Scotland.[90]

Despite Renwick's geopious perception of Scotland's landscape, a new era of intense repression began. Partisans and innocent people alike were forced to submerge into a sea of peasantry that prevailed across Scotland's southwestern Lowlands:[91] "Hard pressed by the official church, often stripped of their livings, such men had become itinerant preachers, taking refuge with their equally fierce Presbyterian Scots brethren in Ulster [where dissenting expressions of Protestantism were tolerated], across the North Channel."[92] Likewise when circumstances in Ireland became unpleasant or when circumstances in Scotland permitted, those who fled to Ireland from Scotland would reverse their sails and venture back across the Irish Sea.[93] They were now outlaws everywhere and were an embarrassment to the Ulster Presbytery because it was keen to show loyalty to the monarchy. The nonpartisan resident in the region was also compelled by the government and his/her own neighbors to keep a low profile or leave.[94] It is, of course, difficult to know how many people immigrated to Ireland simply to stay out of the fray.[95]

In the 1680s Alexander Shields became a leading minister in the region. He held that Scotland was sacred land and its people blessed. In London during January 1685, he preached a sermon entitled "Naphtali is a Hind Let Loose," in which he "equated those suffering in south-west Scotland to the tribe of Naphtali—born with great wrestling, blessed with God's [favor] and beautiful Word, promised lands south and west of the Sea of Galilee, and connected to Judah at the Jordan towards the rising sun."[96] The Irish Sea, too, took on the sacred, geotheological qualities of the Sea of Galilee.[97] The waterway facilitated the perpetuation of interactive social networks among dissenting Presbyterians.

That trans–Irish Sea social networks existed was not dismissed by some among the forces of Charles II who sought to silence conventiclers. In 1682 James Nisbet, a covenanted minister in the southwest of Scotland, was discovered by dragoons after they carefully crafted a deceptive ploy to find him. Upon arriving in Nisbet's home village in the southwest of Scotland, a young soldier shed his military garb, dressed as a woman, and went into the village where he asked residents for help in finding his cousin James Nisbet. The would-be woman assured people that "she" was the preacher's cousin from Ireland and that she was sent by Nisbet's Irish family and friends to offer him refuge among them. Nisbet wrote in his memoirs, "A fair well-favoured young man, in women's clothes, like a gentle-woman, giving out that she was a cousin of our own from Ireland . . . gained credit amongst our friends who knew where we were."[98] Ploys such as this were necessary because of the close-knit and protective nature of the communities in the southwest where trans–Irish Sea kinship and religious ties served as cohesive glue to bind social units together.[99] It also suggests that observers of that community during the last half of the seventeenth century understood the trans–Irish Sea nature of it and were prepared to exploit its structure to their advantage.

According to Nisbet in *Private Life*, on April 26, 1685, "It pleased God in his good providence to send that great man Mr. Alexander Peden to the gentleman's house where I was." The next day, Nisbet records that Peden spoke at great length about the application of biblical truths to the present time. After he finished, Peden seemed to go into a meditative state. "Then with great emotion of spirit, [he] broke silence and said with a loud voice, 'Cursed be those in the name of the Lord that speak of my being come to Scotland' (for he was but come from Ireland a few weeks before)." As it turned out, Nisbet learned afterward that "a wicked, malicious woman did, at the same very hour that he pronounced the curse upon her, go and inform the enemy . . . where he was."[100] Like Nisbet, Peden was chased by dragoons from that and many other places.

Although Nisbet and Peden successfully eluded the king's justice, Nisbet's father, John Nisbet, was not as fortunate. He was executed in the Grassmarket at Edinburgh on December 4, 1685.[101] Prior to his execution, John Nisbet wrote a letter to the Countess of Loudoun, and after mounting the scaffold he gave a testimony in which he warned that the "Covenanted God of Scotland hath a dreadful storm of wrath provided, which he will surely pour out suddenly and unexpectedly like a thunderbolt upon these covenanted lands, for their perfidy, treachery, and woeful apostasy."[102]

Similarly Alexander Peden predicated that a seven-year famine would strike the land for Scotland's apostasy.[103] The famine of the late 1690s must have convinced some residents of the southwest that God had indeed sent his wrath on Scotland. In 1698, Andrew Fletcher of Saltoun estimated that two hundred thousand beggars roamed about in Scotland.[104] Fletcher may have inflated his estimate because, as an East Lothian laird, he advocated turning paupers into serfs.[105]

The Nisbets and Peden were not alone in predicting God's wrath on a sinful Kirk and its nation during the later seventeenth century. Even those who opposed the Covenanting movement in the wake of the execution of Charles I were not against calling upon Scottish geopious sentiments for their own purposes. James Sibbald, acting as sort of a prophet against the Covenanting movement, called upon Scottish geopiety in his published sermons of 1658.

> Lastly, we have yet another pregnant motive to perswade us to sorrow and repentance at this time, that is, the danger of our Church and countrey. Who seeth not a fire kindled in the Wrath of God, which threatneth this Church and Land with desolation. . . . Oftentimes we have foretold you that God would visit for the sinnes committed in this land, and that he would be avenged on such a nation as this.[106]

Unlike Scotland, however, Ireland in the late 1600s was not subject to God's wrath as warned by Puritan-Presbyterian divines. As David Stevenson wrote, "Many accepted and glorified in the developing national myth of their church as the 'best reformed' of all churches, and this myth was becoming attached specifically to the Presbyterian party."[107] The Kirk's reformed offspring, the Presbytery of Ulster, despite not meeting between 1661 and 1690, was alive and flourishing. From 1672 to 1714, which followed a dozen years of discrimination under the restored House of Stuart, dissenting Protestant divines in Ireland, including Presbyterians, were encouraged by their receipt of the regium donum.[108] For some the regium donum[109] was arguably seen as a sign from God that their lives would be blessed in Ulster. As Robert Blair declared, "So careful was the Lord, and bountiful towards that Plantation of his in the north of Ireland, that whoever wanted, they might not want."[110]

In the last half of the seventeenth century and for much of the first decade of the eighteenth, Ireland was indeed regarded by many as a blessed land for dissenting Protestants. The Army Presbytery, which began with five ministers and four elders, had by 1660 grown into the Presbytery of Ulster that consisted of five presbyteries. The new Ulster Presbytery employed seventy ministers who served eighty congregations with an estimated one hundred thousand communicants.[111] Edward Synge, the bishop of Tuam, claimed that between 1690 and 1700, fifty thousand Scots families settled in the north of Ireland.[112] To meet the demand for its ministries, the Synod of Ulster, following the renaming of the Presbytery of Ulster in 1690, was reorganized again in 1702, and nine presbyteries were formed.[113] At that time, the Synod included nearly 120 congregations and employed more than 100 ministers who served an estimated 250,000 Scots immigrants.[114] The number of Presbyterian congregations at the Restoration was doubled by 1715.[115] Most of the recent arrivals had been Covenanters, according to James G. Leyburn, so "the tone of Ulster Presbyterianism, already prevailingly Puritan, took on the added strictness and rigidity of that persuasion."[116] It must be noted, however, that many of the newcomers eventually turned to theological liberalism, enlightenment theology; Aryanism, Deism, and a number of others were decidedly against subscription to the confessions of faith.[117] Of course, many Puritan-Presbyterians continued migrating; and during the eighteen-century, 250,000 Ulster-Scots—mostly Puritan-Presbyterians—resettled in the colonies of North America.[118]

In the minds of the members of Melville's ecclesiastical intelligentsia, Scotland and its Kirk were critical participants, even leaders, of the works of the invisible church, which they hoped to make more visible.[119] The conviction that God had called their country to lead the reformation in the pursuit of true religion was not limited to Scots. That lofty, geoteleological goal was shared by English Puritans, who like their seventeenth-century Scots counterparts believed that greater opportunities to build "a shining city on a hill" existed. Unlike seventeenth-century Scottish Puritans, however, many English Puritans believed a Christian commonwealth was to be built in the wilderness of America. To a number of Scots divines who served in Ulster, it was God who placed them and their country in their role to lead all kirks of every realm in establishing the true Christian faith. That belief was expressed in the National Covenant and sworn to by many Lowlanders.

The underling ethos that influenced the contents of the document was preserved in both the southwest of Scotland and Ulster by the ebb and flow of political pressure that pushed disaffected Puritan Presbyterian ministers back and forth across the North Channel. Being on the fringe of Scottish political and social power, the religious leaders in the area were encouraged to embrace the Covenant's ethnocentric vision of their place in sacred history. The Puritan-Presbyterian vision of Scotland's and Ireland's geotheological significance nurtured, as described by Donaldson, a national conceit among the members of that community that made ecclesiastical compromise difficult, if not impossible, with Episcopalians.

Seventeenth-century Puritanism was a supra-ecclesiastical power and, more importantly, it was a "strong social and political force able to disturb and divide communities with its uncompromising plea for full social and religious reformation."[120] Avihu Zakai further explains that the Puritan failure to achieve reformation through the creation of "a godly, Christian society and the increasing strife between the 'godly' and the 'profane' at the local level caused, in large measure, thousands of English Puritans to emigrate to New England in order to realize in the American wilderness their vision of the holy Christian society."[121] The Scots ministers who served in Ulster were likewise eager to establish a sanctuary for themselves and Christ's kingdom; and while the decimated environs of Ulster presented Scots with something of a wilderness, the geotheological basis of their perception of Scottish land further encouraged them to stay closer to the sacred soil of home. Relocating to New England may have also meant that they would have had to become "New Englishmen," which was an anathema to Scots and Irish folk.[122] At any rate, Zakai's description of the schismatic tendencies of Puritans and of their desire to establish "a shining city on a hill" can also be applied to Scots who settled in Ulster as well as to English pioneers in New England. Irish Protestants have expressed the same desire for sacred space in the American South.

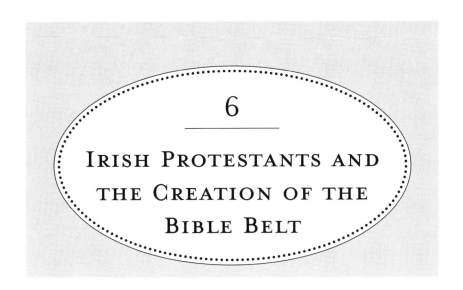

6

IRISH PROTESTANTS AND THE CREATION OF THE BIBLE BELT

As political circumstances changed in Ulster, ministers began to desacralize their country while casting a geotheological view towards America. In 1729 a frustrated Ulster magistrate made an observation of Presbyterian ministers who, he claimed, "have taken shear pains to seduce their poor ignorant hearers, by bellowing from the pulpits . . . that God had appoynted a country for them to dwell . . . and desires them to depart thence, where they will be freed from the bondage of Egipt and goe to ye land of Cannan."[1] Comments such as these were made because under the rule of Queen Anne from 1702 to 1714, high-church Anglicans had gained control of Parliament, and the Test Acts that had been used against Irish Catholics were applied to dissenting groups of Protestants in Ulster, who by 1700 included Quakers; English, German, and Welsh Baptists; and Calvinist French Huguenots.

Beginning in 1699 with the passage of the Woolens Act that was followed by the Test Act in 1703, many Ulster-Scots could see that their lot in Ireland was changing. For some leaders among Puritan-Presbyterians, this situation was especially true when George I suspended the lucrative regium donum, the annual payments to dissenting Protestant ministers.[2] From 1699 to 1717, the plight of all Irish Protestants who remained loyal to their nonestablished churches was made worse by a number of environmental problems, all perhaps symptomatic of the consequences of overpopulation. These problems included a smallpox epidemic, a disease that attacked sheep, and a protracted drought that temporarily paralyzed the flax and linen industry.[3] For Ulster-Scots the thought of returning to

Scotland was dashed by the realization that their home nation had submitted to the rule of Westminster with the union of Parliaments in 1707. With the absorption of Scotland into Britannia, punitive policies were inescapable on the eastern side of the Atlantic. Adverse political and ecological conditions prepared many members of Ulster-Scots Land, the dissenting culture area that straddled the Irish Sea, to look westward to America.

When William Penn traveled to Britain to recruit settlers for his new colony, which Charles II had named Pennsylvania, the catalyst for their migration to America was established, for he hired James Logan, an Ulster Scot, to serve as his provincial secretary in the New World.[4] Logan, whose job included settling newcomers on land in Pennsylvania, was convinced that his countrymen would serve as a buffer against possible Indian attacks because they, as followers of the Calvinist William of Orange, successfully defended Derry and Inniskillen as Billy-Boys (a possible origin of *hillbilly*) against the Catholic forces of James II.[5] Thanks in part to Logan's recruitment efforts, which he later regretted, the first of five waves of Ulster immigration began in 1717 and 1718.[6] The western sea routes that were by now well established across the Atlantic carried thousands of Ulster folk to Philadelphia (and also to Charleston), but disputes between Logan and the family of William Penn, who died in the summer of 1718, interrupted Logan's ability to grant choice lands to immigrants.[7] While some of the immigrants were able to settle down in eastern Pennsylvania, others found their way west along a trail that led to the mountains of Appalachia, which in the Allegheny region are over three thousand feet, and were turned southward into and through the Shenandoah Valley of Virginia. Along the way, they were joined by Germans and smaller numbers of English and Welsh Baptists, French Huguenots, and Quakers.[8]

Because this assemblage of ethnic groups formed the Protestant population in Ireland, it is difficult to determine how many of these immigrants came to America via Great Britain and continental Europe. Nevertheless they were the basic Protestant communities in Ireland and in the Southern Uplands of North America. Among the immaterial aspects of culture that they brought with them were their independent and dissenting expressions of religion. While the larger Irish group was Presbyterian, their neighbors were primarily Baptists. Both, however, were essentially Calvinists. Many Quakers, like Daniel Boone's brother Squire, and Presbyterians converted to the Baptist style of worship.[9] Whether they remained Presbyterian or became Baptist, their Calvinism set them apart from their Quaker counterparts.

In the backcountry of Appalachia, it was difficult for college-trained Presbyterian clergy to find attractive employment opportunities. Because Baptists did not require seminary educations for their ministers, their congregational polity enriched by Calvinist theology flourished among the seed of Ulster: "But for Pennsylvania's Presbyterians who moved to (and through) the unchurched valley, Baptists promised the benefits of vital religion without institutional trappings or delay."[10] Presbyterians, such as Isaac Anderson, Samuel Carrick, Samuel Doak, and William Tennant established churches and colleges in Appalachia.[11] Others, such as Joseph Rhea, who was the second Presbyterian to minister in Tennessee, and Francis Mackemie, the founder of American Presbyterianism, were graduates of the University of Glasgow, which educated most of the divines who brought Presbyterianism to Ireland.[12]

Religion aside, modest employment opportunities in coal-rich areas of the Upper South provided fuel for the expanding steel-based industries farther north in the so-called Rust Belt located along the shores of the Great Lakes, but from the middle of the nineteenth century on to more recent times, the hilly and mountainous landscape attracted relatively few postcolonial newcomers. The coal industry did, however, attract exceedingly small numbers of Jews, eastern and southern Europeans, and African Americans to a restricted number of places, such as Harlan County, Kentucky, and McDowell County, West Virginia. Today, these counties produce regionally anomalous voting patterns. Still, the land lying between northern West Virginia and northeastern Alabama forms one of two Scots-Irish ethnic islands, arguably a culture area of sorts, in the United States.[13] The other Scots-Irish ethnic island is in southern Missouri and northern Arkansas in the Ozark Mountains.[14]

The Cumberland Gap served as the primary conduit for expanding westward the Ulster influence on the American political and religious landscapes, for it must be recognized that a certain kind of Christianity came to Appalachia with its settlers. Whereas America has more than one hundred distinct ethnic groups, ranging in religiosity from Buddhists to atheists to witches, over 90 percent of rural Appalachians, regardless of their ethnic identifications, come from only six parent ethnic groups (Irish, Scottish, English, German, French, and Welsh). Their religious diversity ranges for the most part from High Calvinism to modified Calvinism sprinkled with a little Arminian free will. The power of the Southern Upland church today is similar in significance to the institution that was introduced by the first Ulster, English, and Germanic settlers in the eighteenth century. As it was in 1775, the southern house of worship continues to be an important part of the people's way of life, affecting even their political attitudes, which are influenced by their historic sense of geotheology.[15]

Because education, geotheological thought worlds, and politics played major roles in shaping the character of Presbyterian Church leaders in Ulster, this discussion focuses on how those three institutions coalesced in America to help give the South its well-deserved vernacular title of the Bible Belt.

The Bible Belt

Through natural increase and relative isolation, the American South, which in the late twentieth century was the home of 47 percent of the country's Scots-Irish and 33 percent of the Irish American population (mostly Protestant and most likely products of the same immigrant group), has preserved many colonial traits of the Ulster people who settled across the rugged uplands of the South.[16] Their presence has helped color the South's cultural image and has arguably contributed to its colloquial name. Fuelled in part by lingering geotheological imagings that added to the region's Puritan orientation, the South is perhaps America's most religious and politically influential region, yet this region is in certain respects a spatial extension of the trans–Irish Sea community and its dissenting culture area born in the seventeenth century.[17]

The South and parts of the Midwest have been called the Bible Belt since the 1920s.[18] However, a number of problems are associated with identifying the precise boundaries of culture areas, and the Bible Belt is no exception. In 1961, Wilbur Zelinsky published a study with a map of denominations in the United States, identifying the southern region as a part of the country dominated by Baptist churches. Its northern boundary runs just south of Maryland's and Virginia's northern borders, cuts through central West Virginia, and follows the Ohio River for a short distance at the Indiana-Ohio boundary. It shifts northward and heads west across the southern portions of Indiana and Illinois. Most of Missouri, Oklahoma, and Texas are also included.[19]

Nearly two decades later Charles Heatwole extended and modified Zelinsky's approach by identifying and mapping the locations of denominations that profess a literal interpretation of the Bible.[20] Although his map shows areas in which no clear pattern of affiliation exists, he contends that twelve of the twenty-four fundamentalist groups identified in his study account for 98 percent of the population in the Bible Belt. The northern boundary of his Bible Belt closely resembles the line drawn by Zelinsky.[21]

Perhaps Steve Tweedie provides a more useful approach to identifying and describing the Bible Belt discussed in the present volume. He recognizes that televangelists broadcast their messages across denominational lines and into areas not reached by local congregations. Tweedie identifies two core areas. The eastern core is centered on broadcast locations clustered in North Carolina and Virginia. The western core emanates from Little Rock, Arkansas, and Tulsa, Oklahoma. These areas are close to the migration route that tied together southern Appalachia and the Ozarks.[22]

In terms of the social, political, and religious definitions, Tweedie's characterization is useful: the Bible Belt is a part of the country "in which the literal accuracy of the Bible is credited and clergymen who preach it (whether in restricted localized space or through electronic means) have public influence."[23] His characterization could also be applied to Ulster during the last few decades of the Plantation era. Many of the ancestors of Bible Belt citizens were just as Puritan in their theological imagings as any of the settlers who called Plymouth Rock or the Massachusetts Bay Colony their home, yet scholars interested in the Plantation of Ulster or others interested in colonial America rarely attempt to demonstrate the role of the religious thought worlds of long-dead Irish immigrants in the creation of the Bible Belt.

This upland area encompasses the four hearths of country music, as identified by George Carney, and many of the songs recorded by its artists reflect the beliefs of Bible Belt residents.[24] Most of the listeners of country music hail from this region, according to singer Carrie Underwood, who said, "It's not a secret that so many country listeners come from the Bible Belt. We're just good people who like good music."[25] Underwood's song "Jesus, Take the Wheel" stayed on or near the top of the country chart in 2006 for six weeks. Since Hank Williams's hit "I Saw the Light" (1948) and Merle Haggard's "Jesus, Take a Hold" in 1970, other songs appealing to the morality of the Bible Belt have had success on country charts, including "Unanswered Prayers" by Garth Brooks, which made it to number eleven. "Ten Thousand Angels" by Mindy McCready climbed to number seventeen. Both were released in 1991. In 2001 Martina McBride made the top forty with "Blessed," and Sara Evans made it to number twenty with "Saints and Angels." In 2003, Randy Travis reached number one with "Three Wooden Crosses." In 2005 Craig Morgan had a hit at number one with "That's What I Love about Sunday," a song that depicts a typical Sunday-morning church service in the South. Also in 2005, Tim McGraw reached number sixteen with "Drugs or Jesus," a song that shows that many in the Bible Belt who find themselves living outside the supportive environment of the church fall into the drug trap. In addition to Underwood's number-one hit, Dolly Parton and Brad Paisley reached that position on the country chart in 2006 with their duet, "When I Get Where I am Going."[26]

Few southern artists of Scottish or Irish descent have achieved the level of fame reached by Elvis Presley. His musical style was influenced by his religious upbringing, and his only Grammy was awarded to him for a Gospel album. He is also one of a very few performers who have had a number-one hit on the pop chart with a song featuring a decidedly Christian theme. His "Crying in the Chapel" celebrates the spiritual benefits of being part of a church community. With the exception of Haggard, the last names or their variants of these artists could be easily found in a phone book in Antrim or County Armagh.[27] Lyrics in country songs tie together God and country and reflect theocratic beliefs underlying voting patterns in support of candidates who are strong on defense and traditional American lifestyles—based, of course, on their interpretation of morality, and this will be examined later.

In addition to its musical culture, the Bible Belt also features lucrative religious attractions and programs that appeal to residents and visitors. In Cherokee County, North Carolina, the Church of God built a memorial of sorts to its founder in a valley that features the "world's largest Ten Commandments." It is called the Field of the Woods. In the Ozarks the Passion play at Eureka Springs, Arkansas, an hour's drive from the country-music haven of Branson, Missouri, attracts thousands each summer night to its performances. In Tennessee, Gatlinburg and Pigeon Forge also offer vacationers an opportunity to attend their Smoky Mountain Passion plays. In many respects, these huge gatherings are similar to religious meetings held in open spaces in southwestern Scotland and Ulster in the seventeenth century. Across the Bible Belt, one can observe stickers on bumpers and signs on barns that offer praises about God, admonishments, the need for salvation, and references to the blessed American state. The Bible Belt clearly reflects the culture of a devout people whose ancestors lived in the highlands of Europe's Protestant Celtic fringe.

Natural Features of the Bible Belt

Just as the Irish Sea and its coastal lands formed the physical environment for the creation of a dissenting culture area, the landscape of the Upland South along with poverty and outmigration combined to shape the spatial extent of the Bible Belt. By recognizing the role of the natural setting in the settlement of the Upland South, how southern Appalachia (western North Carolina, eastern Tennessee, and northern Georgia) and the Ozarks (southern Missouri and northern Arkansas) preserved attributes of colonial Irish Protestants while becoming the core of America's most geotheological culture area is understandable.

Appalachia was formed 320 million years ago by the impact of the North American and European plates, which forced the North American one below sea level and submerging much of southern Appalachia. Sediments formed layers of limestone, shale, and sandstone. With the next plate collision, these pliable rock layers were folded and in some places cracked, creating today's beautiful landscape. The pressure and heat from the impacts transformed the core of the mountains into dense, sturdy metamorphic rock. Thousands of caves weakened and collapsed, forming sinkholes and knobby hills. With the exception of the eastern escarpment, the Cumberland-Allegheny Plateau is heavily dissected.

The upland area of the Cumberland Mountain range was formed 245 million years ago as the North American plate collided with the African plate, causing a folding and faulting of eastern North America.

Formed by the same tectonic forces, Appalachia and the Ozarks are separated by the Ohio and Mississippi rivers and their fertile plains. In Appalachia, a plateau stretches from Alabama to New York. From Alabama to West Virginia, this plateau is called the Cumberland Plateau and is the southern portion of Appalachia's westernmost upland area. However, from West Virginia to New York, the plateau is called the Allegheny Plateau; the deeply dissected northern portion of this section of the plateau is also called the Allegheny Mountains. Elevations in the plateau range from two thousand to forty-eight hundred feet. Peaks over six thousand feet occur in both northern and southern Appalachian states: in the south in Tennessee and North Carolina and in the north in New Hampshire. Because of the northeast-southwest trajectory of these uplands, migration flows, including those of Native Americans, were diverted southwestward through valleys, such as the Shenandoah, which divides the Blue Ridge from the Cumberland-Allegheny Plateau.

The centers of the Cumberland-Allegheny Plateau and Ozark Mountains are both roughly on the latitude of 36°30 N to 36°40 N. The physiographic feature that connects these centers is also on the same latitude near where the Tennessee, Kentucky, and Virginia borders meet. The feature is a towering outcrop called the Pinnacle, which is exposed sandstone atop the lengthy Cumberland Mountain or the eastern escarpment of the Cumberland Plateau. The Pinnacle has historically provided armies, bandits, and hunters with an excellent vantage point to watch the intermittent flow of animals and people passing through the Cumberland

Gap, a significant natural pass through the mountain. At 2,440 feet above sea level, the rocky overlook is 800 feet above the Gap. From the Pinnacle it is easy to see the result of the ancient collisions of the Earth's plates. The view to the south and east reveals a landscape resembling a crumpled carpet, for southern Appalachia's ridges and valleys run parallel to each other. As far back as the arrival of Native Americans, these valleys provided the most fertile farm lands while serving as the easiest transportation arteries.

Early pioneers moving through the Gap were easy prey for bandits and vengeful natives and so were keen to clear the mountainsides of woody cover. The Cumberland Mountain is exceedingly steep, and because of many decades of heavy timber harvesting, the soil has become shallower as its denuded slope gave up its soil to gravity and running water. Today the Cumberland Gap portion of the mountain is protected by the United States National Park Service. Because of changes in land use and sound conservation measures, the slopes are once again sheltered by deciduous trees, including oaks, hickories, and maples.

An ancient river most likely formed the Cumberland Gap during the era of plate collisions. As the North American plate buckled, the Appalachian Mountains rose. The Cumberland Gap area, a visually striking place, is one of the most significant places in American migration history. Early pioneers, many of whom were Irish, traveled to the Cumberland Gap where an old, well-worn path stretched northward.

Ancient Trails

Before hunters and gatherers from Asia moved into North America during the Pleistocene ten thousand to forty thousand years ago, wooly mammoths and other animals that would become extinct lived in the southern Appalachians and traveled to and fro through the Gap, leaving a well-marked trail. Later, bison, black bears, beavers, deer, and elk were plentiful when the Cherokee, Shawnee, and Europeans arrived.

In the middle of the fifteenth century, the Cherokee came to southern Appalachia from the northeast where other tribes spoke similar Iroquoian languages[28] and established a capital at Chota (in modern-day Monroe County, Tennessee).

The Shawnee were pushed out of their villages in New York and Pennsylvania by rival Iroquois in the late seventeenth century. Like the Cherokee, the Shawnee built small towns on river banks and farmed low-lying, fertile fields. The Cherokee and Shawnee were rivals, and, as such, the country north of the Cumberland Gap was not peaceful.[29] The Great Warriors' Path ran from the Cherokee capital at Chota and north through the Cumberland Gap. From there the path followed meandering hollows filled with canes and thorns.[30] The path also crossed rapidly flowing creeks and rivers until reaching the rolling blue-grass area of the Kentucky River. This region was Kentucky, which the Cherokee and Shawnee used primarily as a hunting ground. Most of the Shawnee who had an interest in Kentucky lived in towns near the Ohio River in the north. Shawnee settlements near the Ohio, such as Mekoche, Piqua, Chillicothe, Kispoko, and Hathawekela, were independent, patrilineal villages.

The Cherokee and migrating herds of buffalo used the relatively low-lying Powell Valley as a route to the Cumberland Gap and into Kentucky. The trail that they wore into the landscape extends through the Powell Valley of Virginia to Moccasin Gap, near modern-day Kingsport, Tennessee. There a trail, the Great Indian Warpath, split off to the north through the Shenandoah Valley.[31] To the south of Moccasin Gap, a trail cut through East Tennessee to Chota, and other paths provided routes across the mountains of western North Carolina all the way to the Piedmont. The Powell Valley in East Tennessee is also marked by footpaths worn down by natives and wild game alike.

Those ancient paths were widened into roads by Europeans seeking a way around the mountains as they pushed both the native people and the frontier westward. Although the Cherokee had sold Kentucky to the Transylvania Company in 1775, some among them, Dragging Canoe in particular, resisted giving up their hunting grounds to the settlers. Making matters worse, French emissaries had forged an alliance with the Shawnee, who disputed the Cherokee claim of ownership of their long-contested hunting grounds. Those disputes and the fighting that resulted added greatly to Dragging Canoe's declaration to Daniel Boone on the day of the sale that the whites would find Kentucky a "dark and bloody ground."[32] Nonetheless, the trail was used by European immigrants as well as African slaves and freedmen. By 1775 between two hundred thousand and three hundred thousand Scots-Irish were living in America, and nearly half moved to southern Appalachia and later to the Ozark Mountains of Missouri and Arkansas.[33]

> The Scots-Irish were the frontier fighters of the Thirteen Colonies, pushing south and west through the Cumberland Gap, and down the Ohio and Tennessee rivers, in search of better land and prospects. Their descendants live on in the hills of Appalachia, the home of blue grass music, and further west in the Ozark Mountains.[34]

Since those early years of settlement, the descendants of colonial settlers across the upper South[35] began seeing themselves not as British subjects but as part of a new nation of Americans determined to set their blessed nation and land apart from Europe and corrupt Europeans, for much of their Puritan-influenced belief system had changed little since their grandparents boarded overcrowded ships in Ulster harbors.[36]

Irish Protestants and Religious Higher Education

As if Christian higher education in the South were a recent phenomenon aimed at igniting a social revolution, sociologist Anthony Giddens claims that leading preachers on the New Christian Right across the South

> have founded a number of universities to produce a new generation of "counter elite" schooled in fundamentalist Christian beliefs and able to take up prominent positions in the media, academia, politics and the arts. Liberty University, Oral Roberts University, Bob Jones University and others confer degrees in standard academic disciplines, taught within the framework of biblical infallibility.[37]

Perhaps these institutions received attention from Giddens because of their founders' fame and notoriety in the popular press, but Christian colleges with evangelical missions have been continuously functioning in the lands west of the Blue Ridge Mountains since the late 1700s.

As the Irish made their way into southern Appalachia, through the Cumberland Gap, across the Mississippi River, and on into the Ozarks, they were hard pressed to find suitable places to worship in the Presbyterian tradition. An undeterminable number of their progeny had left their church to become part of Baptist congregations, which featured a loose, community-based polity. In response to the inability to provide educated clergy for backcountry settlers, frontier Presbyterian ministers like Isaac Anderson, Samuel Carrick, and Samuel Doak had by the early 1800s built seminaries and colleges west of the Blue Ridge. Greeneville College (later renamed Tusculum College) was founded in 1794 at Greeneville, Tennessee. In that same year, Blount College, which grew into the University of Tennessee, Knoxville, was chartered. At nearby Maryville, Tennessee, Anderson served as the founding president of Maryville College, established in 1819.[38] At least seventy other existing colleges, seminaries, and universities were built by Presbyterians in America. Others such as Washington and Lee in Virginia and the University of Georgia were built by Scots-Irish Presbyterians but no longer maintain an affiliation with the church.

With the Scots-Irish hegemony in the South, the upper South in particular, it would seem reasonable to expect to find that most of the

Presbyterian institutions of higher learning are thus situated. Fifty-five percent of the country's Presbyterian colleges, seminaries, and universities are located along or near the historic migration routes and settlements of the pioneering Scots-Irish (Pennsylvania to the Ozarks and from Charleston, South Carolina, to the Ozarks) (see table 2). When institutions located in the deep or coastal South are added in, the figure rises to 69 percent. With forty-eight colleges, seminaries, and universities in the South, even the much larger Southern Baptist Convention fails to match the number of Presbyterian institutions of higher learning in the South.[39] American Presbyterianism is prominently featured on the religious educational landscape of the South and arguably contributes to the reputation of the region as America's Bible belt.

TABLE 2. Comparison by region of Presbyterian universities, colleges, and seminaries in the United States (N = 74)

Northeast Region (n = 9)

Alma College, Alma, Michigan

Blackburn College, Carlinville, Illinois

Bloomfield College, Bloomfield, New Jersey

College of Wooster, Wooster, Ohio

Hanover College, Hanover, Indiana

Illinois College, Jacksonville, Illinois

Lake Forest College, Lake Forest, Illinois

Monmouth College, Monmouth, Illinois

Muskingum College, New Concord, Ohio

Northwest Region (n = 14)

Albertson College of Idaho, Caldwell, Idaho

Buena Vista University, Storm Lake, Iowa

Carroll College, Waukesha, Wisconsin

Coe College, Cedar Rapids, Iowa

Cook College and Theological School, Tempe, Arizona

Hastings College, Hastings, Nebraska

Jamestown College, Jamestown, North Dakota

Macalester College, St. Paul, Minnesota

Rocky Mountain College, Billings, Montana

Sheldon Jackson College, Sitka, Alaska

Sterling College, Sterling, Kansas

University of Dubuque, Dubuque, Iowa

Westminster College, Salt Lake City, Utah

Whitworth College, Spokane, Washington

Coastal South (n = 10)

Austin College, Sherman, Texas

Belhaven College, Jackson, Mississippi

Eckerd College, St. Petersburg, Florida

Knox Theological Seminary, Ft. Lauderdale, Florida

Reformed Theological Seminary, Jackson, Mississippi

Reformed Theological Seminary, Orlando, Florida

Reformed Theological Seminary, Washington, District of Columbia

St. Andrews Presbyterian College, Laurinburg, North Carolina

Schreiner College, Kerrville, Texas

Trinity University, San Antonio, Texas

Pennsylvania and the Upper South (n = 41)

Agnes Scott College, Decatur, Georgia

Arcadia University, Glenside, Pennsylvania

Barber-Scotia College, Concord, North Carolina

Bethel College, McKenzie, Tennessee

Centre College, Danville, Kentucky

College of the Ozarks, Clarksville, Arkansas

Covenant College, Lookout Mountain, Georgia (near
    Chattanooga, Tennessee)

Covenant Theological Seminary, St. Louis, Missouri

Davidson College, Davidson, North Carolina

Davis and Elkins College, Elkins, West Virginia

Erskine College, Due West, South Carolina

Geneva College, Beaver Falls, Pennsylvania

Greenville Presbyterian Seminary, Taylors, South Carolina

Grove City College, Grove City, Pennsylvania

Hampden-Sydney College, Hampden-Sydney, Virginia

Johnson C. Smith University, Charlotte, North Carolina

King College, Bristol, Tennessee

Knoxville College, Knoxville, Tennessee

Lees-McRae College, Banner Elk, North Carolina

Lyon College, Batesville, Arkansas

Mary Baldwin College, Staunton, Virginia

Maryville College, Maryville, Tennessee

Memphis Theological Seminary, Memphis, Tennessee

Montreat College, Montreat, North Carolina

Peace College, Raleigh, North Carolina

Pikeville College, Pikeville, Kentucky

Presbyterian College, Clinton, South Carolina

Queens University of Charlotte, Charlotte, North Carolina

Reformed Presbyterian Theological Seminary, Pittsburgh, Pennsylvania

Reformed Theological Seminary, Charlotte, North Carolina

Rhodes College, Memphis, Tennessee

Stillman College, Tuscaloosa, Alabama

Tusculum College, Greeneville, Tennessee

University of the Ozarks, Point Lookout, Missouri

University of Tulsa, Tulsa, Oklahoma

Warren Wilson College, Asheville, North Carolina

Washington and Lee University, Lexington, Virginia

Waynesburg College, Waynesburg, Pennsylvania

Westminster College, Fulton, Missouri

Westminster College, New Wilmington, Pennsylvania

Wilson College, Chambersburg, Pennsylvania

Indeed, the rigid form of early American Presbyterianism, like its Ulster counterpart, has witnessed numerous schisms over the centuries. Arminianism and the Great Awakening (the general revival of evangelical religion in the American colonies) weakened the Calvinist theology then taught in some of the denominations formed by those schisms. This is certainly true in the denominations of the Cumberland Presbyterian Church (CPC) and the Presbyterian Church of the United States of America (PCUSA). On the other hand, other southern denominations like the Associate Reformed Presbyterian Church (ARPC) and Presbyterian Church in America (PCA) are more conservative and claim adherence to the Westminster Confession of Faith. Diversity, arguably a continuance of schisms described earlier, exists among denominational affiliations of Presbyterian universities, colleges, and seminaries in the South (see table 3). As compared to the rest of the country, denominational affiliations of colleges and universities in the South are more diverse than their northern counterparts that remain tied to the PCUSA. Of the nine major

Presbyterian denominations in the United States, the central offices of eight of them are located in Pennsylvania and across the Bible Belt.[40]

TABLE 3. Affiliation of Presbyterian universities, colleges, and seminaries in Pennsylvania and across the South (n = 51)

University, college, or seminary	Location	Affiliation
Agnes Scott College	Decatur, Georgia	PCUSA
Arcadia University	Glenside, Pennsylvania	PCUSA
Austin College	Sherman, Texas	PCUSA
Barber-Scotia College	Concord, North Carolina	PCUSA
Belhaven College	Jackson, Mississippi	PCUSA
Bethel College	McKenzie, Tennessee	CPC
Centre College	Danville, Kentucky	PCUSA
College of the Ozarks	Clarksville, Arkansas	PCUSA
Covenant College	Lookout Mountain, Georgia	PCA
Covenant Theological Seminary	St. Louis, Missouri	PCA
Davidson College	Davidson, North Carolina	PCUSA
Davis and Elkins College	Elkins, West Virginia	PCUSA
Eckerd College	St. Petersburg, Florida	PCUSA
Erskine College	Due West, South Carolina	ARPC
Geneva College	Beaver Falls, Pennsylvania	Reformed Presbyterian Church of North America
Greeneville Presbyterian Seminary	Greeneville, South Carolina	favored by the PCA and the Orthodox Presbyterian Church; claims to be "old-school Presbyterian"
Grove City College	Grove City, Pennsylvania	PCUSA
Hampden-Sydney College	Hampden Sydney, Virginia	PCUSA

University, college, or seminary	Location	Affiliation
Johnson C. Smith University	Charlotte, North Carolina	PCUSA
King College	Bristol, Tennessee	PCUSA
Knox Theological Seminary	Ft. Lauderdale, Florida	PCA
Knoxville College	Knoxville, Tennessee	PCUSA
Lees-McRae College	Banner Elk, North Carolina	PCUSA
Lyon College	Batesville, Arkansas	PCUSA
Mary Baldwin College	Staunton, Virginia	PCUSA
Maryville College	Maryville, Tennessee	PCUSA
Memphis Theological Seminary	Memphis, Tennessee	CPC
Montreat College	Montreat, North Carolina	PCUSA
Peace College	Raleigh, North Carolina	PCUSA
Pikeville College	Pikeville, Kentucky	PCUSA
Presbyterian College	Clinton, South Carolina	PCUSA
Queens University of Charlotte	Charlotte, North Carolina	PCUSA
Reformed Presbyterian Theological Seminary	Pittsburgh, Pennsylvania	Reformed Presbyterian Church of North America
Reformed Theological Seminary	Charlotte, North Carolina	favored by the PCA
Reformed Theological Seminary	Jackson, Mississippi	favored by the PCA
Reformed Theological Seminary	Orlando, Florida	favored by the PCA
Reformed Theological Seminary	Washington, District of Columbia	favored by the PCA
Rhodes College	Memphis, Tennessee	PCUSA
St. Andrews Presbyterian College	Laurinburg, North Carolina	PCUSA
Schreiner College	Kerrville, Texas	PCUSA
Stillman College	Tuscaloosa, Alabama	PCUSA
Trinity University	San Antonio, Texas	PCUSA

TABLE 3 (*continued*)

University, college, or seminary	Location	Affiliation
Tusculum College	Greeneville, Tennessee	PCUSA
University of the Ozarks	Point Lookout, Missouri	PCUSA
University of Tulsa	Tulsa, Oklahoma	PCUSA
Warren Wilson College	Asheville, North Carolina	PCUSA
Washington and Lee University	Lexington, Virginia	established 1749 as Augusta Academy by Scots-Irish settlers, not affiliated
Waynesburg College	Waynesburg, Pennsylvania	PCUSA
Westminster College	Fulton, Missouri	PCUSA
Westminster College	New Wilmington, Pennsylvania	PCUSA
Wilson College	Chambersburg, Pennsylvania	PCUSA

NOTE: ARPC, Associate Reformed Presbyterian Church; CPC, Cumberland Presbyterian Church; PCA, Presbyterian Church in America; PCUSA, Presbyterian Church of the United States of America

Many members of the Southern Baptist Church, like their counterparts in the Presbyterian and Primitive Baptist denominations, share a belief in the sovereignty of God. Although some embrace the Arminian view that God allows human free will in matters of salvation, this situation is nonetheless permitted by the sovereign will of God.[41] On matters of sacred space as they relate to the unfolding of God's Providence, Calvinism is prominently placed because geoeschatology and geoteleology, as parts of geotheology, are based on the belief that God overrules human free will to bring about his plans. Ulster-Scots geotheology has mutated into an American geotheology.

Geotheology in the Bible Belt

As heirs to the people of the Old and New Testaments, the conservative religious voices heard in the Bible Belt speak of the belief that God gave humans dominion over the Earth and that his elect was given the reigns of social power and political influence.[42] Many of America's Scots-Irish see themselves as masters of their environment, and the way in which they live in it helps them to preserve their liberty. These folks have historically demonstrated a culture that values closeness to the rural landscape. Their ancestors created a rural-to-rural migration pattern into Ulster, which defies one of Ravenstein's migration laws.[43] Even today, the Ulster-Scots' preference for a rural lifestyle can be heard in the words of any number of country songs. Consider the words to the popular song *A Country Boy Can Survive* by Hank Williams Jr.; the singer lives back in the woods with his family, dog, rifles, shotguns, and a four-wheel-drive. His backwoods home is a place where he can raise "good ole tomatoes and make home-made wine," "catch catfish from dusk till dawn," and "plow a field all day long." As if to provide a Divine endorsement of his way of life, the singer relates that his people "say grace" and "Amen," and "If you ain't into that, we don't give a damn." This song tells of the Scots-Irish view of the good life. Like their pioneering ancestors who left the vanishing rural environs of southwestern Scotland, they sought to preserve a gemeinschaft life-style that their culture continues to romantically nurture and stimulate in their shared memories.

Appalachian and Ozark people of Ulster descent as is evidenced by *A Country Boy Can Survive* and other secular and religious songs in the South clearly express a desire for a lifestyle free from government bureau-cracies that David Hackett Fischer calls natural liberty.[44] As declared by the people of Mecklenberg County, North Carolina, in 1768, "We shall ever be more ready to support the government under which we find the most liberty."[45] As a result, the culture of the Upland South does not often see the government as a proper instrument for preserving or even conserving natural resources. Economics also comes into play when ex-amining the relationship that many people have with the natural world and their resultant attitudes favoring a noninterventionist government. Extractive industries like mining and tobacco farming along with pastoral agriculture and forestry have formed the basis of the economy of many areas in the Upland South. In their way of thinking, polices affecting the environment could make it more difficult to earn a living as well as main-tain a way of life that is rooted in their belief system born in the seven-teenth century.

Just as Robert Blair and John Livingstone believed that God had a plan for them in Scotland, which they felt was a nation chosen by God for the unfolding of his Providence, many in America's Scots-Irish community have demonstrated a sanctified, even geopious view of America and its efforts to ensure a way of life framed by the country's Puritan founders. Underlying this perspective was the conviction that God was sovereign over every aspect of their lives, including in the secular realm and terres-trial space.[46] In 1683 the minister Francis Makemie (McKamey) of the

Laggan District in Donegal brought this understanding with him to the southern colony of Maryland. He believed his work as a minister was performed "in the sight of an all-seeing and omnipresent God."[47] A modern Ulsterman named Billy Kennedy, at the site of the first Presbyterian congregation established in 1782 in the Tennessee Valley, reflected on the Ulster-Scots diaspora and the contribution its participants had on the South's religious landscape.

> Standing beneath the cedar trees and alongside the four pillared plinth which marks the spot of the original Lebanon in the Fork Church . . . one is struck immediately by the awesome reverence in the place. The beauty of the encircling countryside sets it out as a spot close to heaven. This was once a church in the wildwood, a sanctified acre where God's faithful servant Samuel Carrick brought the gospel to a people searching for a new destiny in the wilderness of the frontier but desperately eager to reclaim the Presbyterian faith of their fathers.[48]

One of those searching was an eighteenth-century frontiersman who symbolically led the way in migrating beyond the Mississippi River and into Missouri and the Ozarks.[49] Daniel Boone was not of Ulster-Scots descent, but he was certainly absorbed into its community in Appalachia. Being raised in a devout Quaker family, it is not too difficult to think of Boone as a second-generation Englishmen, but what is often overlooked is that George Boone III, his paternal grandfather, lived in Exeter, which is located in the Celtic southwest of England near the Welsh border, before settling in the Pennsylvania town of the same name.[50] This is the part of England where the legendary Celtic King Arthur kept waves of Saxons from destroying the remnants of Celtic England. Daniel Boone's mother, Sarah Morgan, was Welsh, and many of the people with whom Boone formed relationships were of Irish, Border Anglo-Scottish,[51] or Welsh descent. Each group came from the Celtic fringe in Great Britain and Ireland, and in Ulster, they formed the basic Protestant population. Richard Henderson, Boone's employer and sponsor of the Wilderness Road project, was of Scots-Irish ancestry.[52] Boone married a Welsh lassie named Rebecca Bryan. The man who piqued Boone's interest about Kentucky was a Scots-Irishman named John Finley.[53]

In 1769 Finley led Boone and four others from their homes in the Yadkin Valley of western North Carolina through the Cumberland Gap and into Kentucky. Boone, whose eyes sparkled when listening to Finley talk about Kentucky's beautiful meadowlands and plentiful game,[54] recruited his Ulster-Scots brother-in-law John Stuart to accompany him.[55] The three other men who accompanied Boone on his first visit through the Powell Valley and the Cumberland Gap were of Irish descent.[56]

In 1775 Benjamin Logan, a former friend[57] of Boone's and a rival to Richard Henderson, ignored Henderson's claim of ownership of Kentucky and followed Skaggs Trace, which splits off to the northwest from the Wilderness Road about eight miles north of present-day London, Kentucky.[58] Logan's partner in this adventure was an Ulster Scot named William Gillespie.[59] The path they followed was named for three Irish brothers, Charles, Henry, and Richard Skaggs.[60] On May 1, 1775, Logan, a second-generation Scots-Irishman, began building a settlement near a trace that eventually became Stanford, Kentucky.[61]

Boone, who was unchurched in any formal sense, declared to a Baptist minister who had inquired whether Boone had experienced any change in his feelings toward the Savior, answered, "No, sir, I always loved God ever since I could recollect."[62] Also, possibly he believed in predestination because he unequivocally declared a preference for Presbyterianism.[63] Perhaps John Finley and other Scots-Irish friends and in-laws inspired Boone on a deep, spiritual level. Finley ignited his imagined geography of Kentucky, but little attention has been given to Boone's geotheology.

Boone's beliefs are clearly revealed in a letter he wrote to his sister-in-law Sarah Day Boone, and these beliefs are romantically depicted in his authorized biography that was published in 1784 as an autobiography by John Filson the year Boone celebrated his fiftieth birthday. This seems to have been a happy and reflective time for him. Problems with debtors and his move to Missouri still years ahead. One of his frequent companions in the wilderness was his brother Squire, who had served as a lay Baptist preacher for most of his adult life. In recalling their conversations, Boone revealed his belief in the Providential aspects of place and the peace he felt in recognizing them.

> Thus situated, many hundred miles from our families in the howling wilderness [of Kentucky], I believe few would have equally enjoyed the happiness we experienced. I often observed to my brother, you see now how little nature requires (of us) to be satisfied. Felicity, the companion of content, is rather found in our own breasts than in the enjoyment of external things, and I firmly believe it requires but a little philosophy to make a man happy in whatsoever state he is. This consists of a full resignation to the will of Providence, and a resigned soul finds pleasure in a path strewed with briers and thorns.[64]

Once in the wilderness, Squire became frustrated with Daniel, who insisted that they patiently hunker down to sit out a storm. When the storm
was over, they resumed their trek, and when they soon came upon an
Indian camp vacated because of rising water, Boone turned to Squire,
"See what fretted you so much was really the means of Providence for our
salvation. But for the storm we should have run into the very jaws of our
enemies."[65] This interpretation of a natural event was similar to one written about by Robert Blair after his ship the *Eaglewing* was turned back to
Ireland by a storm.

The views of others, including regional ministers, about Kentucky and
westward expansion clearly reflect an early expression of the sentiment
that underpinned the idea of manifest destiny. Irish American John L.
O'Sullivan in 1845 articulated the belief that God's Providence had
ordained the expansion of the United States from "sea to shining sea."[66]
A Virginia minister wrote, "What a Buzzel is amongst people about Ken-
tuck. To hear people speak of it one would think it was a new found paradise."[67] Kentucky's reputation for being a bountiful, blessed land provided
a metaphor to a frontier divine, who told his congregation, "Heaven is a
Kentucky of a place."[68]

Daniel Boone clearly held a view that God ruled and overruled in
human affairs and secular events. His reflections about the settlement of
Kentucky give a glimpse into his geopious and geoteleological imaginings.

> Curiosity is natural to the soul of man, and interesting objects have
> a powerful influence on our affections. Lo these influencing powers
> actuate, by the permission or disposal of Providence, from selfish or
> social views, yet in time the mysterious will of Heaven is unfolded,
> and we behold our conduct, from whatsoever motives excited, oper-
> ating to answer the important designs of Heaven. Thus we behold
> Kentucky, lately a howling wilderness . . . become a fruitful field; this
> region, so favorably distinguished by nature, now become the habi-
> tation of civilization, at a period unparalleled in history, in the midst
> of a raging war, and under all the disadvantages of emigration to a
> country so remote from the inhabited parts of the continent . . . we
> now hear the praises and adorations of our Creator. . . . We behold
> the foundations of cities laid, that, in all probability, will equal the
> glory of the greatest upon earth. And we view Kentucky, situated on
> the fertile banks of the great Ohio, rising from obscurity to shine
> with splendor, equal to any other star of the American hemisphere.[69]

One might wonder how in more recent times others claiming Scots-Irish
ancestry imagine American space. In 1890 Dr. John S. Macintosh, the

founding president of the Scotch-Irish Society of the United States of America, pronounced:

> Born and naturalized citizens, we give ourselves anew in this organization to the land for which our fathers and friends gave their blood and lives. We are not a band of aliens, living here perforce and loving the other land across the sea. We belong to this land, and only recall the old that we may better serve the new, which is our own.[70]

The Scots-Irish people of the South have contributed their sense of geopiety to the Bible Belt and its conservative orientation to politics. At a meeting of the Scotch-Irish Society in 1889, J. Proctor Knott, an ex-governor of Kentucky, delivered the keynote address.

> The children of the race are now scattered throughout all this broad continent, mingling like drops of water in the mighty ocean, with a vast and wondrous people gathered from many lands; but wherever they may be, they and their descendants will cherish with affectionate veneration the honour of their ancient sires, and keep the sacred fires of family love brightly burning on their domestic alters as long as a drop of the old Scotch-Irish blood shall trickle through their veins; and should the grasping hand of consolidated wealth, the wild fury of communism, or the insolence of foreign power ever menace the fair fabric of constitutional liberty erected by their fathers, they will rush to its defense.[71]

Knott's views are consistent with the continuing conservative forces in the South, yet modern sociologists, such as Anthony Giddens and Ronald L. Johnstone, seem to think that views such as these are the products of the New Christian Right.[72] Although the leaders of this "so-called movement" hail from the Bible Belt, their message is delivered across regional boundaries via electronic means. As a result, casual secular observers, including academics such as these, believe that they are witnessing a "new movement" when the evangelical message and moral concerns of this community are actually older than the United States.

Sweat of the Brow

Taxation and the redistribution of wealth are also issues believed to be the targets of fundamentalist ministers in the so-called New Christian Right. The fundamentalist notions of the New Christian Right stem from Calvinism.[73] However, the position on wealth redistribution is not new among Bible Belt preachers and politicians of Ulster-Scots descent, for, despite regional poverty, their culture embraces the Calvinist-based work ethic (also called the Protestant ethic) that was introduced into Ireland by the Melvillian Scottish ecclesiastical intelligentsia in the seventeenth century. Indeed, some southern politicians sound a great deal like seventeenth-century social leaders in Scotland. As Gordon Donaldson writes about relief for the poor in Scotland during that century, "Neither the church nor the state believed in helping the able-bodied poor, or unemployed, and while solicitude was expressed for the 'poor' and 'impotent,' the 'strang' and 'idle beggar' was to be discouraged or even punished."[74]

In 1698, a weather-related famine caused a significant number of people to roam the Scottish countryside as beggars. An estimated proportion of between one-third to one-half of the people died from starvation or immigrated to Ulster. One proposal involved giving temporary help to the needy. The English, in a manner similar to attitudes in the United States North, had accepted the idea. Some justices in the Scottish Lowlands threatened to strike if it were enacted. At least one Scot remarked that the proposal was "odious and smellis of ane taxatioun" and that is "nathair a credeit ner benefeit" to anyone.[75]

Robert Rollock, one of Scotland's post-Reformation leaders, thought that visitors finding people shamelessly begging was a national embarrassment. It is not surprising then that southern politicians and preachers have made the redistribution of wealth a political issue. While it is tempting to believe that these folk are expressing a stingy, self-interest, their concerns are rooted in the biblical mandate to "earn thy bread by the sweat of thy brow."[76]

The remedy for begging, according to Rollock, is to labor.[77] The doctrine permeates the Bible Belt and even appears in some country-music songs. Country music originates in the Bible Belt, and a fair portion of its residents are consumers of country artists' CDs and DVDs. It is not hard to find so-called secular country songs that suggest a Divine mandate to work. Consider the lyrics to "Give a Damn," written and performed by Hank Williams Jr.[78] The singer tells Americans to "give a damn about your job," insisting that they must give complete and honest effort to their work, for he warns them that failure to do so would be tantamount to letting "the Devil rob." He admonishes them to "take pride in anything you sign your name to." Finally, he tells his listeners to "give a damn about your Maker (because) He may also be a taker."

Alabama, the country band from Fort Payne, Alabama, had a cross-over hit with "Forty-Hour Week," a song that shows appreciation for American workers. Interestingly the song only thanks autoworkers, steel-mill laborers, and coal miners. To the chagrin of lowly college professors who also labor as book authors, the song does not offer thanks to white-collar workers. The lyrics say, "There are people in this country who work hard everyday. Not for fame or fortune do they strive, but the fruits of their labor are worth more than their pay." The use of the word *fruit* is a metaphor for the biblical mandate to be productive in honest and genuine work.[79] In Ulster-Scots Land and the Bible Belt, producing fruit is a sign of—or a means to get—God's blessings.

Aaron Tippin is another country artist who sings about the need to work in his hit "Working Man's Ph.D." The song says that the virtuous man labors:

> With your heart in your hand and the sweat on your brow,
> you build the things that really make the world go around. . . .
> There ain't no shame in a job well done,
> from driving a nail to driving a truck.
> As matter a fact, I'd like to set things straight:
> A few more people should be pullin' their weight.[80]

As a carpenter, Jesus drove nails and no doubt fulfilled the Old Testament mandate to earn his bread by the sweat of his brow.

In 2005 Gretchen Wilson and Merle Haggard teamed up for a hit song "Politically Uncorrect." The lyrics speak of God, the flag, the Bible, and "the low man on the totem pole," especially those "guys still pulling the third shift . . . and the single mom raisin' her kids." The duet further declares that they are "for the preachers who stay on their knees and . . . for the sinner who finally believes." In the chorus the duet reemphasizes their main points:

> And I'm for the Bible and I'm for the flag
> And I'm for the working man, me and ol' Hag
> I'm just one of many
> Who can't get no respect
> Politically uncorrect.[81]

In light of the South's work ethic, one may wonder why parts of the region remain poor. To answer this question, recall that Ulster-Scots people were mostly subsistence farmers (field to table). The migration pattern they produced between Scotland and Ireland was a rural-to-rural phenomenon. The same pattern was formed across the American South, although some of their relatives followed the more typical rural-to-urban migration pattern between the Upland South and the cities of the Rust Belt, for in those cities were found employment opportunities, although low-skill and labor-intensive. Like the songs above, value is placed on physical labor and not on more lucrative occupations that require higher and more advanced levels of education and training that could lead to greater levels of regional economic development. These beliefs and behaviors contributed to economic and population growth in Scotland during the seventeenth century, a time that T. C. Smout calls the prelude to the take-off of the Industrial Revolution.[82] Although it could be argued that immigrants to Ulster held beliefs that would have contributed to Scottish economic growth, they left before their agrarian-based ethic was reshaped into a work model associated with life in industrial cities. In the expansive, upland environs of the American South, they were able to push the frontier westward, and along the way, their bountiful new environment nurtured the continuation of their agrarian, albeit economically poor, lifestyle. Meanwhile, the North experienced the Industrial Revolution, drawing away some of Appalachia's people. The idea of "Appalachian otherness," which is a polite name for the perspective that the Upland South is a place of poverty and backwardness set apart from the rest of America, is a recent expression of earnest scholars.[83] As the audience for some of the country artists mentioned above suggests, the work ethic of the Bible Belt now sees industrial labor in the same sacred light as work on a farm. Unfortunately the manufacturing base of the American economy is disappearing and faces the same fate as the feudal economy of southwestern Scotland. This time, there are no new lands to absorb the excess population. Somehow the work ethic of the Scots-Irish must be redirected to include occupations that require education and training.

Voting Behavior

Irish Protestants, including members of the Ulster-Scots, English, French, and German communities who lived for a time in Ulster, carried their negative feelings about tyranny and a strong central government to America. Their participation in the American Revolution against the British was disproportionately large, and when the country was torn apart during the Civil War, the southern Appalachians and Ozarks quickly fell into Union hands. The Lowland South unsuccessfully fought to retain slavery through the creation of a confederacy that allowed for stronger states' rights relative to that of the national government. Skirmishes in the Upland South were usually fought over access to supplies.[84] However, battles at Lookout Mountain, Wilson's Creek, and Pea Ridge were obvious exceptions, but as the locations of those battlefields suggest, they were strategically important passageways into the Lowland South or the West.[85]

There was a good deal of union support in the Southern Uplands. Partly in recognition of this fact, Abraham Lincoln chose Andrew Johnson as his running mate in 1864. Johnson was an East Tennessean of Ulster-Scots descent.[86] Although he was a Democrat, he was certainly pro-Union and had the support of the mountain people. Johnson assumed the presidency when Lincoln was assassinated in April 1865, but because of the role played by the North's "Radical Republicans" during the Reconstruction (1865 to 1877), regional voting patterns were well established by 1908. From then until the 1970s, the South was squarely in the Democratic camp, and the North routinely went to Republican presidential candidates.[87] In the South, Democrats came to be known as "Dixiecrats," and they insisted on stronger states' rights in federalism.[88] Since the 1980s, the regional appeal of the national parties has changed. The Republicans adopted positions that appealed more to the conservative South, especially to white voters, and the Democratic Party spoke to the interests of minorities, women, and government workers. Nowadays, "the Republican Party sees its role in society as the guarantor of individual freedoms [including states' rights] and tries to avoid promoting programs that differentiate Americans by racial and ethnic groups. This position appeals to white Southerners who have felt that the Democrats do not have their best interests at heart, including support of their cultural values."[89]

Southern voting patterns show that citizens are most likely to cast ballots for candidates who express concern about national defense, lower taxes, and the moral issues of the day, including efforts to legalize gay marriages and provide public support for abortions.[90] Between Governor Knott's time and the recent past, specifically the decades between 1880 and 1980, congressional voting patterns also echo the North-South regional pattern.[91] In recent presidential elections, candidates who have campaigned on issues appealing to the Upland South's sense of geopiety and morality have received most of the votes.

With America at war for the second time in little more than a decade, many of the counties in the South, like others in rural America, cast their votes for George W. Bush at an even higher rate in 2004. In Carroll County, Iowa, for example, Bush received 52 percent of the vote in 2000; in 2004, he received 55 percent.[92] Likewise, in Crowley County, Kansas, 59 percent of the electorate voted for Bush in 2000, but during wartime he received 66 percent of the vote.[93] Perhaps a look at the 2000 election is a clearer picture of the issues that affected voting behavior in the Upper South. Support for using data from the 2000 election is further strengthened because a southern Democrat ran against a southern Republican candidate; thus regional preferences, at least as far as the South is concerned, would have been unbiased by the home of the candidate. While the outcome of the 2000 election was questionable because of the infamous hanging-chad controversy in Florida, there is no question that Vice President Al Gore Jr. lost his home state of Tennessee to Bush.[94] Indeed, even outgoing President Bill Clinton could not deliver his home state of Arkansas to Gore's ticket.

Gore's and Clinton's home states are included in the Scots-Irish ethnic islands of the southern Appalachian and Ozark Mountains. These culture areas are the most conservative places in the United States generally and the South specifically. The conservative undercurrent in the region's political climate has caused a movement away from the Democratic Party as it has embraced the interests and concerns of ethnic and racial minorities, supported gay-marriage legislation, supported abortion, proposed gun-control measures, and appeared as weak on national defense. Mississippi, once a stronghold of the Dixiecrats (southern Democrats), had its first two-term Republican governor during the 1990s, and both of its senators are Republicans.

Tennessee has a Democrat governor who campaigned on a fiscally tight platform that featured a no-state-income-tax plank, but, as with Mississippi, both of its senators are Republicans. While Tennesseans cast 52 percent of their major party vote to Bush, in the Appalachian uplands of East Tennessee, he received a higher percentage. For example, he grabbed 67 percent in Sevier County, 66 percent in Hancock County, and 70 percent in Bradley County.[95]

Alabama and Georgia have flirted with becoming Republican states. In 2000, Alabamans cast 58 percent of their votes for the Republican ticket, but in Winston County, Bush received 70 percent of the ballots. In other Alabama counties classified as Appalachian, for example, St. Claire and Shelby, Bush collected 73 and 78 percent of the votes, respectively. From 1995 to 1999 Georgia representative Newt Gingrich served as Speaker of the House. In the 2000 election, Bush won Georgia with 56 percent of the votes. In some Appalachian counties, Bush won by a much larger percentage. In Gilmer and Forsyth Counties, for instance, Bush received 69 and 81 percent of the major party vote, respectively.[96]

In Kentucky and North Carolina, Bush won with 57 and 56 percent of the major party votes, respectively.[97] In upland Kentucky counties in which coal mining has not been a major employer, Bush received more than 57 percent of the vote. In Adair and Pulaski Counties he received 75 percent of the vote, and in Laurel County he won with 73 percent of the ballots. Among the Appalachian people of Avery, Davie, and Mitchell counties in North Carolina, the Republican ticket received 75, 74, and 76 percent of the ballots.[98]

On the other hand, in Harlan County, Kentucky, where the coal-mining industry has attracted racial and ethnic minorities as well as the United Mine Workers of America (UMWA), Bush lost with only 48 percent of the vote. Similar voting patterns are found in other coal-mining areas. This is seen, for example, in McDowell County, West Virginia, and Buchanan County, Virginia.[99]

Of particular interest to this study are the contrastive regional voting patterns in Maryland, South Carolina, and Mississippi. Each has a small number of counties classified by the Appalachian Regional Commission (ARC) as Appalachian. Among Maryland's twenty-three counties, only Allegany, Garrett, and Washington are classified Appalachian. Whereas Bush with 42 percent of the vote lost to Gore in Maryland, the state's three Appalachian counties cast their ballots for Bush at 57, 72, and 61 percent, respectively.[100] Moving southward, Bush won South Carolina with 58 percent of the vote, but he won all six Appalachian counties with an average of 66 percent of the ballots.[101] Although the ARC classifies twenty-four counties in Mississippi as Appalachian, Woodall Mountain in Tishomingo County, the state's highest point, is only 806 feet above sea level.[102] It follows that geographers do not classify any of Mississippi's counties as Appalachian.[103] In terms of the voting patterns of Mississippi's so-called highland counties, ballots cast for Bush show little, if any, regional difference. While voters across the state cast 59 percent of their ballots for Bush, Tishomingo County produced 60 percent for the Republican ticket. Nearby Alcorn County met the state figure with 59 percent.[104] Excluding Mississippi and a few coal-mining counties, these data show that Appalachian counties have more conservative voting patterns than their states as a whole.

The Ozark counties of Arkansas and Missouri are also conservative areas. This region includes the Third Congressional District, whose seat was held for nearly three decades by John Paul Hammerschmidt. While Bush collected 53 percent of the state's 2000 major-party vote, Benton and Carroll counties cast 67 and 61 percent, respectively, of their major party votes for the Republican. In Boone, Hammerschmidt's home county, voters gave Bush a 66 percent victory.[105] In Missouri, Bush barely won the state with 52 percent of the vote, but in the southern Ozarks, however, he received a much higher percentage. In McDonald County, which is located in the southwestern corner of Missouri, Bush received 71 percent of the vote. In nearby Christian and Douglas counties, he won 60 and 70 percent of the votes, respectively.[106]

Missouri and other states in the Upland and coastal South are not becoming conservative. Indeed, the parties are just switching places on the issues. The geotheological sentiments brought to the region by Irish Protestants have no doubt affected the country's political landscape. As with their Protestant counterparts in modern Ulster, who, when compared to residents in England, Scotland, and Wales, are the most likely people to call themselves British, the United States Census Bureau says that the most likely region in America to find people claiming an "American only" identity is in the upper South.[107] Patrick Griffin has called this transatlantic segment of humanity "the people with no name." In the absence of a sovereign place called Ulster-Scots Land, their sense of namelessness is perhaps connected to a sense of ancestral homelessness, and their association with the loftier identities of empire, both old and new, gives them a sense of belonging and higher purpose.

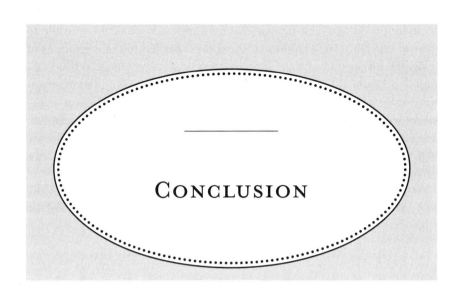

CONCLUSION

The migration of Scottish Puritan-Presbyterians back and forth across the North Channel during the seventeenth century dramatically altered the political and religious landscapes of southwestern Scotland and Ulster. Under differing policies and government administrations, Ireland and Scotland alternated as places of refuge for dissenting ministers who took advantage of existing social ties and well-established transportation and communication arteries that spanned the North Channel. They introduced a new thought world into the area that placed themselves in succession to "old saints" and even Old Testament prophets in the unfolding of God's Providence.[1] Their world was shaped by Puritanism and a participatory polity that were often at odds with the monarchy. To appreciate more fully their impact on southwestern Scotland and Ulster, the current volume describes the geography of southwestern Scotland and the North Channel that encouraged the development of a new regional way of life that was already oriented toward the sea. The current volume also reconstructs the economic, demographic, and institutional ties as well as the political and theological contexts that played important roles in their movements and how these contexts manifested themselves in the American South.

Any research on the overall pattern and extent of seventeenth-century Scottish *lay* migrations to and from Ireland and their subsequent eighteenth-century migrations to America is a difficult subject to pursue because of the limited quantity of extant records. While admitting that glaring weakness, this volume assumes that by reconstructing the theological bases of their leaders' religious, spatial, and political thought worlds, including their real and imagined communities, it would be possible to expand current understanding of the forces that led to the migrations of a significant portion of the "ordinary" people who took part in the Plantation of Ulster. To establish this assumption on a firm foundation, it was necessary to include analyses of their ministers' geotheological belief structure, which must have shaped their interpretations of more immediate external forces that arguably influenced their decisions to relocate across land and sea, as well as their ideas about the Christian governance of space.

Perhaps the most significant contribution this volume makes to the body of work compiled on aspects of the Plantation and the genesis of the Bible Belt is in effect to adopt, extend, and blend Bowen's seaways theory and its capacity to explain interconnectedness between disparate places with the geotheological ideas and nomenclature of John K. Wright. Bowen's theory explains the means by which a culture area could have formed along the North Channel of the Irish Sea, and the concepts of Wright help to reconstruct the thought world that influenced the shaping of it. With respect to cultural geography generally and religious geography specifically, this book departs from the concrete spatial or landscape focus of Zelinskian and Sauerian approaches associated with denominational geography and embraces instead the immaterial aspects of religious thought worlds that may (or indeed may not) have affected the landscapes of southwestern Scotland and Ulster. Although this orientation frames the Plantation-era subject matter examined in this book, the results also provide an important link between the scholarship on the Ulster Plantation and that on colonial and contemporary America. Between two hundred thousand and three hundred thousand Ulster-Scots migrated farther west to America in the eighteenth century, affecting political and religious landscapes of the American South as well as Ulster. In addition to those who claim Scots-Irish ancestry, Americans claiming Irish compose the largest ethnic group in two southern states (Arkansas and Tennessee).[2] Members of this group are also well represented in other southern states, including Georgia, Mississippi, North Carolina, South Carolina, Texas, and Virginia. Indeed, 33 percent of Irish Americans live in the South.[3] Just as this population was instrumental in creating Ulster-Scots Land, the culture area formed in the seventeenth-century, they continue to shape the Bible Belt, its American counterpart.

Plantation Memory in Northern Ireland

Without the politics of the Plantation, it is difficult to know how the religious and political landscapes in Ulster would have developed since the seventeenth century. Possibly the process of centuries-old interchange along the North Channel would have continued amongst the people living on both shores of the Irish Sea. Unfortunately that was not the case. The Stuart policies pitted one ethnic-religious group against another.[4] The Tudors, the Stuarts, and Cromwell were inconsistent in targeting ethnic-religious groups for dispensing tolerance, intolerance, and preferential incentives in the form of grants of land and cash stipends such as the regium donum.

Even without that inconsistency, the practice would have most likely driven wedges between the groups because the king conceived that a loyal church body, which was intended to be a replication of England's Erastian, Episcopalian model, would bring about Anglicization. Michael Perceval-Maxwell metaphorically describes the king's policy and its result: "He [James VI and I] used Scottish earth for his purpose, in which the seeds of Presbyterian doctrine lay buried. Even some of the Scottish gardeners he employed preferred Presbyterian weeds to Episcopalian flowers. Thus what grew . . . bore little resemblance to that image envisioned by the designer."[5] Perceval-Maxwell failed to note that English Puritans and their Congregationalist polity fertilized the Scottish Presbyterian seed. The result among dissenting Irish Presbyterians was a hybridized church structure that empowered the congregation relative to the power of church officers. The congregation in Irish Presbyterianism emerged from that cultural mixture with a power exceeding that held by its counterpart in a Scottish Kirk parish, which, in contrast to Episcopacy, was participatorial, especially when compared to the polity envisioned by Charles I and by William Laud. That idea was informed by the doctrine of the "priesthood of all believers." If the church and its officeholders were not above reproach based on scriptural passages, whose interpretation was clearly influenced by the ethos of Scotland's community of Puritan divines, the Melvillian notion of "two kingdoms" certainly kept the state within reach of a similar reprimand. Certainly adherence to such notions resulted in the deposition of a large percentage of the ministers in the Irish Sea culture area at the Stuart Restoration. As the following comparison of statements show, many of the basic beliefs about God, the state, and their interpretation of scripture have changed little since the seventeenth century.

Plantation-era beliefs among a portion of modern Irish Presbyterian divines have continued to color the manner in which political and social pressures are perceived. In 1993, the General Assembly of the Presbyterian Church in Ireland summarized its thoughts and beliefs on relations with the state and, through inference, its Roman Catholic neighbors:

The reformed tradition has always been wary of revolutionary action, since "the powers that be are ordained by God." Calvin even held that "the worst tyranny is more bearable than no order at all" for it still serves in some sense to hold human society together. Nevertheless God himself may summon his servants to set the oppressed free, hence Calvinists, historically and today, have often been in the forefront of revolutionary movements. But all such action is fraught with moral ambiguity and danger, and violence can be contemplated only as a last resort. In Reformation teaching the Church as such has a spiritual mandate to resist those in power only where they may try to compel the church organisation or membership to act directly contrary to their faith in Jesus Christ as their paramount Lord or to restrict freedom of worship.[6]

As the report confesses, this ethos is fraught with ambiguity. On the one hand, it seems to convey offers of conciliation while, on the other hand, it airs divinely mandated threats against actions that are intended to restrict religious expression. As it was in the seventeenth century, their ethos centers on the belief that the hand of God is responsible for all action and human reaction and that even the state must be submissive to Divine will. As a comparison, the minister Robert Blair in the seventeenth century reflected geotheologically about his settling in Ulster: "The Sovereign Lord, who hath determined the bounds of our habitation, thrust me over to Ireland altogether against my inclination."[7] What is especially unclear about the modern-day version of the ethos is the issue of interpreting God's sovereign will. This is particularly difficult as Northern Ireland and its Presbyterian Church, indeed all of its Protestant Churches, confront an uncertain political future.

Aside from political conflicts and the uncertain future that they create, the problem of national/ethnic identity is another issue plaguing the heirs of the Plantation. Gaelic ethnicity was discriminated against throughout most of the Plantation era, and with the ascent of Queen Anne and the implementation of the Test Act of 1703, nonconforming groups of Protestants were deprived of civil employment, and their marriages and burials were declared illegal. Their loss of lands, language, and other expressions of artistic culture among the natives of Ireland and to some extent also for Scottish Presbyterians are well documented. Government policies underpinning the Plantation left scars on natives and virtually every immigrant group. The examination of Ireland's historical complexities, including in the areas of politics and religion, has relevance to the future governance of Ireland as a whole.[8] Revisionist histories, aimed at re-forming Plantation era identities in Ulster, have colored much of the scholarship on which those rediscoveries are made.[9] Ulster-Scots ethnicity is now anti-British and anti-Irish.[10] Like its Irish counterpart, its appeal is based on the feelings of ethnonationalism.

Perhaps as a means of mitigating painful historical memories, Ulster people today are expected to learn symbols of ethnic / community identity, such as language and musical forms, that could be shared by all who call Northern Ireland their home. Many expressions of music and art, as with religion, have become politicized. As if religious expression were not enough, those symbols signify community allegiance and in-your-face ethnic pride. The Reverend Colin Williamson, a native of County Down who serves as a minister in the Scottish Kirk and is hence an heir to the cross-channel community discussed in this work, states that the adoption of ethnic labels such as Ulster Scot and Scots-Irish among Ulster Protestants and unionists is politically divisive.[11] He also feels that such labels minimize the contribution of Anglo-Irish settlers to both Northern Ireland and America. He prefers the use of "Plantation stock" as a label for those who descend from colonial settlers from Great Britain.[12]

As Williamson points out, there is a real threat that the solidarity of Protestant unionists may weaken as ethnic rediscoveries destroy the illusion of a common Protestant British heritage. A general household survey, for which thousand adults throughout the United Kingdom were questioned about their preferred ethnic/national identity, yielded some interesting data that has important implications for the future of both the United Kingdom and the unionist cause in Northern Ireland. Fifty percent of the participants reported that they were English, Scottish, Welsh, Irish, or other, such as Manx or Nigerian. Only 31 percent of the adults surveyed view themselves as British. In England less than 50 percent of the participants use the British label to describe their ethnicity. Racial minorities are the most likely to prefer the British label, and 42 percent of them use another identity.[13]

Some who would like to see a united Ireland hope that it will only occur with unionist consent.[14] Sinn Fein, the Irish nationalist political party, however, rejects this notion, "claiming when it was negotiating with the British Government in the months, weeks and days prior to the Good Friday Agreement, it was told that fifty percent plus one would be good enough for Irish unity and it had every intention of holding the Brits to that."[15] Assuming that most Protestants would vote against a united Ireland, that 54 percent of the Northern Irish population is Protestant and the other 46 percent is Roman Catholic probably means that a nationalist referendum in the next few years will not be successful. However, according to the journalist Pat McArt,

> There is already a nationalist majority at the school-going level, but the experts also indicate that the unionist population is older than its nationalist counterpart. The outcome here is clear: more Catholics being born, more unionists dying. Statistically, it is that simple.[16]

The Roman Catholic community in Northern Ireland is not uniform in regard to its desire to unite with the Republic of Ireland. An estimated 4 percent of the Catholic population supports unionism. Among those who do support the union with Great Britain are professionals who have done well financially as citizens of the United Kingdom.[17]

Nevertheless there is a very real likelihood that the years of the United Kingdom of Great Britain and Northern Ireland are numbered as demographic changes occur along with a lingering legacy of ethnic strife. A reawakening of Plantation era national/ethnic identities among British Protestants in Ulster will potentially create numerous changes in the beleaguered and divided land. The looming political realignments in Northern Ireland would be unnecessary if it was not for a seventeenth-century Plantation policy that saw one group as inferior while the other was its cultural master. Northern Ireland's continued tense situation, like the geopious landscape in the American South, provides evidence that neither "space of time or distance of place" could destroy the thought world of those who introduced Presbyterianism into the Irish Sea culture area. What, if anything, can be taken from this study that may or may not apply to twenty-first-century America?

The Bible Belt: America's Ulster-Scots Land

It is all too easy and convenient to think of white Americans as one large group. Any number of academic books offer social analysis to see how race and ethnicity can be simplified simplify and inaccurately classified. Many Americans think of African-Americans as one homogeneous group, and the same can be said for Asians and Hispanics. People of European origin are called white, which is perhaps a lingering characteristic of a world in which biological factors were seen as the most powerful force shaping potential while explaining the current state. In reality, humans are not so neatly placed into categories. Among each of the above groups is tremendous diversity.

Throughout human history, people have moved and resettled on lands that were either vacant or occupied. When they arrive in sufficient numbers as compared to others living in an area, the newcomers tend to retain a sense of community or sense of uniqueness. On the other hand, if they arrive in a land ruggedly shaped by tectonic forces over eons of time, a larger sense of community can be lost as the microenvironments of visible spaces create new identities, such as a Big Ridge man or a Haney Hollow girl. This has happened in the South.

Thanks in part to the good work of scholars, it is possible to look beyond those microspaces and see cultural imprints that reveal a larger community. The people of the Upland South can now be seen as an ethnic group with cultural origins that predate the Declaration of Independence. However, even with that recognition, there are problems yet to be resolved. For instance, what do we call these people? Admittedly, Ulster is a small place, roughly the size of Connecticut, and for people who have never been to Ulster or studied the region's past, especially as it relates to human-settlement patterns, they simplify the true ethnic complexity of the place. Perhaps "Ulster American," for some, accomplishes that feat, and for others Ulster means Scots-Irish, Scotch Irish, or Anglo-Irish. These ethnic labels do not recognize the less-visible German and French people who settled in Plantation-era Ulster. Ulster is also the home of Irish Catholics. Of the nine counties that make up Ulster, three (Monaghan, Cavan, and Donegal) had Catholic majorities and opted to leave the United Kingdom and become part of the Republic of Ireland. The other six counties have sizable Catholic populations.

In summary, this book has endeavored to show the ethnic complexity of the ancient province while telling the story of the birth of the Ulster-Scots community, the largest Protestant ethnic group in the north of Ireland. An astute reader could respond to that statement by pointing out that the Irish Sea was a transportation artery, and for centuries it carried Scots and Irish Catholics back and forth across the North Channel. It follows that as a group, Ulster-Scots could include Catholics. As reasonable as that point may sound, it would not be a true statement. Whereas in the past, say prior to 1600, a common religious and linguistic background (Catholic and Gaelic) as well as family ties made ethnic labels unnecessary. The Plantation of Ulster, born in the mind of James VI and I, pushed language and religion to the forefront of social contact in Ireland. After 1600 Scots arriving in Ulster had distinct ethnic ties. They spoke a southwestern version of Lowland Scots, which is close to English, and were Protestants. Ethnic conflict created by the Plantation scheme has left a strained and tenuous political legacy that impacts identities in modern Ireland and America.

When Americans add to their American identities any of the ethnic groups from Ireland, they are taking part in a four-century-old political conflict. For example, Ulster American most likely refers to an Irish Protestant. Because Catholics living in Ulster simply call themselves Irish, it follows that the ethnic label Irish American usually refers to a person of Irish Catholic parentage, regardless of whether their roots are in Cavan in Northern Ireland or Cork in the southern part. Some scholars have argued that Americans of Irish Protestant lineage adopted the Scotch Irish label in the middle of the nineteenth century to distinguish themselves from recent Irish Catholic immigrants who were being treated harshly by workers who saw them as competitors for low-wage jobs. Perhaps the fate of the Protestant descendants of the Plantation of Ulster is to never have a clear ethnic identity. One thing is for certain—those who claim a Scots-Irish or Irish Protestant ancestry can look to Ulster-Scots Land, the dissenting culture area formed on the shores of the North Channel of the Irish Sea, for some of their cultural origins. Because of this migration flow and the inland topography of its eastern seaboard and the Appalachian and Ozark Mountains, America has its own Ulster-Scots Land, and it lives on in the guise of the Bible Belt.

APPENDIX

Birth, Education, and Associations of
Irish Presbyterian Ministers

Table A1

Places of birth and education of Irish Presbyterian (IP) ministers, 1642 to 1661

NOTES: The symbols * and ^ identify sets of brothers.

A minister's name is indicated by his initials and the page number on which he is listed in the *Fasti*; for example, PA4 refers to Patrick Adair, who is found on page 4 of *Fasti*.

In the column Remain/Go: A = America; BF = Back-and-forth; BP = Blood's Plot 1663; CON = Conventicler; DOOR = Providence or ministerial calling; E = England; GA = General Assembly Scotland; GS = General Synod IPC; H = Holland; NC = Nonconformity; OTHER = economic; P = political; PROT = Scottish Protesters; RE = Republican Engagement 1650; RG = Rullion Green; RET = retired; REV = 1689 Revolution; S = Scotland

| | *Birthplace* | | | | *Place of education* | | | | | *Remain/Go* |
	Scot.	Ire.	Eng.	Unknown	Glasgow University	Edinburgh University	Aberdeen University	St. Andrews University	Other	Eng./Scot./Ire.
1	JA4					X				
2	PA4				X					
3	JA5					X				
4	JA5								unknown	
5	FA5				X					SRE
6	RA5				X					P
7	JB5				X					
8				JB6					unknown	
9		EB6							unknown	

No.	Code	Code2							
10	MB6			X					
11	JB6		X						
12	TB6		X						
13	WB7		X						
14	MB7			X				SBF	
15	DB8						unknown		
16	WC8		X					SBF	
17	JC8			X					
18	JC8		X						
19		GC8				X			
20		SC9							
21	RC9			X		X	unknown	SBF	
22	TC9		X						
23	WC10		X						
24	JC10			X				SBP	P
25	WC10				X				
26	HC10		X					SBF	
27	JC11*		X						
28	RC11*			X					
29		RD11					unknown		
30	JD11		X					SBP	P

	Birthplace				Place of education					Remain/Go Eng./Scot./Ire.
	Scot.	Ire.	Eng.	Unknown	Glasgow University	Edinburgh University	Aberdeen University	St. Andrews University	Other	
31	TD12 FM								unknown	
32	JD13				X					SBF
33	AF14							X		
34	JF14*					X				
35	JF14*					X				
36	TF14				X					
37	DG14				X	X				SRE P
38	AG15					X				
39	JG15						X			
40	TG37					X				
41	JG37				X	X				SBF
42	TH38				X					SRE P
43	AH38					X				
44	JH39					X				
45	JH39					X				
46	RH39				X					
47			NH39						unknown	
48			TH39						unknown	ABF

No.	Code							
49	JH39							
50	RH40				X			
51	HH40				X			
52	AH40				X			
53	WJ41	X		X		unknown	SRET	
54	JJ42		X			unknown	SRET	
55	GK42		X					
56	AK43							
57	TK43				X		SBF	
58	JK44			X			SRET	
59	WK44					unknown		
60	JL44					unknown	SCON	P
61	WL44					T.C.D.		
62	JL44				X	unknown	SNC	P
63	HJ45							
64	HM45			X	X		SRE	P
65	JM45					C.C.COL	ENC	P
66	WM45		X					
67	WM46				X			
68	AM46				X	unknown	SBP,RG	P
69	JO46				X			

Place of education

	Birthplace				Glasgow University	Edinburgh University	Aberdeen University	St. Andrews University	Other	Remain/Go Eng./Scot./Ire.
	Scot.	Ire.	Eng.	Unknown						
70	AO46				X					
71	TP46				X					
72	RG47								unknown	
73	MR47				X					
74	WR47				X					
75	DR47				X					
76			AR47*						unknown	
77			RR47*						unknown	
78	JS48								unknown	SRET
79	WS48				X					
80	AS48					X				SRE P
81				JS49^					unknown	SPROT P
82				JS49^					unknown	
83				HS49					unknown	
84				GS49	X					
85				JS49		X				HNC P
86				JS50	X					
87		AS50							unknown	SBF

88	RS50				X				SBF	EDOOR
89		EV50							OXFRD	unknown
90			TV51		X				ADOOR	
91	GW51									
92	JW51					X				
93	JW51									unknown
94		NW51							KNSAL	
95				JW51						unknown
96	AW52				X					
97	JW52				X					
98	HW52				X					
99	RW52								SRET	unknown
Total	71 (72%)	10 (10%)	5 (5%)	13 (13%)	39 (40%)	20 (20%)	5 (5%)	4 (4%)	27 unknown; 31 total (31%)	30 = A(2) + E(2) + S(25) + H(1); S(24) = P(11) + SBF(9) + OTHER(5)

SOURCE: Data generated from McConnell, *Fasti of the Irish Presbyterian Church 1613–1840*, and Scott, *Fasti Ecclesiae Scoticanae*.

Table A2

Places of birth and education of Irish Presbyterian (IP) ministers, 1661 to 1690

NOTES: *A minister's name is indicated by his initials and the page number on which he is listed in* Fasti; *for example, PA4 refers to Patrick Adair, who is found on page 4 of* Fasti.

*Father-in-law of William Tennant "Log College"

Codes for Remain/Go: A = America; AO = Abjuration Oath; BF = Back-and-forth; BP = Blood's Plot 1663; CON = Conventicler; DOOR = Providence or ministerial calling; E = England; GA = General Assembly Scotland; GS = General Synod IPC; H = Holland; NC = Nonconformity; OTHER = economic; P = Political; PROT = Scottish Protesters; RE = Republican Engagement 1650; RET = Retired; RG = Rullion Green; REV = 1689 Revolution; S = Scotland

| | Birthplace | | | | Place of education | | | | | Remain/Go |
	Scot.	Ire.	Eng.	Other	Glasgow University	Edinburgh University	Aberdeen University	St. Andrews University	Other	Eng./Scot./Ire.
1	WA57								Scot	
2	DA57					X				SRET
3	JA57						X			SDOOR
4	JA57					X				
5	DB58				X					
6		JB58				X				SBF
7	DC58				X					SRET
8	JC58				X					
9	RC59				X					SBF
10	JC59					X				SRET

No.	Parent	Code					Scot	Type	P
11	TC59								
12		WC59	X	X					
13		HC59		X				SBF	
14		DC60		X				SBF	
15		JC60		X					
16		JD61		X				SDOOR	
17		AF61		X					
18		AF61			X				
19	JF62				X				
20		JF62		X				SBF	
21	TF62						Scot	SREV	P
22		AG62		X					
23		WG62		X					
24		AG62		X	X			SBF	
25	AG63					X			
26		JG63				X			
27		JG64			X				
28		NG64		X					
29		SH64		X				SBF	
30		JH64		X					
31		MH65		X					

Birthplace | **Place of education** | **Remain/Go**

	Scot.	Ire.	Eng.	Other	Glasgow University	Edinburgh University	Aberdeen University	St. Andrews University	Other	Eng./Scot./Ire.
32		AH65				X				SBF
33		JH65				X				SREV P
34				RH66		X				
35	WH66								X	ADOOR
36				TH67	X					SBF
37				RH67		X			X	SBF
38		RH67				X				
39				WH67	X					
40	DH67				X					SBF
41		JH68			X					SREV P
42				JH68		X				SGA
43	FI68								Ireland	
44		GJ69				X			X	EAO P
45						JJ69			Scotland	P
46		RK69								
47	SK69								X	SREV P
48	GK70*				X					
49		TK70			X					SREV P

No.								
50	JK70				X		SGA	
51	HK70				X			
52	RL71		X				SREV	P
53	GL71		X					
54	JL71		X				SREV,GA	P
55	WL71		X					
56		WL72	X				SBF	
57	JM72		X					
58	JM72		X					
59	AM77			X				
60	JM77			X				
61	FM77		X				A	
62		JM77		X				
63		JM78	X					
64	TM78			X				
65	JM78		X				SREV	P
66	JM78				X		SDOOR	
67	PO78		X				SBF	
68		RP79	X					
69	PP79					X		
70	JP79					X	SDOOR	

Birthplace / **Place of education**

	Scot.	Ire.	Eng.	Other	Glasgow University	Edinburgh University	Aberdeen University	St. Andrews University	Other	Remain/Go Eng./Scot./Ire.
71	JR79				X					
72	RR80					X				
73		JS80			X					SBF
74				PS80					X	
75				WS80	X					
76			AS80		X					EBF
77	AS81						X			SREV P
78	JT81								X	SREV P
79	WT81					X				ABF
80	JW82								X	
81	GW82					X				SBF
82	WW82					X				SBF
83				FW83		X				
84	JW83					X				SREV P
85	JW83					X				
86	RW83					X				
87	TW83							X		ADOOR
88	TW84					X				SPROT P

		X				SREV	P
89	AY84	40 (44%)	27 (30%)	4 (4%)	3 (3%)	11, 4K (16%)	43 = A(4) + E(2) + S(37); S(37) = P(13) + SBF(15) OTHER(9)
Total 54 (61%)	20 (22%) 1 (1%) 14 (16%)						

SOURCE: Data generated from McConnell, *Fasti of the Irish Presbyterian Church 1613–1840*, and Scott, *Fasti Ecclesiae Scoticanae*.

Table A3

Further exploration of ethnic/paternal family origin and institutional affiliation of Irish Presbyterian (IP) ministers 1641 to 1690

NOTES: Though not all of the surnames are exclusive to Scotland, most of these ministers (25/27, or 93%) belong to paternal families that were represented in Scotland before or during the seventeenth century (Black, *Surnames*). The number after each person's name and university information refers to the page number in which he is found in Black's book.

Of the twenty-seven ministers listed, sixteen have a Scottish university connection, one an English university connection, and ten are unknown.

*A minister's name is indicated by his initials and the page number on which he is listed in *Fasti*; for example, PA4 refers to Patrick Adair, who is found on page 4 of *Fasti*.

Minister's name	Fasti reference*	Education	Page
James Baty	JB6	unknown	6
William Cocks	WC59	Glasgow University, M.A., 1662	160
Gabriel Cornwall	GC8	St. Andrews, degree and date unknown	172
Robert Dewar (Denner)	RD11	unknown	207
Robert Hamilton	RH66	Edinburgh University, 1679	340
Thomas Harvey	YH67	Glasgow University, M.A., 1663	346, 357
Robert Henry	RH67	Edinburgh University, M.A., 1670	353
William Henry	WH67	Glasgow University, M.A., 1663	353
John Hutcheson	JH68	Edinburgh University, M.A., 1681	371
James Johnston	JJ42	unknown	385
James Johnston	JJ69	unknown	385
William Liston	WL72	Glasgow University, M.A., 1659	431
John Mair	JM77	Edinburgh University, M.A., 1676	574
John Malcom	JM78	Glasgow University, M.A., 1672	576

Jeremiah Marsden	JM45	Christ Church College, England	not listed
Robert Patton	RP79	Glasgow University, M.A., 1654	650
James Shaw	JS49	unknown	720
John Shaw	JS49	unknown	720
Patrick Shaw	PS80	unknown	720
William Shaw	WS80	Glasgow University, M.A., 1651	720
Hope Sherrid	HS49	unknown	not listed
Gilbert Simpson	GS49	Glasgow University 1646	727
James Simpson	JS49	Edinburgh University 1635	727
John Sommerville	JS50	Glasgow University, M.A. 1642	737
Thomas Vesey	TV51	unknown	794
John Weldwood	JW51	unknown	808
Fulk White	FW83	Edinburgh University, M.A., 1672	811

SOURCE: George Black, *Surnames of Scotland,* Edinburgh, 1996; McConnell, *Fasti of the Irish Presbyter Church 1613–1840;* and Scott, *Fasti Ecclesiae Scoticanae*

Table A4

Push-and-pull factors of back-and-forth (BF) Irish Presbyterian (IP) ministers

NOTE: Of the twenty-four ministers listed, fifteen left Scotland for political reasons, nine because of SGA and DOOR, and none for criminal reasons.

Minister's name	IPC Fasti reference	Cause(s) for moves to/from Scotland
James Bruce	JB58	(1) Revolution of 1689
Michael Bruce	MB7	deposed for nonconformity 1661; conventicler
Robert Campbell	RC59	DOOR
John Colthart	JC8	personal leave 1659; deposed for nonconformity 1661
Robert Craghead	RC9	deposed for nonconformity 1661; preached illegally

Minister's name	IPC Fasti reference	Cause(s) for moves to/from Scotland
Hugh Crawford	HC59	(1) deposed for nonconformity 1662
David Cunningham	DC60	retirement and return DOOR
Hugh Cunningham	HC10	refused to take Republican Engagement (1650); deposed for nonconformity
John Drysdale	JD13	refused Republican Engagement (1650); deposed for nonconformity; Blood's Plot 1663 (prison)
John Freeland	JF62	DOOR
Alexander Gordon	AG63	served in Scots General Assembly; retired to Ireland
John Greg	JG37	refused Republican Engagement (1650); Blood's Plot 1663 (prison)
Samuel Halliday	SH64	DOOR
Archibald Hamilton	AH65	(1) deposed for nonconformity 1662
Thomas Harvey	TH67	DOOR
David Houston	DH67	(1) Covenanter societies
Thomas Kennedy	TK43	(1) deposed for nonconformity 1661
John McBride	JM72	DOOR
Peter Orr	PO78	DOOR
James Scott	JS80	Revolution 1689; DOOR back to Ireland 1690
Andrew Stewart	AS50	refused Republican Engagement (1649); deposed for nonconformity 1661;
Robert Stirling	RS50	DOOR
George Waugh	GW82	deposed for nonconformity; retirement and DOOR in Ireland
William Weir	WW82	(1) deposed for nonconformity 1673

SOURCE: McConnell, *Fasti of the Irish Presbyterian Church 1613–1840*, and Scott, *Fasti Ecclesiae Scoticanae*.

NOTES

Introduction

1. Vann, *Rediscovering*. For an identification of southern Appalachia and the Ozarks as Scotch-Irish ethnic islands, see Fellman, Getis, and Getis, *Human Geography*, 189. See also Gerlach, *Settlement Patterns*, 41.

2. Webb, *Born Fighting*. See the opening quote for part 1 by Vernon Louis Parrington. Even the seminal work by James G. Leyburn is somewhat guilty of this simplistic summation of seventeenth-century Scots. See his *Scotch-Irish*.

3. Hazlet, *Reformation*. Presbyterianism is a representative form of church government. An Episcopalian polity relies on the supervision of the church by bishops and uses more Catholic-like elements in their services (for example, Holy Communion). Both, however, can be Calvinist in their theology, and both can be agents of the government, suggesting an Erastian (monarchy-controlled) authority structure. Elizabeth I attempted to make a small but unsuccessful planting of Protestants in Ireland. She also established Trinity College at Dublin as a Protestant institution.

4. This is debatable because even Puritan Separatists thought that a moral society would control government and serve as a beacon for other realms.

5. Zakai, *Exile and Kingdom*; Fischer, *Albion's Seed*, 13–206.

6. Mullan, *Scottish Puritanism*.

7. Vann, "Presbyterian Social Ties," 227–54.

8. The name *Ulster-Scots Land* is used to identify the new, dissenting, trans–Irish Sea culture area that formed during the seventeenth century. The concept of culture area is explored later in this chapter.

9. Fischer, *Albion's Seed*, 622. To see the contrasts among the regions of Scotland, refer to Ian D. Whyte, *Scotland before the Industrial Revolution*.

10. Fischer, *Albion's Seed*, 606.

11. Blair, *Life of Mr. Robert Blair*, 145.

12. Webb, *Born Fighting*, 1–8.

13. Donaldson, *Scotland: James V–James VII*, 149; Donaldson and Morpeth, *Who's Who*, 93.

14. Westerkamp, *Triumph of the Laity*.

15. Griffin, *People with No Name*. Subsequent chapters in the current volume explore the geographical errors mentioned here.

16. Montgomery, "The Scotch-Irish Element"; C. Williams, "Who Are the Southern Mountaineers?," 493–506. See also Montgomery, "How Scotch-Irish Is Your English?"

17. R. Gillespie, *Colonial Ulster*, 32–33; see also Robinson, *Plantation of Ulster*.

18. Blaustein, *Thistle and Brier*, 42. Campbell, *Southern Highlander*.

19. K. Miller, *Emigrants and Exiles*, 156–57.

20. Bell, *Book of Ulster Surnames*, 1, contends that the Scottish Gaels were essentially assimilated into Irish society through closely related cultures. The Protestant religion and English language of the Lowlanders drove a cultural barrier between the Catholic Irish and the Protestant Scots, helping to create a discrete community of Ulster-Scots.

21. Smout, Landsman, and Devine, "Scottish Emigration," 89.

22. See Robinson, *Plantation of Ulster*; R. Gillespie, *Colonial Ulster*; Perceval-Maxwell, *Scottish Migration*; J. M. Hill, "The Origins of the Scottish Plantation"; Brady and Gillespie, eds., *Natives and New Comers*; Perceval-Maxwell, "Ireland and the Monarchy"; and Falls, *Birth of Ulster*.

23. See A. W. Parker, *Scottish Highlanders in Colonial Georgia*; Landsman, *Scotland and Its First American Colony*; Blethen and Wood, *Ulster and North America*; Wokeck, "Irish Immigration to the Delaware Valley"; Cullen, "The Irish Diaspora"; "Westerkamp, *Triumph of the Laity*; Griffin, *People with No Name*; and K. Miller, *Emigrants and Exiles*.

24. See Moore, *Our Covenant Heritage*; Fitzpatrick, *God's Frontiersmen*; and Kennedy, *Scots-Irish in the Hills of Tennessee*.

25. I. B. Cowan, *Scottish Covenanters*.

26. They were Andrew MacCormick and John Cruickshank.

27. See his *Covenanters*.

28. R. Gillespie, *Colonial Ulster*; Perceval-Maxwell, *Scottish Migration*.

29. R. Gillespie, *Colonial Ulster*; Falls, *Birth of Ulster*; Leyburn, *Scotch-Irish*; and Perceval-Maxwell, *Scottish Migrations*.

30. Lockington, *Robert Blair of Bangor*.

31. Leyburn, *Scotch-Irish*.

32. Leyburn, *Scotch-Irish*, 108.

33. R. Gillespie, *Colonial Ulster*, 35.

34. I. D. Whyte, *Scotland before the Industrial Revolution*, 120.

35. Griffin, *People with No Name*, 18.

36. Schama, *History of Britain: The British Wars*, 36.

37. Smout, Landsman, and Devine, "Scottish Migration," 87–89.

38. Zelinsky, "The Hypothesis of Mobility Transition," 219–49. A delineation of this theory is provided in chapter 1, and an analysis of its relationship to Scottish migration flows to Ireland is presented in chapter 3.

39. Murdoch, "The Scots and Ulster in the Seventeenth Century," 87.

40. Young, *Ulster and Scotland*, 11–22.

41. Fitzgerald, "Black '97," 74.

42. Young, *Ulster and Scotland*, 13.

43. Clearly an undetermined number of Scots in Ulster joined the Church of Ireland, and a number of Scots served as ministers in its pulpits. Still, the growth in Irish Presbyterianism throughout the seventeenth century is striking in contrast to memberships in the Church of Ireland.

44. Leyburn, *Scotch-Irish*, 101–7.

45. Dissenting Protestants after the Restoration in 1660 were denied access to economic opportunities in high-growth areas such as those found in the Central Belt because of their failure to obtain Kirk-issued testimonials that would have permitted them to relocate to a new parish in Scotland. See Houston, "Geographical Mobility in Scotland."

46. Todd, *Culture of Protestantism*, 12.

47. Houston, "Geographical Mobility in Scotland," 379–94.

48. Houston, "Geographical Mobility in Scotland," 379–94.

49. This situation hints at a distinctive regional religious culture.

50. This analysis is the product of deduction employed by this researcher.

51. For a variety of reasons, including changes in land tenancy, Whyte offers a similar conclusion on the motive for many migrating Scots (*Migration and Society*, 108).

52. Huw Jones, "Evolution," 151–64.

53. Whyte, *Migration and Society*, 106–13.

54. Mackinder, *Britain and the British Seas*, 21.

55. Crawford, "Distribution," 184–304.

56. Fox and Chitty, *Personality of Britain*.

57. Bowen, *Saints, Seaways, and Settlements*, 3.

58. Bowen, *Saints, Seaways, and Settlements*, 25.

59. Bowen, *Britain and the Western Seaways*, 16.

60. Bowen, *Britain and the Western Seaways*, 16.

61. Blair, *Life of Mr. Robert Blair*, 52–53.

62. These comments were made to this author during phone conversations in 2003. A review of the archives reinforced the professors' remarks, so this book is focused on the formation of the Presbyterian community in a trans –Irish Sea context. The best work on familial settlement of Ulster is by Raymond Gillespie, *Colonial Ulster*. He used extant land records in Ulster, and his primary source for assigning Scottish homeplaces for those settling families is George Fraser Black, *Surnames of Scotland*. See R. Gillespie, *Colonial Ulster*, 32–34.

63. "The Contribution of Geography," 6, in Philo, "History," in Gregory, Martin, and Smith, *Human Geography*, 255.

64. Ibid.

65. Richard Hartshorne felt that past events belonged exclusively to historians, and topics of a spatial nature were in the purview of geographers (*Nature*

of Geography, 135). In his famous address to the Association of America Geographers in 1941, Carl O. Sauer expressed his dissatisfaction with Hartshorne's way of thinking and clearly felt that history and geology were critical parts of academic geography.

66. William Row, quoted in Blair, *Life of Mr. Robert Blair,* 145

67. David Calderwood's description of the members of congregations expressing themselves to ministers shows that the divines in his circle were inclined to listen to members of their flocks (*History of the Kirk,* 7.356). Edward Brice, for instance, was recruited to Ulster by a Stirlingshire friend named William Edmonston (McCartney, *Nor Principalities Nor Powers,* 21–22).

68. Baker, *Geography and History,* 177.

69. Ibid. The author later demonstrates a way to weaken this difficulty.

70. Sauer, *Agricultural Origins and Dispersals,* 1.

71. Baker, *Geography and History,* 166.

72. "Geography of Religion," 1; Park, *Sacred Worlds,* 78–79.

73. Of particular note is the fundamentalist-dominated southern (Bible Belt) region. Here Zelinksy's spatial categorization depends on patterns in the numbers of adherents in Christian churches (dominated by various Baptist denominations) that make membership data available. In the case of the South, membership in the evangelical Southern Baptist Convention far outnumbers other organizations. His study dismisses, however, the influences of theological thought worlds that Presbyterians and Church of Christ congregations, among others, have had on the creation of the Bible Belt. Had he paid more attention to theologies of colonial southerners, he would have recognized the influence of Irish Presbyterians (Park, *Sacred Worlds,* 79–81). See also Vann, *Rediscovering,* 116–38.

74. Sauer, "Foreword to Historical Geography," 24. On the links between Sauer and Bowen, see Thomas, "Landscape with Figures."

75. Bowen, "Le Pays de Galles."

76. The inscriptions were written in Old Irish. Bowen believed that the use of these stones originated on the continent in the Lyon-Vienne area in central France (*Britain and the Western Seaway,* 72–73).

77. Bowen, *Saints, Seaways, and Settlements,* 28–29.

78. The "saints" whom he discusses as central to the making of the seaways culture area are usually regarded as bearers of a form of Celtic Christianity that, though varying from the Catholic orthodoxy stemming from Rome, was in various ways conformable (and in retrospect these saints are indeed venerated within a Catholic tradition).

79. Ogborn, "Historical Geographies," 52.

80. Ibid.

81. *Saints, Seaways, and Settlements* and *Britain and the Western Seaways.*

82. Cooper, "New Directions"; Holloway and Valins, editorial; Kong, "Geography and Religion"; Pacione, "The Relevance of Religion"; and Valins, "Identity, Space, and Boundaries."

83. Holloway and Valins, editorial, 5.

84. Ibid., 6.

85. "Four Traditions of Geography," 211–16. Pattison identified the area-studies, man-land, earth-science, and spatial traditions.

86. "Towards a Spatial Theory," 62.

87. Naylor and Ryan, "The Mosque in the Suburbs."

88. Pacione, "The Geography of Religious Affiliation." See also Sauer, "The Agency of Man."

89. Sauer, "Forward to Historical Geography."

90. In Scotland and Ulster they were called conventicles. Todd (*Culture of Protestantism*, 109) gives an example of how Robert Blair used the outdoors, as an extension of sacred space, in communion services.

91. See Stump (1986) below.

92. Tuan, "Humanistic Geography."

93. Kong, "Geography and Religion," 355–71. See also Kong, "Religion and Technology," 404–13. Kong's reference to Stump (1986) is his "Geography and Religion—Introduction," 358.

94. Kong, *Lily* (1990).

95. J. K. Wright, "Terrae Incognitae."

96. Donaldson describes Melville's followers as an ecclesiastical intelligentsia, which this research has adopted in the use of the name Scottish Ecclesiastical Intelligentsia. This label is used precisely in reference to a community of antiprelatic divines and the learned members of their congregations who are described as Puritan-Presbyterians by Mullan, *Scottish Puritanism*. This community does not include Scottish intellectuals of Roman Catholic, Congregational, Quaker, or Episcopalian orientations (Donaldson, *Scotland: James V–James VII*, 149; Donaldson and Morpeth, *Who's Who in Scottish History*, 93).

97. Johnstone, *Religion in Society*, 28.

98. A *reference group* is a social categorization of people, which may or may not be composed of personal acquaintances, and is constructed by an individual to provides standards of personal conduct and social expectations. See Vann, "Learning Self-Direction."

99. In this instance, imagined geographies of Puritans in Southwest Scotland and Ulster included Palestine, England, the continent (especially Calvin's Geneva), and New England.

100. M. Savage, "Spatial Differences in Modern Britain" (1988), 267.

101. Thrift, "Taking Aim," 225.

102. Donaldson, *Scotland: Church and Nation*, 74.

103. Holloway and Valins's editorial provides a recent analysis on studies that have conjoined geography and religion. For an in-depth look at nonbelief attributes of the geography of religions, see Park, *Sacred Worlds*.

104. J. K. Wright, "Terrae Incognitae," 68–88; Kirk, "Problems of Geography."

105. Philo, "History, Geography, and the Still Greater Mystery of History and Geography," 261–62.

106. W. D. Baillie, *Six Mile Water Revival*, 21.

107. This description captures the cultural aspects of the demographic, economic, and political changes that took place in Ulster during the seventeenth and early eighteenth centuries. See Leyburn, *Scotch-Irish*.

108. John Livingstone, an Ulster minister and colleague of Robert Blair, had a number of communications with Massachusetts's governor John Winthrop. Livingstone and other Ulster Presbyterians made at least two attempts to resettle in New England during the 1630s (Lockington, *Robert Blair of Bangor*, 21).

109. P. Miller, *Errand into the Wilderness*, 11.

110. See chapter 3 in Bozeman, *To Live Ancient Lives*.

111. Carroll, *Puritanism and the Wilderness*; Heimert, "Puritanism, the Wilderness, and the Frontier;" G. H. Williams, *Wilderness and Paradise in Christian Thought*; and Zakai, *Exile and Kingdom*, 120–31.

112. Cotton, *Brief Exposition*, quoted in Zakai, *Exile and Kingdom*, 120–31.

113. It is interesting that Park does not offer any substantive discussion on the themes and topics advanced by Wright and even erroneously suggests that Tuan is the person associated with coining *geoteleology* (*Sacred Worlds*, 19).

114. Park, *Sacred Worlds*, 251–67.

115. Wright, "Terrae Incognitae."

1. On the Eve of the Exodus to Ulster

1. Brereton, *Travels in Holland*, 118.

2. Shakespeare, *Comedy of Errors*, 3.2.

3. G. Marshall, *Presbyteries and Profits*. The border region benefited from the king's peace that was brought about by the ascension of James VI of Scotland to the throne of England as James I. See R. Gillespie, *Colonial Ulster*.

4. R. Gillespie, *Colonial Ulster*, 40. See also how this explanation fits with the theory advanced by Jones, "Evolution of Scottish Migration Patterns."

5. Throughout Scotland's history, there were years in which population grew and other periods of time in which it declined. This is revealed in the following estimates. Michael Lynch reports a population estimate of between one-half million to one million people for the year 1300 (*Scotland*, 54). Scotland's population is estimated to have been one-million in 1700, so the demographic pattern, at least for four hundred years, was stable (Smout, *History of the Scottish People*, 240).

6. This point is developed later in this chapter.

7. Brereton, *Travels in Holland*, 119.

8. Megaw, "Date of Pont's Survey," 71–73; R. Gillespie, *Colonial Ulster*, 35.

9. Alexander, "Encouragement to the Colonies," 38.

10. Perceval-Maxwell, *Scottish Migration*, 27.

11. *Calendar of the Clarendon State Papers*, 426.

12. *British Museum Additional Manuscripts*, 33–34.

13. Schama, *History of Britain: The British Wars 1603–1776*, 89. The Church of England also provided Monday services.

14. Smout, Landsman, and Devine, "Scottish Migration," 78–79, 85, 87–88. See also R. Gillespie, *Colonial Ulster*. See also Perceval-Maxwell, *Scottish Migration*, 17; and Schama, *History of Britain:The British Wars, 1603–1776*, 36.

15. Smout, Landsman, and Devine, "Scottish Migration," 78–79, 85, 87–88. An estimated forty thousand to fifty thousand Scots were living in Ulster during the Cromwellian Interlude (Carlyle, *Oliver Cromwell's Letters and Speeches*, 3:178).

16. Schama, *British Wars*, 36.

17. This topic is further examined in chapters 5, 6, and 7.

18. To appreciate the sentiment that the Puritan-Presbyterians in the region had toward the sacredness of Scottish earth, see the letter from James Renwick to Loudoun, September 1683 (Moore, *Our Covenant Heritage*, 102–3).

19. Todd, *Culture of Protestantism*, 250.

20. This was a common view in medieval Catholicism as well as in the Old Testament.

21. Emigration was seen as an acceptable means to escape the wrath of a magistrate (see subsequent chapters).

22. Flinn, *Scottish Population History*.

23. Smout, *History of the Scottish People*, 143.

24. Ibid.

25. Ibid.

26. Ibid.

27. Ibid., 144.

28. Ibid., 143–44.

29. Ross, *Chronology of Scottish History*, 70.

30. There are several conflicting population estimates for Scotland prior to 1755. The population figures used here are taken from Ross, *Chronology of Scottish History*, 70, and Smout, *History of the Scottish People*, 240.

31. Smout, *History of the Scottish People*, 240. Sinclair, *Analysis*, 1.148–49.

32. Whyte, *Scotland before the Industrial Revolution*, 115.

33. Leyburn, *Scotch-Irish*, 3. Scotland's population in 1500 has been estimated at between five hundred thousand and seven hundred thousand (Whyte, *Scotland before the Industrial Revolution*, 113). Donaldson estimates "perhaps 800,000" for the year 1560 (*Scotland: James V–James VII*, 133).

34. See Sinclair. Alexander Webster did not examine population data with respect to this geographic configuration. A Lowland and coastal-strip zone set against a Highland region establishes a dichotomy to illustrate the pattern of population settlement in Scotland as well as to reflect the cultural regions of the country. Webster divides Scotland into a Central Belt that includes the counties of Ayr, Dumbarton, Lanark, Renfrew, Clackmannan, Stirling, the Lothians, Fife, and the City of Dundee. The Highland region includes all areas, including the low-lying coastal strip, north of the Central Belt. The Lowland region is limited to all areas to the south (Kyd, *Scottish Population Statistics*, xviii).

35. See Sinclair and Smout.

36. Leyburn, *Scotch-Irish*, 3; Lynch, *Edinburgh and the Reformation*, 3, 9–14; Todd, *Culture of Protestantism*, 10.

37. Figures are calculated from data provided by Lynch, *Scotland*, 367; Sinclair, *Analysis*, 1:148–49; and Leyburn, *Scotch-Irish*, 3. The basis for using 90 percent is calculated on population data for 1755. The equation is $(1,265,000 - 115,000) / 1,265,000$ $(100 / 1) = 90$. The numerator is Webster's total population minus Lynch's Highland population figure. The Central Belt, which is within the Lowland region of Scotland, would have had a higher population density than the border counties and the southwest of the country.

38. Sinclair, *Analysis*, 1:148–49.

39. Whyte, *Scotland before the Industrial Revolution*, 115.

40. As many as twenty-five thousand Scottish soldiers served in Scandinavia and another thirty thousand families, presumably from eastern Scotland, lived in Poland (Whyte, *Migration and Society*, 114).

41. Whyte, *Migration and Society*, 116.

42. Ibid.

43. See Leyburn, *Scotch-Irish*, 3; Sinclair, *Analysis*, 1:148–49.

44. See Leyburn and Sinclair.

45. The figure of 4.75 is based on the changes of the estimates published in Lynch, *Edinburgh and Reformation*; Todd, *Culture of Protestantism*; and the 1755 data. Lynch estimates that the city's population tripled during the less-expansive period of 1560 to 1660 (*Edinburgh and the Reformation*, 3).

46. Whyte, *Scotland's Society and Economy*, 115.

47. Ibid., 117.

48. Donaldson, *Scotland: James V–James VII*, 391.

49. *Feuing* refers to a change in land tenancy that effectively killed the man-rent basis of Scotland's feudal society. Money rent replaced labor as the means by which nonlandowners were allowed to stay on the lord's estate.

50. Tyson, "The Population of Aberdeenshire."

51. Donaldson, *Scotland: James–V James VII*, 391.

52. Smout, *History of the Scottish People*, 223.

53. Houston, "Geographical Mobility in Scotland."

54. *Calendar of the Clarendon State Papers*, 426.

55. Fitzpatrick, *God's Frontiersmen*, 9.

56. Ibid. Fitzpatrick's comments about the relative size of the Lowland population fails to recognize distinct areas within the Lowlands, such as the Borders, Fife, the Lothians, the Central Belt, the Clyde estuary region, and the southwest. There were marked differences in population in these areas. Those differences are explored in chapter 4.

57. Whyte, *Scotland's Society and Economy*, 33.

58. This thought is captured in Knox's Scots Confession (1560) and many other extant documents. See chapter 6 for a discussion on the geotheological attributes of the Puritan-Presbyterian community.

59. Leyburn argues that the Covenanter strife, especially in the wake of their defeat at the battle of Bothwell Bridge, forced many to migrate to Ireland. See Leyburn, *Scotch-Irish.* The immaterial aspects of religious culture are explored in subsequent chapters.

60. A casual relationship between Calvinism and capitalism is a highly contested topic. See Smout, *History of the Scottish People,* 88.

61. The replacement of manrent with money rent was called *feuing.* See Whyte, *Scotland's Society and Economy,* 29–30.

62. The theological points underlying the mindset of the members of the community are covered in subsequent chapters.

63. This topic is addressed in the next section of this chapter.

64. Weber, *Protestant Ethic.*

65. G. Marshall, *Presbyteries and Profits,* 280–81. Such a mindset would clearly undermine the resilience of the feudal social structure. Profits by feuing provided landowners with evidence of God's blessings.

66. Ibid., 284–319.

67. Smout, *History of the Scottish People,* 88.

68. Ibid.

69. Ibid., 90.

70. J. B. Torrance, *Westminster Confession in the Church Today,* 40–55.

71. Weber, *Protestant Ethic.*

72. Dickson, *Truth's Victory over Error,* 253; G. Marshall, *Presbyteries and Profits,* 91. Dickson is important in Southwest Scotland and Ulster for his communion services were attended by Presbyterian ministers and parish friends from Ulster (J. Livingstone, *A Brief Historical Relation,* 97).

73. Dickson and Durham, *Sum of Saving Knowledge,* 28.

74. While the bilateral-covenant construct originated on the continent with Ulrich Zwingli and Heidelberg Reformed theologians such as Wolfgang Musculus, Rollock was heavily influenced by English Puritanism (J. B. Torrance, *Westminster Confession in the Church Today,* 48). Later chapters explore the concept of bilateral covenants.

75. Rollock, *Lectures,* epist. 1:71.

76. Ibid.

77. Smout, *History of the Scottish People,* 81–88.

78. Ross, *Chronology of Scottish History,* 69.

79. A. W. Parker, *Scottish Highlanders in Colonial Georgia.* The scheme included planting a Scottish colony on the Isthmus of Panama. Its purpose was to transport goods between the Atlantic and Pacific coasts.

80. Ross, *Chronology,* 69.

81. In this letter of June 16, 1637, Rutherford is referring to political persecution (*Rutherford Letters,* 90–93).

82. Todd, *Culture of Protestantism,* 34.

83. Poverty was also a judgment on the rich—in the biblical prophetic tradition.

84. Todd, *Culture of Protestantism,* 174.

85. Rollock, *Lectures,* epist. 1:71.

86. Blair, *Life of Mr. Robert Blair,* 55.

87. Stewart quoted in Adair, *True Narrative,* 2.

88. Rollock, *Lectures,* epist. 1:71.

89. Dickson and Durham, *Sum of Saving Knowledge,* 28.

90. See Houston, "Geographical Mobility in Scotland."

91. Leyburn, *Scotch-Irish,* 1–30.

92. Ibid.

93. Whyte, *Scotland's Society and Economy,* 94–114.

94. Leyburn, *Scotch-Irish,* 1–30.

95. See Bowen, *Saints, Seaways, and Settlements,* 22–27.

96. Whyte, *Scotland's Society and Economy,* 94–114.

97. This idea is supported by Whyte (*Scotland before the Industrial Revolution,* 114), although his comparison pertains to Border counties, which would have had an even higher carrying capacity than the southwestern districts.

98. Whyte, *Scotland's Society and Economy,* 141.

99. Ibid., 116–17.

100. Ibid.

101. Smout, *History of the Scottish People,* 144.

102. Bowen, *Britain and the Western Seaways,* 124.

103. Ibid.

104. Cited in Bourne. Bowen provides a good analysis of the work of Bourne, who lived from about 1535 to 1582. *Britain and the Western Seaways,* 125–26. For an examination of Mediterranean navigation in the sixteenth century, see Fernand Braudel, *Mediterranean and the Mediterranean World in the Age of Philip II* (New York, 1972), originally published in French in 1966.

105. Bowen, *Britain and the Western Seaways,* 40.

106. Blair's experience is discussed in chapter 5.

107. Blair's description of a trip that included overnight travel suggests the passage of a cold front. He does not mention whether the moon was high (*Life of Mr. Robert Blair,* 53).

108. Donaldson and Morpeth, *Who's Who,* 134.

109. Rutherford, *Fourteen Communion Sermons,* 198.

110. Rutherford, February 20, 1637, letter to Lady Cardoness, *Rutherford Letters,* no. 100.

111. James G. Leyburn (1902 to 1993) served as dean and as the head of the Sociology Department at Washington and Lee University in Virginia from 1947 to 1972. As a sociologist, he was not tied to disciplinary expertise of a single nation. Instead, his focus was on social and cultural diffusion across large bodies of water and national boundaries.

112. Leyburn, *Scotch-Irish,* 101.

113. R. Gillespie, *Colonial Ulster,* 24–25.

114. Brereton may well have been charged more than local people.

115. R. Gillespie, *Colonial Ulster,* 24–25.

116. Houston, "Geographical Mobility in Scotland."

117. MacHaffie, *Portpatrick to Donaghadee.*

118. Although Wesley's crossing was fifty-seven years beyond the time frame of this study, sailing technology probably had not improved much during the ensuing years.

119. MacHaffie, *Portpatrick to Donaghadee,* 12.

120. Bardon, *History of Ulster,* 122.

121. MacHaffie, *Portpatrick to Donaghadee,* 8.

122. Ibid., 7–8.

123. Blair, *Life of Mr. Robert Blair,* 57.

124. Ibid.

125. D. Woodward, quoted in R. Gillespie, *Colonial Ulster,* 72.

126. Ibid.

127. McConnell, *Fasti,* 10.

128. *Jubilee of the General Assembly,* 42.

129. J. Livingstone, *Life of John Livingstone,* 104.

130. K. Miller, *Emigrants and Exiles,* 34.

131. Fry, *Scottish Empire,* 10.

132. MacHaffie, *Portpatrick to Donaghadee,* 8–10.

2. Ethnic Politics in the Plantation of Ireland

1. Ohlmeyer, "Civilisinge Those Rude Partes." The process of adopting English cultural traits, including loyal dispositions, is sometimes called *Anglicization* (D. Stevenson, *Covenanters,* 18).

2. Perceval-Maxwell, *Scottish Migration,* 254.

3. Ross, *Chronology of Scottish History,* 57.

4. J. Stevenson, *Two Centuries of Life,* in Fraser G. MacHaffie, *Portpatrick to Donaghadee,* 8.

5. Ohlmeyer, "Civilizinge Those Rude Partes," 124–47.

6. K. A. Miller, *Emigrants and Exiles,* 19; Ohlmeyer, "Civilizinge of Those Rude Partes," 130–43.

7. Quoted in Fitzpatrick, *God's Frontiersmen,* 9.

8. Blenerhasset, "A Direction for the Plantation of Ulster," 317–18.

9. Blair, *Life of Mr. Robert Blair,* 56–57. A *widcairn* was a native Irish guerrilla/terrorist fighter.

10. *Calendar of the State Papers,* 276.

11. Perceval-Maxwell, *Scottish Migration to Ulster,* 17.

12. Whyte, *Migration and Society,* 108.

13. Figures are calculated from data provided by Lynch, *Scotland,* 367; Sinclair, *Analysis,* 148–49; and Leyburn, *Scotch-Irish,* 3.

14. Whyte, *Migration and Society,* 109.

15. Patrick Griffin cites Smout, Landsman, and Devine but gives a figure that is seventy thousand to eighty thousand people higher than theirs. It may

be that he mistakenly quoted the larger figure of approximately one hundred thousand that they cite to account for all of Scots emigration (Poland, Ireland, Scandinavia, and elsewhere) (Griffin, *People with No Name*). See also Smout, Landsman, and Devine, "Scottish Migration." An estimate of between forty thousand and fifty thousand Scots living in Ulster was made during the Cromwellian Interlude (Carlyle, *Oliver Cromwell's Letters and Speeches*, 3:178). The rate of population increase, of course, would be somewhat reduced if these data are used relative to the estimates for 1715.

16. Ogilvie, *Presbyterian Churches*, 87. At least ten more ministers were installed by 1665, for during the early years of the Stuart Restoration, seventy-two ministers were deposed for nonconformity, and eight conformed to Episcopacy (McConnell, *Fasti*, 4–52).

17. Quoted in P. Livingstone, *The Monaghan Story*, 132.

18. Lecky, *Ireland in the Eighteenth Century*, 2:400–401; Perry, *Scotch-Irish in New England*, 7.

19. Woodburn, *Ulster-Scot*, 172; Griffin, *People with No Name*. However, Griffin provides a date of 1690 for the establishment of the Ulster Synod and its nine presbyteries (*People with No Name*, 19). He further provides a figure of 150,000 Ulster-Scots by that date. The figure of 250,000 is based on an additional 50,000 Scots families (assuming a conservative figure of two persons per family) as presented in Lecky, *Ireland in the Eighteenth Century*, 2:400–401, and Perry, *Scotch-Irish in New England*, 7.

20. Dunlop, *Precarious Belonging*, 24.

21. Leyburn, *Scotch-Irish*, 132.

22. K. A. Miller, *Emigrants and Exiles*, 20.

23. Bell, *Book of Ulster Names*, 106. See the discussion on the Jordan family in Bell, *Book of Ulster Surnames*, 106.

24. Ohlmeyer, "Civilizinge Those Rude Partes," 124–47.

25. Quoted in Magnusson, *Scotland*, 408.

26. Donaldson, *Scotland: James V–James VII*, 228, 252.

27. Ohlmeyer, "Civilizinge Those Rude Partes," 124–47.

28. *Register of the Privy Council of Scotland*, First Series, 7.706.

29. Ohlmeyer, "Civilizinge Those Rude Partes," 127.

30. Chapter 4 explores the ethnic politics of the Plantation of Ulster, and, in that context, monarchical attitudes toward the Irish are also considered in greater detail.

31. Smout, *History of the Scottish People*, 104.

32. Monaghan, Cavan, and Donegal are Ulster counties, but being the farthest Ulster counties from the fertile source of colonists, they were not heavily settled by Scots or English pioneers.

33. James VI and James I, quoted in John MacLeod, *Dynasty*, 149. The same quote is found in Magnusson, *Scotland*, 408.

34. Leyburne, *Scotch-Irish History*, 114, 120–21.

35. Falls, *Birth of Ulster*.

36. Blair, *Life of Mr. Robert Blair.* The word *laity* would not have been used in the seventeenth century; however, modern scholars have used it with respect to nonordained members of the church. See for example, Westerkamp, *Triumph of the Laity.*

37. Perceval-Maxwell, *Scottish Migration,* 45.

38. Anderson, *Imagined Communities.* To see the intricacies of the English and Scottish linkages in the imagined community of Puritan divines, which Mullan calls a "Puritan brotherhood," refer to his *Scottish Puritanism,* 13–44; see also Vann, "Presbyterian Social Ties."

39. Unlike the established, legal Kirk of Scotland, this church organization was until 1690 dissenting and voluntary, so it operated somewhat outside the law. As a result, it was a self-governing polity.

40. Calderwood's description of the members of the congregation expressing themselves to wayward ministers was a clear departure from the source of discipline associated with Erastianism. In Erastianism, corrective discipline was dispensed by bishops, archbishops, and ultimately the monarch (*History of the Kirk of Scotland,* 7:356).

41. Mullan, *Scottish Puritanism,* 13–44.

42. The chief architect of this doctrine was Theodore Beza, Melville's teacher in Geneva. See Ian Hazlett, *The Reformation in Britian and Ireland,* 34, 64.

43. *Submissive* means to Christ's kingdom.

44. Melville, in Herron, *Kirk by Divine Right,* 30.

45. Donaldson, *Scotland: Church and Nation,* 77–78.

46. A *theocracy* is formed when a group of devote believers insist on controlling morality based on divine law through the apparatus of government (Johnstone, *Religion in Society,* 171–72).

47. Knox, Scots Confession: 1560, chapter 18. The Book of Confessions, PCUSA, 20.

48. The magistrate, or secular government, according to the Scots Confession, chapter 24, is responsible for ensuring the practice of true religion.

49. Ulster's prominence in Irish Presbyterianism is significant. The ecclesiastical body referred to here actually grew out of the Synod of Ulster. The name Irish Presbyterian Church (IPC) was adopted in 1840. Records for the Army Presbytery (1642–1646), Presbytery of Ulster (1646–1690), and the Synod of Ulster are maintained by the IPC.

50. Herron, *Kirk by Divine Right.*

51. Makemie, in Barkley, *Francis Makemie,* 10.

52. Ibid.

53. Macinnes, *Clanship,* 59.

54. MacLeod, *Dynasty,* 141.

55. Perceval-Maxwell, *Scottish Migration,* 254.

56. James VI, *Basilikon Doron,* 71.

57. Lynch, *Scotland,* 241.

58. Donaldson, *Scotland: James V–James VII*, 230–32.

59. Ibid.

60. Donaldson, *Scotland: James V–James VII*, 228–32. James's wife died a Roman Catholic. His son Charles, an Arminian, married a Catholic woman, a union the king endorsed. Nonetheless Mullan insists that James was a Calvinist (*Scottish Puritanism*, 215).

61. McKerrall, *Kintyre*. MacDonnell is an alternate form of MacDonald in Ireland (Bell, *Book of Ulster Surnames*, 154).

62. Nothing really came of the earl's initial efforts, but one of his kinsmen, the dashing twenty-one-year-old Alasdair McColla MacDonald, went to the aid of the Covenanter-turned-Royalist the Marquis of Montrose. MacDonald served the king with as many as two thousand native Irish fighters (Macleod, *Dynasty*, 204).

63. This is the author's assessment.

64. Ibid.

65. Ibid., 125.

66. Bardon, *History of Ulster*, 143.

67. Ford, *Scotch-Irish in America*, 152–53.

68. Rubenstein, *Cultural Landscape*, 140.

69. Leyburn, *Scotch-Irish*, 92.

70. *Register of the Privy Council of Scotland*, 8:267–68. Leyburn, *Scotch-Irish History*, 92–93.

71. Perceval-Maxwell, *Scottish Migration*.

72. Packer, *Knowing God*, 26.

73. J. Stevenson, *Two Centuries of Life in Down*, cited in MacHaffie, *Portpatrick to Donaghadee*, 8.

74. Fry, *Scottish Empire*, 8–9.

75. Blair, *Life of Mr. Robert Blair*, 58–59; J. Livingstone, *Life of John Livingstone*, 142; Pearson, *Puritan and Presbyterian Settlements*, 69.

76. W. D. Baillie, *Six Mile Water Revival*, 21.

77. Ibid.

78. Lockington, *Robert Blair of Bangor*, 22–23.

79. Mullan, *Scottish Puritanism*, 13–44.

80. J. Livingstone, *Life of John Livingstone*, 108.

81. Ibid.

82. Blair, *Life of Mr. Robert Blair*, 148.

83. Sprott, *Worship of the Church of Scotland*, 8.

84. W. D. Baillie, *Six Mile Water Revival*, 21.

85. Todd, *Culture of Protestantism*, 75–76.

86. W. D. Baillie, *Six Mile Water Revival*, 21–22.

87. For an example of how Robert Blair used the outdoors as an extension of sacred space in communion services, see Todd, *Culture of Protestantism*, 109.

88. Perceval-Maxwell, *Scottish Migration*, 268.

89. Westerkamp, *Triumph of the Laity*, 22–23.

90. Mullan, *Scottish Puritanism,* 79.

91. W. D. Baillie, *Six Mile Water Revival,* 9–10.

92. Leyburn, *Scotch-Irish,* 106–7.

93. Fry, *Scottish Empire,* 13.

94. Ibid.

95. The annual payment was subsequently suspended two times prior to the close of Scottish migrations to Ulster, once under Queen Anne and the last time in 1714 under George I (Bardon, *History of Ulster,* 162).

96. In numerous discussions the author and Colin Williamson, the secretary of the Irish ministers' fraternal organization within the Scottish Kirk, pondered this topic. From Williamson's perspective, a congregational session in Ulster has much more authority over ecclesiastical affairs than its counterpart in the Kirk. In addition the Kirk being a national church body and Irish Presbyterianism an independent denomination, the interaction between English Congregationalists and Scots Presbyterians in Ulster during the seventeenth century tended to democratize the Irish Presbyterian polity. These discussions were held in the Strathearn Parish in Perthshire, Scotland, between June 2002 and November 2003.

97. Scholars such as Raymond Gillespie and T. C. Smout argue that economic issues created by overpopulation caused most of the migrations to Ireland. A full discussion on their views appeared earlier.

98. For a discussion on the migration of English Puritans to America, as opposed to Ulster, see Zakai, *Exile and Kingdom.* The rise of Brownism is an even more pronounced example of the empowerment of congregations relative to overarching governing bodies (W. D. Baillie, *Six Mile Water Revival,* 21–22).

99. Vann, *Rediscovering.* Also, see Fischer, *Albion's Seed.*

100. Leyburn, *Scotch-Irish History.*

101. Graham of Claverhouse, Viscount Dundee, was relentless in his pursuit of Scottish Covenanters among whom he gained the nickname of "bloody Clavers." In the twentieth century, parents in America's Southern Uplands continued to warn their children, "Behave yourself, or Clavers will get you" (Bolton, *Scotch-Irish Pioneers,* 300). See also Leyburn, *Scotch-Irish,* 129.

102. Bardon, *History of Ulster,* 150.

103. Leyburn, *Scotch-Irish,* 128. With Presbyterian-minded Scots in the path of Claverhouse, an undetermined number of the families who left Ulster may well have immigrated to America.

104. The University of Tennessee was founded as Blount College in 1794 by Americans of Ulster Presbyterian descent. The Presbyterian minister Rev. Samuel Carrick was the main force behind the establishment of Blount College and served as its founding president. See Kennedy, *Scots-Irish in the Hills of Tennessee.* As later generations of Tennesseans moved westward across the southern landscape, they established new colleges and universities. Like Oklahoma, Texas was heavily settled by Tennesseans. The social and cultural connections between Tennessee and Texas are strong. For instance, the small East

Tennessee community served by Blount College was the childhood home of Sam Houston (born March 2, 1793), an American of Ulster-Scots descent, who served as a member of Congress from Tennessee (1823 to 1827) and governor of Tennessee (1827 to 1829). After living for a time again with the Cherokee, he went to Texas where he led the Texas army for independence from Mexico. He was the first president of the short-lived Republic of Texas (1836 to 1838 and 1841 to 1844). The University of Texas was established during Houston's political career in Texas. When Texas became a state in 1845, Houston was elected to the United States Senate (1846 to 1859). He later served for two years as governor (1859 to 1861). Like his East Tennessee counterparts, he resisted secession from the Union in 1861 and was forced out of office. He died on his farm in Huntsville, Texas, in 1863 (James, *Raven;* see also Day and Ullom, *Autobiography of Sam Houston*).

105. Leyburn, *Scotch-Irish,* 167.

106. Ibid. Anne, under pressure from her Anglican-dominated court, began a campaign of political repression against Ulster's dissenting Christians. The Test Act of 1703, which was primarily aimed at the civil workforce, gave strength to the enforcement of the already established illegal status of Presbyterian marriages.

107. Bardon, *History of Ulster,* 173.

108. Ibid., 174.

109. R. L. Marshall, "The Commemoration Sermon," in "Tercentenary Committee of the Presbyterian Church in Ireland," *Three Hundred Years of Presbyterianism,* 7–9.

110. Connolly, *Religion, Law, and Power,* 166.

111. Bardon, *History of Ulster,* 173.

112. Hayton, "Presbyterians and the Confessional State," 12.

113. Leyburn, *Scotch-Irish.*

114. Whyte, *Migration and Society,* 105.

115. Hayton, "Presbyterians and the Confessional State," 16.

116. Barry, "Historical Introduction," ix–xii.

117. Whyte, *Migration and Society,* 111; Bardon, *History of Ulster,* 122–23.

3. The Birth of Ulster-Scots Land

1. For a discussion on the use of sea routes by ministers during this time— the Age of the Saints—see Bowen, *Saints, Seaways, and Settlements,* and Landsman, *Scotland and Its First American Colony,* 9.

2. John K. Wright, "Notes on Early American Geopiety," defines the term *geoapocalyptic* as relating to the spatial aspects of divine retribution and the concept of *geoeschatology* as the relationship between space and providential outcomes.

3. The religious ethos of this community was not only anti-Erastian and anti-Episcopalian, it was also anti-Arminian, which was seen as a Catholicizing theology of salvation. See Tyacke, *Anti-Calvinists;* Walker, *Theology and Theologians.*

4. J. B. Torrance provides valuable information on this ethos in his lecture notes, "Covenant or Contract."

5. In this instance, the "invisible church" consists of those called by God. The "visible church" includes the physical presence of the elect (those chosen by God) and reprobates (those not chosen).

6. Unless otherwise noted, social connections are put together from Mullan, *Scottish Puritanism*, 13–44.

7. Major, in *Disputationes de Potestate Papae et Concilii* (1519), argues that political power emerges from the people and is not vested in kings.

8. J. B. Torrance, *Westminster Confession in the Church Today*, 40–53.

9. This innovation was misidentified with Calvinism. See J. B. Torrance, *Westminster Confession in the Church Today*, 48.

10. T. F. Torrance, *Scottish Theology*.

11. Ibid. T. F. Torrance regards both Dickson and Durham as high Calvinists, which suggests that Christ's atoning death applies only to the elect and that the doctrine of irresistible grace reduces the need for evangelism. Under such a situation, the elect are under greater psychological and social pressure to behave piously.

12. Dickson and Durham, *Sum of Saving Knowledge*. See T. F. Torrance, *Scottish Theology*, 103. Semi-pelagianism is a somewhat diluted version of the doctrine of natural salvation espoused by Pelagius (b. 354) and opposed by Aurelius Augustus (354 to 430). Pelagius argued that salvation was attainable through willfully following God's commands and that grace was not necessary for salvation. For a thorough discussion on Pelagius in the context of the debate over free will and salvation, see Sproul, *Willing to Believe*, 33–45.

13. For an in-depth discussion on the sociological aspects of this religious community, see chapter 3.

14. Buchan and Smith, *Kirk in Scotland*.

15. J. B. Torrance, *Westminster Confession in the Church Today*, 40–53; Mullan, *Scottish Puritanism*.

16. Dickson and Durham, *Sum of Saving Knowledge*.

17. This notion is developed in later chapters. The present chapter describes the social structure of the community leaders.

18. Donaldson, *Scotland: James V–James VII*, 149; the remark concerning Melville as the founder of Scottish Presbyterianism is from Donaldson and Morpeth, *Who's Who*, 93; the concept of a community of imagination was introduced by Anderson in *Imagined Communities*.

19. Though both men wrote autobiographies that provide valuable insights into the events that surrounded them, excellent biographical information on these men can be found in Cameron, et al., *Dictionary of Scottish Church History and Theology*.

20. Mullan, *Scottish Puritanism*, 23.

21. Lockington, *Robert Blair of Bangor*, 2.

22. J. Livingstone, *Brief Historical Relation*, 66.

23. Mullan, *Scottish Puritanism*, 13.

24. *Life of Robert Boyd*, quoted in Mullan, *Scottish Puritanism*, 13.

25. W. K. Tweedie, *Select Biographies*, 1:140. In his autobiography, John Livingstone is quite clear on who he felt were his spiritual role models. They included both men and women. Among them were Puritan-Presbyterians such as Robert Bruce, Lady Banton, Lady Culross, Robert Boyd, Robert Blair, Patrick Simpson, Robert Scott, the Countess of Wigton, Lady Lillias Graham, John Dick of Anstruther, John Ker of Prestonpans, James Greg of New-milns, Josias Welsh, Robert Rollock, the Countess of Eglintoun and Loudoun, and William Wallace (*Life of Mr. Livingstone*, 64–65, 74–75).

26. From 1642 to 1646, the name Army Presbytery was used, and from 1646 to 1690, the Presbytery of Ulster was employed as the name of the body of Presbyterian churches in Ireland.

27. Moffatt, *Presbyterian Churches*, 39. See this chapter and the next, this volume, for discussions on the differences between Episcopalian and Presbyterian polities with respect to spatial patterns and varying orientations toward Erastianism.

28. Hazlett, *Reformation in Britain and Ireland*, 105.

29. Blair, *Life of Mr. Robert Blair*, 57–58.

30. Ibid.

31. W. D. Baillie, *Six Mile Water Revival*, 4–5.

32. J. Livingstone, *Life of John Livingstone*, 1.143. However, the two English ministers whom Livingstone mentions were included in the eight whose English origins can be confirmed among the 188 divines who served in Ireland as Presbyterians. This topic is discussed later in this chapter.

33. Culverwell, *Treatise of Faith*.

34. Rogers, *Seven Treatises*.

35. Rogers, "Diary of Richard Rogers."

36. Blair, *Life of Blair*, 32.

37. Dickson, *Short Explanation of the Epistle of Paul to the Hebrews*, 3:4.

38. Donaldson and Morpeth, *Who's Who*, 125–26.

39. Johnston, *Diary*.

40. Hazlett, *Reformation in Britain and Ireland*, 105. See also Donaldson, *Scotland: Church and Nation*, 74.

41. Tracy, *Europe's Reformations*, 270.

42. Donaldson, *James V–James VII*, 149.

43. Cameron, et al., *Dictionary of Scottish Church History*; Durkan and Kirk, *University of Glasgow*. See also Donaldson and Morpeth, *Who's Who*, 93–95.

44. Quoted in Herron, *Kirk by Divine Right*, 30.

45. J. Melville, *Memoirs*.

46. Blair, *Life of Blair*, 5. Dickson, too, had troubles with Episcopal courts, especially the one headed by Archbishop Law of Glasgow, and was temporarily banished from Irvine to Turriff for his nonsupport of the Perth Articles. Dickson

also served as a professor at both Glasgow and Edinburgh (Blair, *Life of* Blair, 5n). See chapter 2 for a discussion on transportation across the Irish Sea.

47. McConnell, *Fasti*, 6–8. See also McCartney, *Nor Principalities nor Powers*, 30.

48. Lockington, *Robert Blair of Bangor*, 5.

49. Mullan, *Scottish Puritanism*, 148.

50. Rutherford, letter to James Lindsay, *Letters of Samuel Rutherford*, 131–34.

51. Mullan, *Scottish Puritanism*, 19.

52. Ibid., 20.

53. Perceval-Maxwell, *Scottish Migration*, 269; *Jubilee of the General Assembly*, 41; McConnell, *Fasti*, 5.

54. McConnell, *Fasti*, 5. See also McCartney, *Nor Principalities nor Powers*, 21–22.

55. Donaldson and Morpeth, *Who's Who*, 133–34. See chapters 4 and 7 for a discussion about the National Covenant.

56. Fleming, *Fulfilling of the Scripture*, 353.

57. Rutherford was ordered into exile by Thomas Syderf, the high-church bishop of Galloway. The order was precipitated by Rutherford's anti-Arminian work entitled *Exercitationes Apologeticae*.

58. Rutherford, letter to James Lindsay, *Letters of Samuel Rutherford*, 131–34.

59. James Hamilton was recruited into the ministry by Blair, but he had already earned his credentials (M.A.) at the University of Glasgow in 1620 (McConnell, *Fasti*, 8).

60. An Engager was a royalist Scot who, when faced with Cromwell's New Model Army, offered Charles I military support in exchange for the king's promise to make England Presbyterian for a trial period of three years (Donaldson, *James V–James VII*, 336).

61. Mullan, *Scottish Puritanism*, 38–39; Donaldson and Morpeth, *Who's Who*, 133–34.

62. Mullan, *Scottish Puritanism*, 39.

63. Rutherford, letter to James Lindsay, *Letters of Samuel Rutherford*, 131–34. In his letter to David Dickson, he speaks of the joy he had when he learned that Dickson employed ousted ministers from Ireland, which most likely referred to Blair and Livingstone (letter to David Dickson, *Letters of Samuel Rutherford*, 59–60).

64. Young, *Life of John Welsh*, 10.

65. Kirkton, *Secret and True History*, 18.

66. Ibid., 37.

67. J. Livingstone, *Life of Mr. Livingstone*, 74.

68. W. K. Tweedie, *Select Biographies*, i, 160–61.

69. Foote, *Sketches of North Carolina*, 98.

70. *Jubilee of the General Assembly,* 41.

71. The Five Articles of Perth called for (1) kneeling during communion, (2) private baptism, (3) private communion for the sick or infirm, (4) confirmation by a bishop, and (5) observance of holy days. The requirement to kneel at communion suggested veneration of the elements, a Catholic doctrine. This created quite a reaction among Protestants who feared a reversion to Catholicism (Donaldson, *Scotland: Church and Nation,* 81–82). For Welsh's opinion of the Perth Articles, see also J. S. Reid, *History of the Presbyterian Church,* 1:112.

72. McConnell, *Fasti,* 7.

73. Ibid., 46; J. S. Reid, *History of the Presbyterian Church,* 2.291; Adair, *True Narrative,* 283.

74. McConnell, *Fasti,* 7; J. S. Reid, *History of the Presbyterian Church,* 2.291; Adair, *True Narrative,* 283.

75. Leyburn, *Scotch-Irish,* 92.

76. Beckett, *Protestant Dissent in Ireland,* 86.

77. Schama, *History of Britain: The British Wars,* 89.

78. See chapter 4.

79. Leyburn, *Scotch-Irish,* 87–88.

80. It can be argued that a cultured Scot in the seventeenth century was conversant in theology, and educated gentry were no exception (Packer, *Knowing God,* 26, see below).

81. On May 12, 1635, Robert Blair married Katherine Montgomery, Hugh Montgomery's daughter (Blair, *Life of Blair,* 104).

82. Lockington, *Robert Blair of Bangor,* 5–6.

83. Ibid.

84. Barkley, *Francis Makemie,* 7.

85. Perceval-Maxwell, *Scottish Migration,* 268.

86. Ulster's almost-obliterated population that resulted from the Tudor Wars is discussed in chapter 4. Robert Blair described Ulster as a place where the wolf and woodkern played havoc with the first essayers, which suggests that the absence of Anglo civilization created a wilderness environment. James I certainly regarded Ireland as "rude" and in need of being civilized (Blair, *Life of Blair,* 56–57). See also Ohlmeyer, "Civilising those rude partes," 124–47.

87. *Jubilee of the General Assembly,* 41. These reflections, written 275 years later, may reflect some romanticizing of the Revival. For modern studies on the Revival, see Westerkamp, *Triumph of the Laity;* McKee, "Revival, Revivalism, and Calvinism," 87–100; and W. D. Baillie, *Six Mile Water Revival.*

88. Perceval-Maxwell, *Scottish Migration,* 271.

89. Blair, *Life of Blair,* 83.

90. W. D. Baillie, *Six Mile Water,* 1. See also Couper, *Scottish Revivals,* 26–39.

91. Blair, *Life of Blair,* 82.

92. King, *Reeves Copy Book of Visitations.*

93. In 1683, Ulster's Laggan Presbytery planted the Presbyterian Church in Maryland. See Barkley, *Francis Makemie.*

94. R. Gillespie, "Dissenters and Nonconformists," 11–28.

95. This point is a central theme of subsequent chapters, especially chapter 7.

96. McCartney, *Nor Principalities nor Powers,* 38.

97. Ibid. Blair was in attendance at the meeting because the assembly voted to have him translated from Ayr to St. Andrews (Lockington, *Robert Blair of Bangor,* 22–23). See also Stevenson, *Scottish Covenanters and Irish Confederates.*

98. W. D. Baillie, *Six Mile Water Revival,* 16.

99. Lockington, *Robert Blair of Bangor,* 23; McCartney, *Nor Principalities nor Powers,* 53–54.

100. McCartney, *Nor Principalities nor Powers,* 53.

101. Pearson, "Origins of Irish Presbyterianism," 14.

102. Lockington, *Robert Blair of Bangor,* 23.

103. The Baptist ministers saw Ulster as a place where dissenting religious views, as long as they belonged to loyal Protestants, could be expressed. See chapter 6 for a discussion on diversity among Protestants, especially by the end of the plantation. See also Adair, *True Narrative,* 98.

104. McCartney, *Nor Principalities nor Powers,* 53.

105. Ibid., 55.

106. Ibid., 54.

107. This idea is developed in the next two chapters.

108. See chapter 7 and the appendixes.

109. Hew Scott, *Fasti Ecclesiae Scoticanae,* v, 136.

110. McConnell, *Fasti,* 84.

111. This shift in polity can be seen in the context of a political-theory continuum. If centralized power and Erastianism are compatible, representative democracy and Presbyterianism are similarly matched. Direct democracy and congregationalism are likewise parallel ideas on governance. In an interview in November 2003, Colin Williamson, the secretary of the Irish ministers' fraternal society within the Kirk, expressed an interpretation on this difference in polity by noting that the Kirk is a national church, and the Presbyterian Church in Ireland is only a denomination. See also W. D. Baillie, *Six Mile Water Revival,* 21; Herron, *Westminster Confession in the Church Today.* See chapter 4 for a discussion on the politics of religion inherent in the plantation scheme.

112. Rutherford, *Due Right of Presbytery.* The logic behind this statement rests with Rutherford's conviction that Christ's kingdom is sovereign over that which is governed by the magistrate.

113. Ibid.

114. Barry, "Historical Introduction." See also Whyte, *Migration and Society,* 105.

115. Mullan, *Scottish Puritanism,* 79.

116. Perceval-Maxwell, *Scottish Migration,* 268.

117. McConnell, *Fasti.*

118. Ibid.

119. Ibid. See also appendixes 2, 3, and 4 for data on IPC ministers.

120. Black, *Surnames of Scotland.* Raymond Gillespie also uses Black's book. See R. Gillespie, *Colonial Ulster,* 32–34.

121. McConnell, *Fasti.* See also appendixes 2, 3, and 4.

122. Circuit-riding conventiclers were ministers who conducted illegal field meetings in various remote places in the southwest of Scotland and Ulster (at least up to 1672 at which time Charles II moderated his policy against dissenting Protestants in Ireland).

123. When Cromwell's forces took control of Ireland, ministers were required to take the Republican engagement, which required their submission to the new government.

124. In 1663 Colonel Thomas Blood developed a plot that required Presbyters and others to take Dublin Castle in the name of defending the Covenant. See McConnell, *Fasti.*

125. After the defeat of Scottish forces under Hamilton at Preston in 1648, anti-engagers took control of parliament. They passed the Act of Classes, which excluded all engagers from every public office. Within a week of the passage of the act, Charles I was executed. In 1650, Charles II was crowned at Scone, and on September 3 of that year, he suffered a major defeat at Dunbar. Those Scots who wanted to allow former engagers into the military, which conceivably would have strengthened their position against Cromwell, were called Resolutioners. Those who opposed the idea were Protesters or Remonstrants (Burleigh, *Church History,* 231–32).

126. See the appendix, tables A1 and A2.

127. Vallance, "Holy and Sacramentall Paction."

128. Ibid.

129. This topic is explored in chapter 7.

130. McConnell, *Fasti,* 50. For a more thorough examination of Irish Presbyterianism outwith the North Channel culture area, see R. L. Greaves, *God's Other Children;* Irwin, *History of Presbyterianism.*

131. McConnell, *Fasti,* 39.

132. Ibid., 44, 59.

133. This statement is based on the known Scottish birthplaces of the divines as well as the origins of family names of Irish-born ministers. See Black, *Surnames of Scotland.*

134. Burrell, "The Apocalyptic Vision."

4. Toward a Theocratic World View

1. Johnston and Henderson, *Confession of Faith.* The National Covenant, also known as confession, was signed February 28, 1638.

2. According to the traditional story, Jenny Geddes etched her protest on the ears of the dean conducting the service by asking, "Dost thou say mass at my lug [ear]"? (Macleod, *Dynasty*, 181). The protestation at St. Giles was the occasion but not the cause of the revolt. The events at St. Giles appealed to popular feelings against popery, English interference in Scottish affairs, and arbitrary rule (Donaldson, *Scotland: Church and Nation*, 83).

3. Burleigh, *Church History*, 215–17.

4. The key issue is that the National Covenant was engrossed in statutory law. The geotheological attributes of the document are discussed in chapter 6.

5. See the appendix, tables A1 and A2.

6. D. Stevenson, *Covenanters*, 6.

7. Tracy, *Europe's Reformations*.

8. Presbyterian Church, USA, Book of Confessions, 10.

9. Quoted in McNeil, *History and Character of Calvinism*, 178.

10. This document did not have equivalent legal status with the National Covenant, because the King's Confession was not approved by Parliament.

11. Torrance, *Westminster Confession in the Church Today*, 41.

12. "Westminster Confession of Faith," Book of Confessions, 23.

13. Torrance, *Westminster Confession*, 45–50.

14. Ibid., 45.

15. Ibid., 49.

16. Scots Confession, 3, 16, and 8.

17. Torrance, *Westminster Confession*, 47.

18. Calvin, *Institutes of the Christian Religion*, 2:926.

19. Tracy, *Europe's Reformations*, 95.

20. The inability to turn aside from God's decrees is determined by the doctrine of irresistible grace (ibid., 314n61).

21. This action was not universally accepted in Scotland. It was actions such as this that drove James Graham, the Marquis of Montrose, from the ranks of the leading Covenanters. In his absence, leadership went to Montrose's rival Archibald Campbell, the Marquis of Argyle. See Cowan, *Montrose*.

22. Five Scottish clergymen were present for discussions, but they could not vote. The English Parliament did approve the document with the addition of scripture proofs. However, the ascension of Oliver Cromwell stopped its adoption in England. Pride's Purge of 1648 forcibly removed Presbyterians from parliament in 1648. The next year, Cromwell's Puritan parliament executed Charles I. See Book of Confessions, 122.

23. While the Calvinism of the Scots Confession is softer than its replacement, interactionist sociologists such as George Herbert Meade and Harold Garfinkel point out that words and communication carry with them assumptions and shared understandings. The choice of words used in the Scots Confession show the nation's concern for godly management of the magistrate's affairs in relation to the Kirk's frequently failed mission (Giddens, *Sociology*, 87–88.

24. Knox, Scots Confession, chapter 17 in the Book of Confessions, 819.

25. Ibid, chapter 18, p. 19.

26. Ibid., chapter 20, p. 21.

27. Such words have also been used by Arminians as a means to create a sense of guilt among people. People who feel guilty, according to the Arminian notion of free will, would exercise it to abandon their sinful ways.

28. Westminster Confession of Faith, 4.

29. Buchan and Smith, *Kirk in Scotland.*

30. Westminster Confession of Faith, 7.

31. G. Marshall, *Presbyteries and Profits,* 88.

32. Dickson and Durham, *Sum of Saving Knowledge,* 28.

33. The Scottish divines who attended the assembly were George Gillespie, Alexander Henderson, Samuel Rutherford, Lord Loudoun, and Robert Baillie. See chapter 5 for more biographical information on these men.

34. Burleigh, *Church History,* 215.

35. Donaldson and Morpeth, *Who's Who,* 132.

36. Buchan and Smith, *Kirk in Scotland,* 21.

37. G. Gillespie, *Dispute Concerning the English Popish Ceremonies,* 269.

38. D. Stevenson, *Covenanters,* 7.

39. Ibid.

40. McGrath, *Reformation Thought,* 216. This was also a medieval Catholic doctrine.

41. See Burleigh, *Church History,* 262–63 for a perspective on the society folk.

42. Mullan, *Scottish Puritanism,* 38.

43. D. Stevenson, *Covenanters,* 2. *Arminianism* refers to a theological doctrine named for Jacobus Arminius, who argued against the predestinarian interpretation of strict Calvinism. Specifically Arminius took issue with the incompatibility between predestination and human free will. In essence, this meant that people are able to reject God's offer of salvation. See Nicholas Tyacke, *Anti-Calvinists.*

44. Mullan, *Scottish Puritanism,* 79.

45. Ibid., 262.

46. McConnell, *Fasti,* 57–58.

47. Ibid.

48. Blair, *Life of Mr. Robert Blair,* 146.

49. Buchan and Smith, *Kirk in Scotland,* 53. Thomas Hobbes, who had served as tutor to Charles I, was an advocate of the headship of the king over both secular and ecclesiastical affairs. Hobbes referred to the king as "supreme pastor." See Thomas Hobbes, *Leviathan.*

50. Buchan and Smith, *Kirk in Scotland,* 54.

51. Dunlop, *Precarious Belonging,* 28–29.

52. Fry, *Scottish Empire,* 13.

53. Buchan and Smith, *Kirk in Scotland*, 54. The three reasons are discussed and expanded upon in this section. The author adds a fourth.

54. G. Gillespie, *Wholesome Severity Reconciled*, 39–40.

55. Durham, *Dying Man's Testament*, 311.

56. Moore, *Our Covenant Heritage*, 41.

57. D. Stevenson, *Covenanters*, 3.

58. Scots Confession, chapter 16, p. 18.

59. Ibid., chapter 24, p. 24.

60. Johnston and Henderson, *Confession of National Covenant Faith*.

61. "Of the Civill Magistrate," Westminster Confession, chapter 25 in the Book of Confessions, p. 3.

62. A. G. Reid, *Annals of Auchterarder*, 211–52. After the Stuart Restoration in 1660, an era began that produced "one of the largest witch crazes in Scottish history" (Lynch, *Scotland*, 297).

63. Todd, *Culture of Protestantism*.

64. This provides a consequence of sin in the "if then, what then" nature of English contract law. The consequence of waywardness of the elect could have macro social and political ramifications.

65. Rutherford, *Exercitationes Apologeticae*. The Scots divines who participated in the assembly as advisers were Calvinists. Rutherford was among the more vocal opponents of the new doctrine of Arminianism, and his views, reflected in *Exercitationes Apologetcae*, caused him political problems with Bishop Thomas Sydserf of Galloway.

66. Buchan and Smith, *Kirk in Scotland*, 25. *Donatism* was an early fourth-century movement, primarily led by the Berber Christian Donatus in North Africa and which refused to recognize church officers who turned aside from the faith during the persecutions of Diocletion (303 to 305).

67. Weber, *Protestant Ethic*.

68. Kyle, *Encyclopaedia of the Reformed Faith*, 209.

69. Ibid.

70. Knox, Scots Confession, chapter 24, in the Book of Confessions, p. 24.

71. Westminster Confession of Faith, chapter 25 in Book of Confessions, p. 23.

72. Knox, Scots Confession, chapter 11, in the Book of Confessions, p. 15.

73. Westminster Confession of Faith, chapter 25 in Book of Confessions, p. 23.

74. "Of the Civill Magistrate," Westminster Confession of Faith, chapter 25, p. 3.

75. The issue of ecclesiastical power was at the heart of the problems that befell Archbishop Thomas Beckett (c. 1118 to 1170) and Henry II (1133 to 1189).

76. M'Crie, *Life of Andrew Melville*, 181.

77. A. Fraser, *Mary, Queen of Scots*, 342.

78. J. B. Torrance, "Covenant or Contract."

79. Rollock, *Five and Twenty Lectures,* 98.

80. Mullan, *Scottish Puritanism.*

81. J. B. Torrance, Westminster Confession, 40.

82. M. F. Graham, *Uses of Reform.* See also G. Parker, *Empire, War, and Faith,* 253–87.

83. Todd, *Culture of Protestantism,* 11.

84. Lynch, *Scotland,* 250.

85. D. Stevenson, *Covenanters,* 62–63. The Engager movement was a dialogue among some Scots and Charles I to keep him as monarch. As will be seen later in this chapter, most of the ministers in Galloway lost their charges for failing to conform to Episcopacy at the Restoration. Changes in land tenancy created a surplus of displaced laborers in the region (see chapter 3). Given those two situations, it is arguable that the nobility simply lost its ability to manipulate local residents through economic and/or spiritual means.

86. By the late seventeenth century, the Covenanters no longer represented the Melvillian intelligentsia, though they certainly believed that they were representing the true religion.

87. "Preservation of the Kirk," Scots Confession, chapter 5 in the Book of Confessions, p. 12.

88. MacLeod, *Dynasty,* 224–25.

89. See D. Stevenson, *Covenanters,* 66.

90. This was especially true because the restored monarch was an Episcopalian and the heir was a Roman Catholic.

91. Smout, *History of the Scottish People;* Leyburn, *Scotch-Irish.*

92. Donaldson, *Scotland: James V–James VII,* 367.

93. Recall that to those who regarded the National Covenant as a perpetually binding oath sanctioned by the Scottish Parliament and king, they were acting within the law of the land. They saw the actions of the restored monarchy as immoral and those who supported its policies as immoral and illegal agents.

94. Burrell, "The Apocalyptic Vision," 6.

95. D. Stevenson, *Covenanters,* 62. See also I. B. Cowan, *Scottish Covenanters.*

96. Ross, *Chronology of Scottish History,* 65.

97. Concerning the biography of Alexander Peden, see Robert Simpson, *Traditions of the Covenanters* (Edinburgh, c. 1900). See also Alexander Smellie, *Men of the Covenant: The Story of the Scottish Church in the Years of the Persecution* (Edinburgh, 1975).

98. Nisbet, *Private Life of the Persecuted,* vii. Nisbet also describes interacting with Alexander Peden, who made numerous crossings to Ireland.

99. Peden, *Lord's Trumpet.*

100. The Society People were alternatively called the Cameronians in recognition of Richard Cameron (D. Stevenson, *Covenanters,* 70–71). See also Cowan, *Scottish Covenanters.* By 1743 they established a Reformed Presbytery.

Aided by Scottish ministers and reflecting a limited yet continued orientation toward religious dissension in the culture area, a Reformed Presbytery was formed in Ireland in 1763.

101. Donaldson, *James V–James VII,* 366.

102. Ibid.

103. This conclusion is strengthened by the results of two chi-square tests. By calculating a chi-square statistic for Glasgow and Ayr with respect to Galloway ($X2 = 7.894$), it is clear that the rates of depositions (categorized as deposed and nondeposed) are different ($X2 \{1, N = 158\} = 6.64, p < .01$). On the other hand, a comparison between Galloway and Ulster ($X2 = 0.139$) reveals that those deposition rates were generated from the same population because the variable regions (Ulster and Galloway) made no difference in the respective deposition rates ($X2 \{1, N = 109\} = 2.71 < .10$). Chi-square is a nonparametric test that can be used in comparing frequency data between two variables, in this case, the region and the total number of ministers. The total number of ministers is divided into deposed and nondeposed. The two chi-square tests show that region is related to the rate of deposition among ministers (Spatz, *Basic Statistics,* 278–96). See also Chapman and Monroe, *Introduction to Statistical Problem Solving in Geography.*

5. Sacred Space for a Chosen People

1. John K. Wright, "Notes on Early American Geopiety."

2. Mullan, *Scottish Puritanism,* 244–84.

3. For an excellent work on this as it relates to English settlers in New England, see Zakai, *Exile and Kingdom.*

4. Mullan, *Scottish Puritanism,* 13–44. See also Foster, *Church before the Covenants.* Presbyterians were especially fearful of a reversion to Roman Catholicism, and the order of worship in Laud's liturgy certainly fueled that anxiety.

5. *Geotheology* refers specifically to the role of space or place in the worship of God, but because most places in seventeenth-century Britain were the homes of people with a common past and a psychological bond with each other—a community—and perhaps a nation (for example, a Scottish, English, or British one), place was a key part of cultural identity. Practical theology in Scotland at the time was set in a context that appealed to the identity of the people and their land; however, it is doubtful that the theologians of the time consciously knew this, for their writings suggest that they themselves felt Scotland was especially chosen by God for work in the unfolding drama of Providence. Several geotheological concepts and their contexts are discussed in this chapter. For a discussion on the conception of the terms used by scholars to describe geotheological aspects of space, see John K. Wright, "Notes on Early American Geopiety." Zakai in *Exile and Kingdom* provides a further discussion on Wright's ideas concerning the relationship between seventeenth-century English Puritanism and space. Unlike geotheology, *contextual theology*

is a relatively modern method by which preachers design the presentation of their understanding of God to fit into the cultural context of the congregation, especially those in non-Western places, such as Asia and Africa. For a discussion on contextual theology, refer to Healey and Farmer, "On Doing Theology."

6. Donaldson, *Scotland: James V–James VII,* 316. The Puritan Oliver Cromwell was a complex man who believed in Providence and often compared England to the children of Israel. Like his Scottish counterparts, he believed that if the nation backslid, it would find itself once more under the binding yoke of the Stuarts and their religion directed by ungodly bishops like Archbishop William Laud (Macleod, *Dynasty,* 198).

7. See chapter 5. John Ridge and Henry Colwart were Englishmen. Ridge, at least, was a Cambridge graduate. The Church of Ireland under Lord Deputy Arthur Chichester was especially receptive to Puritan ministers such as Ridge and Colwart. The specific reasons for their relocation to Ireland and settlement among Scots in Antrim are not known.

8. From the description in Robert Blair's autobiography of the motives behind the initial settlement of these ministers, it seems that filling pulpits in Ulster was the only employment option they had. Blair believed that their coming to Ulster was by God's design. Ulster's prominence in Irish Presbyterianism is significant. The ecclesiastical body referred to here was called the Army Presbytery (1642 to 1646) but was renamed the Presbytery of Ulster in 1646. By 1690 the organization, which did not meet between 1661 and 1690, was reorganized and called the Synod of Ulster. That name was used until 1840 when mergers with churches in the south of Ireland led to the adoption of the name Presbyterian Church in Ireland (PCI). For an excellent work on General Robert Munro and the establishment of the Army Presbytery, see D. Stevenson, *Scottish Covenanters and Irish Confederates.*

9. Mullan, *Scottish Puritanism,* 303.

10. With the appointment of Lord Deputy of Ireland Thomas Wentworth in 1632, the Church of Ireland increasingly insisted upon Episcopal conformity among its ministers. These ministers were deposed for their lack of support of this change in polity.

11. Mullan, *Scottish Puritanism,* 303.

12. Ibid., 285–317.

13. See earlier in this chapter.

14. See chapter 4, this volume.

15. J. Livingstone, *Brief Historical Relation,* 112–50.

16. McConnell, *Fasti,* 7; Reid, *History of the Presbyterian Church,* 2:291; Adair, *True Narrative,* 283.

17. Mullan states that it is easier to discuss the community of Presbyterians than it is Episcopalians because of the scarcity of extant sources for the latter. Although many Presbyterians were Puritans, Presbyterianism should not be regarded monolithically as a Puritan religion. It was, according to Mullan, a

religion beset by "cults of personalities" driven by the intensity of religion and by its self-perceptions as a persecuted group (*Scottish Puritanism,* 13–44).

18. D. Stevenson, *Covenanters,* 4.

19. Wandycz, *Price of Freedom,* 5. Geographers have produced a sizable body of scholarship about ethnoregional identifications, states, and nations.

20. Mullan, *Scottish Puritanism,* 265.

21. E. G. Bowen, *Britain and the Western Seaways,* 19.

22. Leyburn, *Scotch-Irish,* 74–75. Leyburn is comparing the seafaring orientation of the Scots to the Hebrews. His point is that they were not particularly known for traveling vast distances across oceans or seas in a manner consistent with the Phoenician, Greek, Portuguese, or Spanish fleets.

23. Archibald Johnston of Wariston, quoted in D. Stevenson, *Covenanters,* 1.

24. Schama, *History of Britain: The British Wars,* 89.

25. J. K. Wright, "Notes on Early American Geopiety."

26. Johnston and Henderson, *Confession of Faith.*

27. Henderson, Scots Confession *of 1560.*

28. T. F. Torrance, *Scottish Theology,* 28.

29. J. Knox et al., Scots Confession, 18.

30. Desacralization of place was fairly common among Puritans, including those in England (see later in this chapter).

31. Struther, *Scotland's Warning,* cited in Mullan, *Scottish Puritans,* 273.

32. Rutherford, letter to J. R., June 16, 1637, *Rutherford Letters,* 200.

33. G. Gillespie, *Dispute Concerning the English Popish Ceremonies,* 269. The doctrines, regiment, and policies to which George Gillespie refers are written in the King's Confession, or Negative Confession, and are used extensively in the National Covenant.

34. Zakai in *Exile and Kingdom* argues that English Puritans partly justified moving to New England because they convinced themselves that God had lost favor with England and was sending them on an errand into the wilderness. See also *Rutherford Letters,* quoted in Mullan, *Scottish Puritanism,* 279. Rutherford was unclear about the location of such an inn, but Mullan believes that he may have had New England in mind. It is also possible that he was thinking of Ireland, for in a letter to Fulk Ellis in Ireland on September 7, 1637, Rutherford wrote about the plight of God's workers in "our lovely and beloved church in Ireland" and that he believed that the Lord was only "lopping the vine-trees" and that he had no intention of "cutting them down or rooting them out" (*Rutherford Letters,* no. 44).

35. Rutherford, *Rutherford Letters,* no. 28.

36. Quoted in Mullan, *Scottish Puritanism,* 272.

37. Johnston, *Short Relation,* 301.

38. A. Henderson, *Sermons, Prayers, and Pulpit Addresses,* 381.

39. The Scots Confession assumes a godly prince would head the church. In the absence of one, a national assembly provided oversight of the Kirk.

40. Johnston and Henderson, *Confession of Faith*. The Five Articles of Perth required parishioners to kneel to receive communion, provided for private administration of communion to the sick in their homes, allowed infants to receive baptism at home, required bishops to confirm members, and required the Kirk to observe holy days. The articles were approved by the General Assembly on August 24, 1618, and by Parliament on August 4, 1621. Many Scots, however, felt the five articles signified a return to the papacy. See chapter 4 for additional remarks.

41. Unlike Calvin and Knox, many of the Scottish ecclesiastical intelligentsia, including some Episcopalians, adopted the controversial Bezan and post-Reformation doctrine of limited atonement (J. B. Torrance, Westminster Confession in the Church Today, 47).

42. Johnston, *Diary*, 344; quoted in Mullan, *Scottish Puritanism*, 299.

43. Brightman, Apocalypsis *Apocalypseos*, 139–40, 142–45, 155.

44. Johnston, *Diary*; D. Stevenson, *Covenanters*, 1. For a reference in a popular work, see also Magnusson, *Scotland*, 424.

45. Schama, *History of Britain: The British Wars*, 92.

46. D. Stevenson, *Covenanters*, 65.

47. Vallance, "Holy and Sacramentall Paction."

48. Johnston and Henderson, *Confession of Faith*.

49. Ibid.

50. Ibid.

51. Narne, *Christs Starre*, 1.

52. Mullan, *Scottish Puritanism*, 273.

53. Rollock, *Certaine Sermons*, 272.

54. Rutherford, *Fourteen Communion Sermons*, 149.

55. Struther, *Scotland's Warning*, 39.

56. Blair, *Life of Mr. Robert Blair*, 76.

57. Ibid.

58. It is not accurate that the English minister who impressed young Robert Blair as he awaited transportation to Ulster was banished to Ireland. He was deposed, but Blair provides no evidence that he was banished to Ireland. He possibly went there of his own accord (Blair, *Life of Mr. Robert Blair*, 5).

59. Andrew Knox was a nephew of John Knox.

60. Larne's minister, George Dunbar, who was deposed in July 1624 from his charge at Ayr, initiated his recruitment to Ireland (*Life of John Livingstone*, 77).

61. Blair, *Life of Mr. Robert Blair*, 65.

62. McConnell, *Fasti*, 8.

63. Quoted in M'Crie, *Life of Andrew Melville*, 181.

64. Quoted in Macleod, *Dynasty*, 149.

65. Quoted in Leyburn, *Scotch-Irish*; Blair cites the king's "No bishop, no King" comment, which he refers to it as being grounded in "conceit" (*Life of Mr. Robert Blair*, 28). See also Lockington, *Robert Blair of Bangor*, 19.

66. W. D. Baillie, *Six Mile Water Revival*, 21.

67. Mullan, *Scottish Puritanism*, 303.

68. D. Dickson, *Life of Livingstone*, 96–107.

69. As evidence of the existence of geographies and communities of imagination among Scottish Puritan Presbyterians, Livingstone, through communication with John Winthrop in Massachusetts, was offered land in New England. The promise of land and religious freedom in New England were the pull factors at work in this situation (Lockington, *Robert Blair of Bangor*, 21).

70. Livingstone, *Life of Livingstone*, 87. According to John Lockington, Lord Deputy Wentworth was motivated by the need to cultivate Protestant interests in the 1634 Irish Parliament (*Robert Blair of Bangor*, 19).

71. Livingstone, *Life of Livingstone*, 85–7.

72. In January 1635, John Winthrop's son visited Livingstone and Blair in Ulster. Winthrop once again encouraged their immigration to New England (Lockington, *Robert Blair of Bangor*, 21).

73. Lockington, *Robert Blair of Bangor*, 21.

74. John K. Wright, "Notes on Early American Geopiety," 251–52. Most of the usage of these concepts in regard to migration studies is limited to English Puritan movements ("Errand in the Wilderness," in Zakai, *Exile and Kingdom*, 143–54). John Morrill argues that the Scots were indirect in sharing the origins of their Puritan ideas with Englishmen ("National Covenant," 18–19).

75. Quoted in Blair, *Life of Blair*, 145.

76. Ibid., 145–46.

77. Ibid., 146.

78. Livingstone, *Life of John Livingstone*, 103.

79. Ibid., 88.

80. Ibid., 103.

81. Ibid., 160–61.

82. Ibid., 139.

83. Ibid. Many of Ireland's ministers were deposed at this time, so a return to Ireland would not have been practical for Livingstone. Interestingly, however, Charles II initiated the regium donum in 1672, which renewed the appeal of Ireland as an inviting place for dissenting ministers (Fry, *Scottish Empire*, 13).

84. Rutherford, *Rutherford Letters*, no. 33.

85. Ibid., no. 40.

86. Smout, *History of the Scottish People*, 63.

87. Shields, *Hind Let Loose*, 742, in Donaldson, *James V–James VII*, 316. While the word *covenant* is used for its sacred symbolism, in this instance it means a bilateral contract. In exchange for Scotland's submission and humility before God, the sovereign Lord would abide with and bless the nation and its land.

88. D. Stevenson, *Covenanters*.

89. See chapter 4.

90. Renwick to Loudoun, September 1683, in Moore, *Our Covenant Heritage,* 102–3.

91. David Stevenson, *Covenanters,* 66.

92. Schama, *History of Britain: The British Wars,* 89.

93. McConnell, *Fasti,* 4–84. As shown in chapters 5 and 6, when political pressure was applied evenly throughout England, Ireland, and Scotland, mobility among them was suppressed.

94. Renwick, *Apologetical Declaration.* In addition to religious tensions in the southwest that reverberated across the North Channel, the economic impact of raising rents on land was a destabilizing factor in the region and most likely contributed to radical Presbyterianism and the Covenanter conflict.

95. Although most likely many left the southwest in search of a peaceful lifestyle in Ireland, growth in the Ulster Presbytery and the formation of dialect regions in Ulster suggest that most who did so were not anti-Presbyterian.

96. Quoted in Moore, *Our Covenant Heritage,* 114. See also chapter 2 of the current volume for a discussion on the use in sermons of metaphors involving the sea.

97. Shields, *Hind Let Loose,* 316.

98. Nisbet, *Private Life of the Persecuted,* vii. Nisbet also describes interacting with Alexander Peden, who made numerous crossings to Ireland.

99. D. Stevenson, *Covenanters,* 66–67.

100. Nisbet, *Private Life of the Persecuted,* 102–3.

101. See Nisbet, "True Relation," 24. See also Moore, *Our Covenant Heritage,* 130.

102. Nisbet, "True Relation," 24. Moore, *Our Covenant Heritage,* 130.

103. Moore, *Our Covenant Heritage,* 181.

104. Quoted in Ross, *Chronology of Scottish History,* 70.

105. Donaldson and Morpeth, *Who's Who,* 209.

106. Sibbald, *Diverse Select Sermons,* 183. For a standard text on the Apocalyptic tradition in the Covenanter movement, see Firth, *Apocalyptic Tradition.* Sibbald's remarks reveal that Scottish geopiety was not limited to one doctrinal grouping.

107. D. Stevenson, *Covenanters,* 8.

108. Fry, *Scottish Empire,* 13; Bardon, *History of Ulster,* 162.

109. See chapter 4 for a discussion on the regium donum.

110. Blair, *Life of Mr. Robert Blair,* 76. The immigration of Scots Irish Presbyterians to America, which began in earnest in 1718, certainly diffused geopiety to the American South, also a vernacular region called the Bible Belt. It is a politically powerful section of the country, and in many respects it is a driving force in American foreign policy.

111. Ogilvie, *Presbyterian Churches,* 87. See McConnell, *Fasti,* 4–52.

112. Lecky, *Ireland in the Eighteenth Century,* 2:400–401; A. L. Perry, *Scotch-Irish in New England,* 7.

113. This was the era of the Williamite Revolution Settlement. With the death of Catholic political power in Ireland and Britain, the social climate was stable and secure.

114. Woodburn, *Ulster-Scot,* 172; Griffin, *People with No Name,* 19. Griffin gives a figure of 150,000 Scots by 1690. The estimate of 250,000 is based on the addition of 50,000 Scots families (assuming two-person families). See Lecky, *Ireland in the Eighteenth Century,* 400–401, and Perry, *Scotch-Irish in New England,* 7.

115. Dunlop, *Precarious Belonging,* 24.

116. Leyburn, *Scotch-Irish,* 132.

117. Leyburn, of course, was concerned about the element of the Scottish population that by 1718 began migrating to North America where they were known as the Scotch Irish. For a discussion on that movement, see Vann, *Rediscovering.*

118. Leyburn, *Scotch-Irish.*

119. The invisible church includes only the elect of God. It is invisible because no one knows the names of the members.

120. Zakai, *Exile and Kingdom,* 211.

121. Ibid.

122. In the American South, especially in Appalachia and far away from New England, they called themselves Irish Protestants and/or Scotch Irish. See Vann, *Rediscovering,* 1–60.

6. Irish Protestants and the Creation of the Bible Belt

1. Quoted in K. Miller, *Emigrants and Exiles,* 159.

2. Leyburn, *Scotch-Irish,* 167.

3. Vann, *Rediscovering,* 124.

4. Griffin, *People with No Name,* 65–98.

5. Ian Adamson, cited in Kennedy, *Scots-Irish in the Hills of Tennessee,* 14.

6. Leyburn, *Scotch-Irish,* 169. Leyburn contended that poor economic conditions in Ulster precipitated the five migration flows of 1717 to 1718, 1725 to 1729, 1740 to 1741, 1754 to 1755, and 1771 to 1775.

7. Griffin, *People with No Name,* 104.

8. Mitchell, "Shenandoah Valley Frontier," 151.

9. Faragher, *Daniel Boone,* 310.

10. Griffin, *People with No Name,* 165.

11. Kennedy, *Scots-Irish in the Hills of Tennessee,* 27, 146–47. Isaac Anderson established Maryville College, Samuel Carrick served as the first president of Blount College, which later grew into the University of Tennessee, and Samuel Doak is associated with establishing Tusculum College. See below.

12. Ibid. See also Vann, "Presbyterian Social Ties."

13. While the Scots composed the largest Protestant group in Ulster, English and French Calvinists and German Baptists were living in proximity to

Presbyterian settlements. It is likewise interesting that these same ethnic groups became the basic white population in southern Appalachia and the Ozarks. Being the larger and dominant cultural group, the Ulster-Scots were able to exert their ways on these smaller populations, assimilating their members while borrowing certain practices that served them well in their new environments. A group's culture is not necessarily affected by the various and subjectively determined ethnic identities of its members. Blaustein terms or calls those who try to recapture lost ethnic ways "cultural missionaries." See Blaustein, *Thistle and the Brier.*

14. Areas of ethnic concentration (hegemony over a parcel of space) compose ethnic islands. See Fellman, Getis, and Getis, *Human Geography,* 189. See also Gerlach, *Settlement Patterns in Missouri,* 41. This provides a further explanation of ethnic island.

15. Vann, *Rediscovering,* 88.

16. Vann, *Rediscovering,* 19. See also United States Bureau of the Census.

17. Westerkamp provides a description of this process in *The Triumph of the Laity: Scots-Irish Piety and the Great Awakening.* The percent figure (in reference to the Scotch Irish in the South) is taken from the 1990 Census of the United States. See also Vann, *Rediscovering,* 136–38.

18. Park, *Sacred Worlds,* 87.

19. Zelinsky, "Approach to the Religious Geography," 80.

20. Charles Heatwole, "The Bible Belt."

21. For a comparison of the maps, see Park, *Sacred Worlds,* 82, 88.

22. S. Tweedie, "Viewing the Bible Belt," 873.

23. Ibid., 865.

24. Carney, "Blue Grass Grows All Around"; see also his book *Sounds of People and Places.* See also Alanna Nash, "Songs of Faith."

25. Quoted in Nash, *Country Weekly,* 40.

26. Ibid.

27. See also MacLysaght, *Surnames of Ireland;* Bell, *Book of Ulster Surnames.*

28. Mithun, *Languages of Native North America.*

29. Kincaid, *Wilderness Road,* 99.

30. Ibid., 31.

31. Ibid.

32. Ibid., 99.

33. Leyburn, *Scotch-Irish,* 180.

34. McCrum, McNeil, and Cran, *Story of English,* 164.

35. The area called the Upper South runs from the borders of Pennsylvania and Maryland through extreme southern Ohio into and across southern Indiana and Illinois, cuts southwest and includes the southern third of Missouri, and enters Oklahoma, roughly following Interstate 44. Just south of Oklahoma City, the area cuts west and includes the southern two-thirds of the Texas

Panhandle (Rubenstein, *Cultural Landscape,* 106). This area closely resembles the Bible Belt.

36. This point is often overlooked by those who focus their attention on the recreation of ethnic identities and its political implications. See Blaustein, *Thistle and the Brier.* For the idea that America was to be a model for wayward Europeans, see P. Miller, *Errand into the Wilderness;* and A. Zakai, *Exile and Kingdom.*

37. Giddens, *Sociology,* 562.

38. Kennedy, *Scots-Irish in the Hills of Tennessee.*

39. *Directory of the Southern Baptist-related Colleges and Schools 2006.* The Association of Southern Baptist Colleges and Universities supports fifty-three institutions across eighteen states. Forty-eight of them are in Missouri, Oklahoma, and other southern states.

40. McGeveran, *World Almanac and Book of Facts 2006,* 714–15.

41. Vann, *Rediscovering,* 116–38.

42. Johnstone, *Religion in Society,* 171. In this reference Johnstone is discussing the Calvinist basis of the New Christian Right. As a sociologist he pays little attention to the region in question. The New Christian Right, in my opinion, is the electronic use of the airwaves by Bible Belt preachers. Their message is no different than it has always been. It is just being heard in places where people are not accustomed to hearing it.

43. These are discussed in the introduction and chapter 1.

44. Fischer, *Albion's Seed,* 777–83.

45. Preyer, *Hezekiah Alexander,* 66.

46. Herron, *Kirk by Divine Right.*

47. Makemie, *Answer to George Keith's Libel,* cited in Barkley, *Francis Makemie,* 10. Makemie made his statement in 1694.

48. Kennedy, *Scots-Irish in the Hills of Tennessee,* 145.

49. Randell Jones's *In the Footsteps of Daniel Boone* is an interesting read of Boone's travels.

50. Ibid., 5–6. Randall Jones, in *The Footsteps of Daniel Boone* (Winston-Salem, N.C.: John F. Blair, 2005), 1–6.

51. The Anglo-Scottish label used here includes both northern English folk and Lowland Scots.

52. Bell, *Book of Ulster Surnames,* 93–94.

53. Kincaid, *Wilderness Road,* 70–73.

54. Ibid.

55. According to MacLysaght, the Scottish name Stuart or Stewart is the most common nonindigenous name in Ireland. "More than 90 percent of the families so called are located in Ulster" (*Surnames of Ireland,* 279).

56. Ibid., 73. The ethnic affiliations of the four companions were determined by the surnames (per Kincaid) of Cooley, Holden, Mooney, and Stuart (MacLysaght, *Surnames of Ireland,* 57, 159, 221, 279).

57. Benjamin Logan seems to have fallen out with Boone and even accused the famous frontiersmen of collaborating with British authorities and their allies the Shawnee.

58. Kincaid, *Wilderness Road,* 113–15.

59. According to Bell in his *Book of Ulster Surnames,* nine out of ten Irish people named Gillespie live in Ulster (77–78). The name derives from the Gaelic word *easpuig,* which means "bishop."

60. Kincaid, *Wilderness Road,* 113.

61. Ibid., 114.

62. Quoted in Faragher, *Daniel Boone,* 311. For unstated reasons, Faragher seems to believe Boone was insincere in making this comment.

63. Ibid.

64. Boone, *Daniel Boone,* 4. Faragher uses some of this passage, but for unstated reasons, he excludes Boone's next sentence that assigns his felicity to his faith in Providence (*Daniel Boone,* 84).

65. Quoted in Faragher, *Daniel Boone,* 84.

66. Goldfield et al., *American Journey,* 267.

67. Quoted in Faragher, *Daniel Boone,* 70.

68. Ibid., 71.

69. Boone, *Daniel Boone,* 1–2. Filson edited the archaic language that Boone would have used, but Boone was quite able to read. He signed an affidavit endorsing the work as authentically his thoughts (Faragher, *Daniel Boone,* 7).

70. See www.scotch-irishcentral.org and Vann, *Rediscovering,* 85.

71. Knott, *Scotch-Irish Race,* 18.

72. Giddens, *Sociology,* 562; Johnstone, *Religion in Society,* 172–73.

73. Johnstone, *Religion in Society,* 171.

74. Donaldson, *Scotland: James V–James VII,* 398–99.

75. Vann, *Rediscovering,* 87–88.

76. This a paraphrase of Genesis 3:19, in the *New Geneva Study Bible,* "In the sweat of your face you shall eat bread." A footnote for Genesis 2:2 argues that the seven-day creation story provides a work model for humanity. The Apostle Paul makes a similar point about the relationship between work and the opportunity to eat in 2 Thessalonians 2:10.

77. See chapter 1 for discussion of the Calvinist-based work ethic.

78. Hank Williams, Jr., "Give a Damn," (Burbank, Calif., 1990).

79. In Luke 13:7, Jesus tells of seeking figs for three years. He never finds the tree baring fruit, so he orders it to be cut down. It is, of course, a metaphor for and parable about being a fruitful Christian.

80. "Working Man's PhD," Aaron Tippon and Donny Kees (New York: RCA, 2002).

81. "Politically Uncorrect," Gretchen Wilson and Merle Haggard (New York: Sony Records, 2005).

82. Smout, *History of the Scottish People,* 223.

83. See for example, Shapiro, *Appalachia on Our Mind*, 32–112.

84. Steele and Cottrell, *Civil War in the Ozarks*.

85. For a well-written look at the Western theater, see Shea and Hess, *Pea Ridge*.

86. Kennedy, *Scots-Irish in the Hills of Tennessee*, 59.

87. Fischer, *Albion's Seed*, 854–89.

88. Goldfield et al., *American Journey*, G-5, 561.

89. Vann, *Rediscovering*, 89.

90. Ibid. Because amnesty for illegal aliens is such a new political issue and at the time of writing this book, voters have not had to consider it, the author contends that it will be a hot-button topic across the South. As amnesty and social programs to support poor immigrants, whether they are legal or not, can be viewed as supporting the able-bodied, the South's electorate will not support it.

91. Bensel, *Sectionalism and American Political Development*. See also Fischer, *Albion's Seed*, 865.

92. McGeveran, *World Almanac*, 615–16.

93. Ibid., 612–13.

94. Ibid., 630–31.

95. Ibid., 630–31.

96. Ibid., 612–13.

97. Ibid., 617.

98. Ibid., 626.

99. Ibid., 617, 634, 635.

100. Ibid., 619.

101. Ibid., 630.

102. Ibid., 545.

103. *Webster's Geographical Dictionary*, 58.

104. McGeveran, *World Almanac*, 621.

105. Ibid., 609.

106. Ibid., 622.

107. Vann, *Rediscovering*, 17–23. For British-identity data, see Womack, "Majority Do Not Feel British."

Conclusion

1. E. G. Bowen called early Celtic divines saints. Their movements along the coast helped to create southwestern Scotland and Ulster. See his *Saints, Seaways, and Settlements in Celtic Lands*.

2. United States Bureau of the Census, Statistical Abstract of the United States, 1990. For a discussion on the religious aspects of this population, see Vann, *Rediscovering*, 17–23.

3. Ibid.

4. Martin N. Marger, *Race and Ethnic Relations*.

5. Perceval-Maxwell, *Scottish Migration*, 45.

6. Presbyterian Church in Ireland, "Presbyterian principles," 18; Dunlop, *Precarious Belonging,* 18.

7. Blair, *Life of Mr. Robert Blair,* 52–53.

8. B. Graham, *In Search of Ireland.*

9. B. Graham, "Identity, Heritage, and Place in Ulster," 82.

10. Ibid., 85.

11. Some Protestants in Northern Ireland fear political assimilation into the Republic of Ireland, which is more than 90 percent Roman Catholic.

12. Colin Williamson, personal interview, November 26, 2003, Dunning, Scotland.

13. Womack, "Majority Do Not Feel British," 3.

14. Thanks in part to those who support the Good Friday Agreement and to Loyalists such as the Ulster-Scots, unionism is a divided and somewhat diluted movement. See B. Graham, "Identity, Heritage, and Place in Ulster."

15. Womack, "Majority Do Not Feel British," 3.

16. McArt, "View from the Far Side," 8.

17. Ibid.

BIBLIOGRAPHY

Acts and Proceedings of the General Assemblies of the Kirk of Scotland. Vol. 3. 1127.

Adair, Patrick. *A True Narrative of the Rise and Progress of the Presbyterian Church in the North of Ireland.* Edited by W. D. Killen. Belfast, 1866.

Alexander, William. "An Encouragement to the Colonies." In *Royal Letters, Charters, and Tracts Relating to the Colonization of New Scotland . . . 1621–1638,* edited by D. Laing. Edinburgh, 1867, 38.

Anderson, Benedict. *Imagined Communities: Reflections on the Origin and Spread of Nationalism.* London: Verso, 1983.

Baillie, Robert. *The Letters and Journals.* Edited by David Lang. 3 vols. Edinburgh, 1841.

Baillie, W. D. *The Six Mile Water Revival of 1625.* Belfast: Presbyterian Historical Society, 1976.

Baker, Alan R. H. *Geography and History: Bridging the Divide.* Cambridge: Cambridge University Press, 2003.

Bardon, Jonathon, ed. *A History of Ulster.* Belfast: Blackstaff, 1992.

Barkley, J. M. *Francis Makemie of Ramelton: Father of American Presbyterianism.* Belfast: Presbyterian Historical Society, 1981.

Barry, Michael V. "Historical Introduction to the Dialects of Ulster." *A Concise Ulster Dictionary,* edited by C. I. Macafee. Oxford: Oxford University Press, 1996, ix–xii.

Beaujeu-Garnier, Jaqueline. "The Contribution of Geography." In Philo, "History, Geography and the Still Greater Mystery of Historical Geography," in Gregory, Martin, and Smith, *Human Geography,* 255–57.

Beckett, J. C. *Protestant Dissent in Ireland, 1687–1780.* London: Faber and Faber, 1948.

Bell, Robert. *Book of Ulster Surnames.* Belfast: Blackstaff, 1988.

Bensel, Richard Franklin. *Sectionalism and American Political Development, 1880–1980.* Madison: University of Wisconsin Press, 1984.

Biggers, Jeff. *The United States of Appalachia: How Mountaineers Brought Independence, Culture, and Enlightenment to America.* Emeryville, Calif.: Shoemaker and Hoard, 2006.

Binchy, D. A. "Patrick and His Biographers: Ancient and Modern." *Studia Hibernica* 2 (1962): 7–173.

Black, George Fraser. *The Surnames of Scotland.* New York: Birlinn, 1946.

Blair, Robert. *Life of Mr. Robert Blair: Containing His Autobiography, from 1593 to 1636.* Edited by T. M'Crie. Edinburgh, Woodrow Society, 1848.

Blaustein, Richard. *The Thistle and the Brier: Historical Links and Cultural Parallels between Scotland and Appalachia.* Jefferson, N.C.: McFarland and Company, 2003.

Blenerhasset, T. "A Direction for the Plantation of Ulster." In *A Contemporary History of Affairs in Ireland, from A.D. 1641 to 1652 . . .* Vol. 1, part 1. Edited by J. T. Gilbert. Dublin: Irish Archaeological Society, 1879.

Blethen, H. T., and C. H. Wood, eds. *Ulster and North America: Transatlantic Perspectives on the Scotch-Irish.* Tuscaloosa: University of Alabama Press, 1997.

Boettner, Lorraine. *The Reformed Faith.* Phillipsburg, N.J.: Presbyterian and Reformed Company, 1983.

Bolton, Charles Knowles. *Scotch-Irish Pioneers in Ulster and America.* Boston, 1910.

Boone, Daniel. *Daniel Boone: His Own Story and the Adventures of Daniel Boone,* edited by Francis Lister Hawks. Bedford, Mass.: Applewood, 1995. First published 1784 by author John Filson as *The Adventures of Col. Daniel Boon.*

Bourne, William, of Gravesend. Preface. In *A Regiment of the Sea and Other Writings on Navigation, 1535–1582.* The Hakluyt Society, 2nd ser., 121. Edited by E. G. R. Taylor. Cambridge: Hakluyt Society, 1963.

Bowen, E. G. *Britain and the Western Seaways.* London: Thames and Hudson, 1972.

———. "Le Pays de Galles." *Transactions and Papers of the Institute of British Geographers* 26 (1959): 1–23.

———. *Saints, Seaways, and Settlements in Celtic Lands.* Cardiff: University of Wales Press, 1969.

Bozeman, Theodore D. *To Live Ancient Lives: The Primitivist Dimension in Puritanism.* Chapel Hill: University of North Carolina Press, 1988.

Brady, C., and Raymond Gillespie, eds. *Natives and New Comers: Essays on the Making of Irish Colonial Society 1534–1641.* Dublin: Irish Academic, 1986.

Brereton, William. *Travels in Holland, the United Provinces, England, Scotland and Ireland.* Edited by E. Hawkins. Manchester, 1844.

Brightman, Thomas. Apocalypsis *Apocalypseos, or a Revelation of the Revelation.* Leyden, 1616.

Bruce, Robert. *The Mystery of the Lord's Supper.* Edited by T. F. Torrance. London: James Clarke, 1958.

———. *Sermons by the Rev. Robert Bruce with Collections for His Life by Robert Wodrow.* Edited by W. Cunningham. Edinburgh, 1843.

Buchan, John, and A. G. Smith. *The Kirk in Scotland, 1560–1929*. Edinburgh: Hodder and Stoughton, 1930.

Burleigh, J. H. S. *A Church History of Scotland*. London: Oxford University Press, 1973.

Burns, David M. *Gateway: Dr. Thomas Walker and the Opening of Kentucky*. Middlesboro, 2000.

Burrell, S. A. "The Apocalyptic Vision of the Early Covenanters." *Scottish Historical Review* 43.135 (1964): 1–24.

Calderwood, David. *Altare Damascenum*. Amsterdam, 1619.

——. *The History of the Kirk of Scotland*. Edited by T. Thomson. 8 vols. Edinburgh, 1842–1849.

Calvin, John. *Institutes of the Christian Religion*. Translated by Ford Lewis Battles. Edited by J. T. McNeil. 2 vols. Philadelphia: Westminster, 1960.

Cameron, Nigel M., et al., eds. *Dictionary of Scottish Church History and Theology*. Downers Grove, Ill.: Intervarsity, 1993.

Campbell, John C. *The Southern Highlander and His Homeland*. New York: Russell Sage Foundation, 1921.

Canny, Nicholas, ed. *Europeans on the Move: Studies in European Migration, 1500–1800*. Oxford: Oxford University Press, 1994.

Carlyle, Thomas. *Oliver Cromwell's Letters and Speeches*. Edited by S. C. Lomas. 3 vols. London, 1904.

Carney, George. "Blue Grass Grows All Around: The Spatial Dimensions of a Country Music Style." *Journal of Geography* 73 (1974): 34–55.

——. *The Sounds of People and Places: A Geography of American Folk and Popular Music*. Lanham, Md.: Rowan and Littlefield, 1994.

Carroll, Peter N. *Puritanism and the Wilderness: The Intellectual Significance of the New England Frontier, 1629–1700*. New York: Columbia University Press, 1969.

Chadwick, Owen. *A History of Christianity*. New York: St. Martin's, 1995.

Chapman, J., and Charles B. Monroe. *Introduction to Statistical Problem Solving in Geography*. New York: McGraw-Hill, 1999.

Clarendon, Edward Hyde. *Calendar of the Clarendon State Papers Preserved in the Bodleian Library, 1621–1623*. Oxford: Clarendon Press, n.d.

Connolly, S. J. *Religion, Law, and Power: The Making of Protestant Ireland*. Oxford: Oxford University Press, 1992.

Cooper. A. "New Directions in the Geography of Religion." *Area* 24 (1992).

Cotton, John. *A Brief Exposition with Practicall Observations upon the Whole Book of Ecclesiastes*. London: W.W. for Ralph Smith, 1654.

Couper, W. J. *Scottish Revivals*. Dundee: James P. Mathew, 1918.

Cowan, Edward J. *Montrose: For Covenant and King*. London: Weidenfeld and Nicolson, 1977.

Cowan, Ian B. "Church and State Reformed? The Revolution of 1688–9 in Scotland." In *The Anglo-Dutch Moment: Essays on the Glorious Revolution and Its World Impact,* edited by David Israel. Cambridge: Cambridge University Press, 1991, 163–84.

———. "The Covenanters: A Revision Article." *Scottish Historical Review* 47 (1968): 35–51.

———. *The Scottish Covenanters, 1660–1688.* London: V. Gollancz, 1976.

Crawford, O. G. S. "The Distribution of Early Bronze Age Settlements in Britain." *Geography Journal* 40 (1912): 184–304.

Cullen, M. "The Irish Diaspora of the Seventeenth and Eighteenth Centuries." In Canny, *Europeans on the Move,* 113–49.

Culverwell, Ezekiel. *Treatise of Faith.* 1623.

Cushman, Robert. "A Sermon Preached at Plimmoth in New England, December 9, 1621." In Zakai, *Exile and Kingdom,* 124–25.

Day, Donald, and Harry Herbert Ullom, eds. *The Autobiography of Sam Houston.* Norman: University of Oklahoma Press, 1947.

Devine, T. M., and S. G. E. Lythe. "The Economy of Scotland under James VI." *Scottish Historical Review* 50 (1971): 91–106.

Dickson, David. *A Short Explanation of the Epistle of Paul to the Hebrews.* Aberdeen, 1635.

———. *Truth's Victory over Error.* Edinburgh, 1684.

Dickson, David, and James Durham. *The Sum of Saving Knowledge.* Edinburgh, 1871.

Directory of the Southern Baptist-related Colleges and Schools 2006. Nashville, Tenn., 2006.

Donaldson, Gordon. *Faith of the Scots.* London: Batsford, 1990.

———. "Reformation to Revolution." In *Studies in the History of Worship in Scotland,* edited by Duncan Forrester and Douglas Murray. Edinburgh: T and T Clark, 1984, 49–64.

———. *Scotland: Church and Nation through Sixteen Centuries.* London: SCM, 1960.

———. *Scotland: James V–James VII.* Edinburgh: Oliver and Boyd, 1965.

———. *The Scottish Reformation.* Cambridge: Cambridge University Press, 1960.

Donaldson, Gordon, and Robert S. Morpeth. *Who's Who in Scottish History.* Cardiff: Welsh Academic Press, 1996.

Duffy, Sean, ed. *Atlas of Irish History.* Dublin: Gill and Macmillan, 1997.

Dunlop, John. *A Precarious Belonging: Presbyterians and the Conflict in Ireland.* Belfast: Blackstaff, 1995.

Durham, James. *The Dying Man's Testament to the Church of Scotland; or, A Treatise Concerning Scandal.* Edinburgh, 1659.

Durkan, John, and James Kirk. *The University of Glasgow 1451–1577.* Glasgow: University of Glasgow Press, 1977.

Durkheim, Emile. *The Elementary Forms of Religious Life.* Translated by Karen E. Fields. New York: Routledge, 1995.

Falls, Cyril. *The Birth of Ulster.* London: Methuen, 1936.

Faragher, John M. *Daniel Boone: The Life and Legend of an American Pioneer.* New York: Henry Holt, 1992.

Fellman, Jerome D., Arthur Getis, and Judith Getis. *Human Geography: Landscapes of Human Activities.* 9th ed. New York: McGraw-Hill, 2007.

Firth, Katherine. *The Apocalyptic Tradition in Reformation Britain, 1530–1645.* Oxford: Oxford University Press, 1979.

Fischer, David Hackett. *Albion's Seed: Four British Folkways in America.* Oxford: Oxford University Press, 1989.

Fisk, William Lyons. *The Scottish High Church Tradition in America.* Lanham: University Press of America, 1995.

Fitzgerald, Patrick. "Black '97: Reconsidering Scottish Migration to Ireland in the Seventeenth-Century and the Scotch-Irish in America," in Kelly and Young, *Ulster and Scotland,* 71–84.

Fitzpatrick, Rory. *God's Frontiersmen: The Scots-Irish Epic.* London: Weidenfeld and Nicholson, 1989.

Fleming, Robert. *The Fulfilling of the Scripture.* London, 1693.

Flinn, Michael W. *Scottish Population History: From the Seventeenth Century to the 1930s.* Cambridge: Cambridge University Press, 1977.

Flint, Wayne J. *Dixie's Forgotten Poor: The South's Poor Whites.* Bloomington: Indiana University Press, 1980.

Foote, William Henry. *Sketches of North Carolina, Historical and Biographical, Illustrative of the Principles of the Early Settlers.* New York: R. Carter, 1846.

Ford, Henry Jones. *The Scotch-Irish in America.* Princeton: Princeton University Press, 1915.

Forrester, Duncan, and Douglas Murray, eds. *Studies in the History of Worship in Scotland.* Edinburgh: T and T Clark, 1984.

Foster, Walter Roland. *The Church before the Covenants: The Church of Scotland 1596–1638.* Edinburgh: Scottish Academic, 1975.

Fox, Cyril, and Lily F. Chitty. *The Personality of Britain: Its Influence on Inhabitant and Invader in Prehistoric and Early Historic Times.* Cardiff: University of Wales Press, 1932.

Fraser, Antonia. *Mary Queen of Scots.* London: Mandarin, 1969.

Fraser, George MacDonald. *The Steel Bonnets: The Story of the Anglo-Scottish Border Reivers.* London: Barrie and Jenkins, 1971.

Fry, Michael. *The Scottish Empire.* East Linton, Lothian, Scotland: Tuckwell, 2001.

Geree, John. *The Character of an Old English Puritane or Noncomformist.* N.p.: W. Wilson for Christopher Meredith, 1646.

Gerlach, Russel. *Settlement Patterns in Missouri.* Columbia, 1986.

Gibson, A. J. S., and T. C. Smout. *Prices, Food, and Wages in Scotland, 1550–1780.* Cambridge: Cambridge University Press, 1995.

Giddens, Anthony. *Sociology.* 4th ed. Cambridge: Blackwell, 2001.

Gillespie, George. *Dispute Concerning the English Popish Ceremonies Obtruded upon the Church of Scotland.* 1637.

————. *Wholesome Severity Reconciled with Christian Liberty or, the True Resolution of the Present Controversie Concerning Liberty of Conscience.* London, 1644.

Gillespie, Raymond. *Colonial Ulster: The Settlement of East Ulster, 1600–1641.* Cork: Cork University Press, 1985.

————. "Dissenters and Nonconformists, 1661–1700." In *Irish Dissenting Tradition, 1650–1750,* edited by Kevin Herlihy. Dublin: Irish Academic, 1995, 11–28.

————. "The Presbyterian Revolution in Ulster, 1642–1690." In *The Churches, Ireland, and the Irish: Papers Read at the 1988 Summer Meeting and the 1988 Winter Meeting of the Ecclesiastical History Society,* edited by W. J. Sheil and Diana Wood. Oxford: Oxford University Press, 1989, 159–70.

Goldfield, David, et al. *The American Journey: A History of the United States.* Upper Saddle River, N.J.: Prentice Hall, 2006.

Graham, Brian. "Identity, Heritage and Place in Ulster." In *Home and Colonial: Essays on a Landscape, Ireland, Environment and Empire in Celebration of Robin Butlin's Contribution to Historical Geography,* edited by Alan R. H. Baker. Historical Geography Research Series, 39. London: Historical Geography Research Group, Royal Geographical Society, 2004, 77–83.

————, ed. *In Search of Ireland: A Cultural Geography.* London: Routledge, 1997.

Graham, Michael F. *The Uses of Reform: Godly Discipline and Popular Behaviour in Scotland and Beyond, 1560–1610.* New York: Brill Academic, 1996.

Greaves, Richard. *God's Other Children: Protestant Nonconformists and the Emergence of Denominational Churches in Ireland, 1660–1700.* Stanford: Stanford University Press, 1997.

Gregory, Derek, Ron Martin, and Graham Smith, eds. *Human Geography: Society, Space, and Social Science.* Minneapolis: University of Minnesota Press, 1994.

Griffin, Patrick. *The People with No Name: Ireland's Ulster Scots, America's Scots-Irish, and the Creation of a British Atlantic World, 1689–1764.* Princeton: Princeton University Press, 2001.

Hanna, C. A. *The Scotch-Irish, or the Scot in North Britain, North Ireland, North America.* 2 vols. 1902; reprint, Baltimore: Genealogical, 1968.

Hartshorne, Richard. *The Nature of Geography: A Critical Survey of Current Thought in Light of the Past.* Lancaster, Penn.: Association of American Geographers, 1939.

Hayton, David. "Presbyterians and the Confessional State: The Sacramental Test Act as an Issue in Irish Politics." *Bulletin of the Presbyterian Historical Society of Ireland* 26 (1997): 11–31.

Hazlett, Ian. "Playing God's Card: John Knox and Fasting." In *John Knox and the British Reformations,* edited by Roger Mason. London: Ashgate, 1998. 176–200.

————. *The Reformation in Britain and Ireland: An Introduction.* London: T and T Clark, 2003.

Healey, F. G., and Herbert Henry Farmer. "On Doing Theology: A Contextual Possibility." In *Prospect for Theology: Essays in Honour of H. H. Farmer,* edited by Healey and Farmer. Welwyn, Herts: J. Nisbet, 1966, 90–103.

Heatwole, Charles. "The Bible Belt: a Problem in Regional Definition." *Journal of Geography* 77 (1978): 50–55.

Heidelberg Catechism. Heidelberg, 1562.

Heimert, Alan. "Puritanism, the Wilderness, and the Frontier." *New England Quarterly* 26 (1953): 361–82.

Henderson, Alexander. *Sermons, Prayers, and Pulpit Addresses, 1638.* Edited by R. Thomson Martin. Edinburgh, 1867.

Henderson, G. D. "The Covenanters." In *Religious Life in Seventeenth-Century Scotland.* Cambridge: The University Press, 1937.

Herron, Andrew. *Kirk by Divine Right, Church and State: Peaceful Co-Existence.* Edinburgh: St. Andrew Press, 1985.

————, ed. *The Westminster Confession in the Church Today: Papers Prepared for the Church of Scotland Panel on Doctrine.* Edinburgh: St. Andrew Press, 1982.

Hill, George. *An Historical Account of the Plantation of Ulster at the Commencement of the Seventeenth Century, 1608–1620.* Shannon, Ireland: Irish University Press, 1970.

————. *Plantation Papers: Containing a Summary Sketch of the Great Ulster Plantation in the Year 1610.* Belfast, 1889.

Hill, J. M. "The Origins of the Scottish Plantation in Ulster to 1625: A Reinterpretation." *Journal of British Studies* 32 (1993): 40–70.

Hobbes, Thomas. *Leviathan, or the Matter, Forme, and Power of a Commonwealth, Ecclesiasticall and Civill.* London, 1651.

Holloway, Julian, and Oliver Valins. Editorial. "Placing Religion and Spirituality in Geography." *Social and Cultural Geography* 3 (2002): 5–10.

Holmes, R. F. G. *Our Irish Presbyterian Heritage.* Belfast: Presbyterian Church in Ireland, 1985.

Houston, Rab. "Geographical Mobility in Scotland, 1652–1811: The Evidence of Testimonials." *Journal of Historical Geography* 11 (1985): 379–94.

Hutchinson, John, and Anthony D. Smith, eds. *Ethnicity.* Oxford: Oxford University Press, 1996.

Irish Evangelist 1.9 (June 1860).

Irwin, Clarke Huston. *A History of Presbyterianism in Dublin and the South and West of Ireland.* London: Hodder and Stoughton, 1890.

James, Marquis. *The Raven: A Biography of Sam Houston.* Indianapolis: Bobbs-Merrill, 1929.

James VI (James I). *Basilikon Doron.* Edinburgh, 1598.

Jarvis, Peter. *Paradoxes of Learning: On Becoming and Individual in Society.* San Francisco: Jossey-Bass, 1992.

Johnston, Archibald of Wariston. *Diary, 1632–1639.* Edited by G. M. Paul. Edinburgh: Scottish Historical Society, 1911.

———. *Scotland: The Story of a Nation,* edited by Magnus Magnusson. London: Grove, 2001, 424.

———. *A Short Relation on the State of the Kirk of Scotland.* Edinburgh, 1638.

Johnston, Archibald of Wariston, and Alexander Henderson. *The Confession of Faith of the Kirk of Scotland: Or the National Covenant with a Designation of Such Acts of Parliament as Are Expedient for Justifying the Union after Mentioned.* Edinburgh, 1640.

Johnstone, Ronald L. *Religion in Society: A Sociology of Religion.* 7th ed. Upper Saddle River, N.J.: Prentice Hall, 2004.

Jones, Huw. "Evolution of Scottish Migration Patterns: A Social-Relations-of-Production Approach." *Scottish Geographical Magazine* 102 (1986): 151–64.

Jones, Randell. *In the Footsteps of Daniel Boone.* Winston-Salem: Robert F. Blair, 2005.

Jubilee of the General Assembly of the Presbyterian Church in Ireland 1890. Belfast, 1890.

Kelly, William, and John R. Young, eds. *Ulster and Scotland 1600–2000: History, Language, and Identity.* Dublin: Four Courts Press, 2004.

Kennedy, Billy. *The Scots-Irish in the Hills of Tennessee.* Belfast: Ambassador Productions, 1995.

Kilroy, Phil. *Protestant Dissent and Controversy in Ireland 1660–1714.* Cork, Ireland: Cork University Press, 1994.

Kincaid, Robert. *The Wilderness Road.* 4th ed. Middlesboro, Ky.: Lincoln Memorial University, 1973.

Kirk, William. "Problems of Geography." *Geography* 48 (1963): 357–71.

Kirkton, James. *The Secret and True History of the Church of Scotland.* Edinburgh, 1817.

Knott, J. Proctor. *The Scotch-Irish Race: An Address before the Scotch-Irish Society of America.* Cincinnati, 1889.

Knox, Buick R. "The Church in Celtic Ireland: Its Life and Legacy." *Bulletin of the Presbyterian Historical Society of Ireland* 26 (1997): 2–25.

Knox, John, et al. The Scots Confession of 1560. In the Book of Confessions, Presbyterian Church U.S.A. Louisville: Office of the General Assembly, 1994.

Kong, Lily. "Geography and Religion: Trends and Prospects." *Progress in Human Geography* 14.3 (1990): 355–71.

———. "Religion and Technology: Refiguring Place, Space, Identity and Community." *Area* 33.4 (2001): 404–13.

Kuby, Michael, John Harner, and Patricia Gober. *Human Geography in Action.* 3rd ed. New York: Wiley, 2004.

Kyd, James Gray, ed. *Scottish Population Statistics Including Webster's Analysis of Population, 1755.* Edinburgh: T. and A. Constable, 1952.

Kyle, Richard G. *Encyclopedia of the Reformed Faith.* Edited by Donald K. McKim. Edinburgh: Westminster John Knox, 1992.

Landsman, Ned C. *Scotland and Its First American Colony, 1683–1765.* Princeton: Princeton University Press, 1985.

Lecky, William E. H. *Ireland in the Eighteenth Century.* Vol. 2. London: Longmans Green, 1883.

Leyburn, James G. *The Scotch-Irish: A Social History.* Chapel Hill: University of North Carolina Press, 1962.

Livingstone, John. *A Brief Historical Relation of the Life of Mr. John Livingstone, Minister of the Gospel, Containing Several Observations of the Divine Goodness Manifested in Him, in the Several Occurrences Thereof.* Edited by Thomas Houston. Edinburgh, 1848.

———. *Life of John Livingstone: Memorable Characteristics.* Edinburgh: Wodrow Society, 1845.

Livingstone, Peadar. *The Monaghan Story: A Documented History of the County Monaghan from the Earliest Times to 1976.* Enniskillen: Clogher Historical Society, 1980.

Lockington, John W. *Robert Blair of Bangor.* Belfast: Presbyterian Historical Society, 1996.

Love, Dane. *Scottish Covenanter Stories: Tales from the Killing Times.* Glasgow: Neil Wilson, 2002.

Lowry, T. K., ed. *The Hamilton Manuscripts.* Belfast, 1867.

Lynch, Michael. *Edinburgh and the Reformation.* Edinburgh: Humanities, 1981.

———. *Scotland: A New History.* 1992; reprinted, London: Pimlico, 2001.

Lythe, S. G. E. *The Economy of Scotland in Its European Setting, 1550–1625.* West Port, Conn.: Greenwood, 1960.

Macafee, C. I., ed. *A Concise Ulster Dictionary.* Oxford: Oxford University Press, 1996, 46–63.

Macafee, W., and V. Morgan. "Population in Ulster, 1660–1760." In *Plantation to Partition: Essays in Ulster History in Honor of J. L. McCracken,* edited by P. Roebuck. Belfast: Blackstaff, 1981.

MacDonald, Fraser. "Towards a Spatial Theory of Worship: Some Observations from Presbyterian Scotland." *Social and Cultural Geography* 3 (2002): 62–80.

MacHaffie, F. G. *Portpatrick to Donaghadee: The Original Short Route.* Stranraer, Scotland: Stranraer and District Local History Trust, 2001.

Macinnes, Alan I. *Clanship, Commerce and the House of Stuart, 1604–1788.* East Lothian, Scotland: Tuckwell, 1996.

Mackinder, H. J. *Britain and the British Seas.* Oxford: D. Appleton, 1902.

Macleod, John. *Dynasty: The Stuarts 1560–1807.* London: St Martin's, 2001.

MacLysaght, Edward. *The Surnames of Ireland.* Dublin: Irish Academic Press, 1991.

Magnusson, Magnus, ed. *Scotland: The Story of a Nation.* London: Grove, 2000.

Mahoney, Ropert P. *Calendar of the State Papers Relating to Ireland, 1606–1608.* Great Britain Public Record Office. N.p.: Mackie and Company, 1963.

Major, John. *Disputationes de Potestate Papae et Concilii.* 1519.

Marger, Martin N. *Race and Ethnic Relations: American and Global Perspectives.* Belmont, Calif.: Wadsworth, 1985.

Marshall, Gordon. *Presbyteries and Profits: Calvinism and the Development of Capitalism in Scotland 1560–1707.* Edinburgh: Edinburgh University Press, 1980.

Marshall, R. L. "The Commemoration Sermon." In "Tercentenary Committee of the Presbyterian Church in Ireland," in *Three Hundred Years of Presbyterianism: Sermon and Addresses.* Belfast: Presbyterian Church in Ireland, 1943.

Massey, Douglas. "An Evaluation of International Migration Theory: The North American Case." *Population and Development Review* 20 (1994): 699–752.

Massey, Douglas, J. Arango, G. Hugo, A. Kouaouci, A. Pellegrino, and J. E. Taylor. "Theories of International Migration: A Review and Appraisal." In Weeks, *Population,* 431–66.

Mayr-Harting, Henry. *The Coming of Christianity to Anglo-Saxon England.* University Park: Pennsylvania State University Press, 1991.

McArt, Pat. "A View from the Far Side." *News Letter* [Belfast] (December 17, 2002): 8.

McCartney, D. J. *Nor Principalities nor Powers: A History (1621–1991) of First Presbyterian Church. Carrickfergus.* Carrickfergus, Northern Ireland: First Presbyterian Church, 1991.

McConnell, James. *Fasti of the Irish Presbyterian Church 1613–1840.* Belfast: Presbyterian Historical Society, 1951.

M'Crie, Thomas. *Life of Andrew Melville.* Edinburgh: W. B. Lackwood, 1899.

McCrum, Robert, Robert McNeil, and William Cran. *The Story of English.* 3rd ed. rev. New York: Penguin, 2002.

McGeveran, William J., Jr., ed. *The World Almanac and Book of Facts 2006.* New York: World Almanac, 2006.

McGrath, Alistair. *Reformation Thought: An Introduction.* 2nd ed. Oxford: Blackwell, 1993.

McKee, John. "Revival, Revivalism and Calvinism with Special Reference to Ireland." In *Essays in Church History in Honour of R. Finlay Holmes,* edited by W. Donald Patton. Belfast: Presbyterian Historical Society of Ireland, 2002.

McKerrall, A. *Kintyre in the Seventeenth Century.* Edinburgh: Oliver and Boyd, 1948.

McNeil, John T. *The History and Character of Calvinism.* Oxford: Oxford University Press, 1967.

McWhiney, Grady. *Cracker Culture: Celtic Ways in the Old South.* Tuscaloosa: University of Alabama Press, 1988.

Megaw, B. R. S. "The Date of Pont's Survey and Its Background." *Scottish Studies* 8 (1969): 71–74.

Meldrum, Neil. *Forteviot: The History of a Strathearn Parish.* Paisley, 1926.

Melville, Andrew. *Kirk by Divine Right, Church and State: Peaceful Co-existence.* Edinburgh: St. Andrew Press, 1985.

Melville, James. *Memoirs of Sir James Melville of Halhill.* Edited by Gordon Donaldson. London: Folio Society, 1969.

Miller, G. Tyler. *Living in the Environment: Principles, Connections, and Solutions.* 11th ed. Belmont, Calif: Wadsworth, 1999.

Miller, Kerby. *Emigrants and Exiles: Ireland and the Irish Exodus to North America.* Oxford: Belknap Press, 1985.

Miller, Kerby, et al. *Irish Immigrants in the Land of Canaan: Letters and Memoirs from Colonial and Revolutionary America, 1675–1815.* Oxford: Oxford University Press, 2003.

Miller, Perry. *Errand into the Wilderness.* Cambridge, Mass., 1976.

Milton, John. "On the New Forcers of Conscience under the Long Parliament." In *The Works of John Milton,* edited by F. A. Patterson and French R. Fogle. New York, 1931.

Mitchell, Robert D. "The Shenandoah Valley Frontier." In *Geographic Perspectives on America's Past: Readings on the Historical Geography of the United States,* edited by David Ward. New York, 1979. 148–66.

Mithun, Marianne. *The Languages of Native North America.* Cambridge: Cambridge University Press, 1999.

Moffatt, James. *The Presbyterian Churches.* London: Methuen, 1928.

Montgomery, Michael B. "How Scotch-Irish Is Your English?" *Journal of East Tennessee History* 77 (June 2006): 65–91.

———. "The Scotch-Irish Element in Appalachian English: How Broad? How Deep?" In *Ulster and North America: Transatlantic Perspectives on the Scotch-Irish,* edited by H. T. Blethen and C. H. Wood. Tuscaloosa: University of Alabama Press, 1997, 189–212.

Moodie, Wayne. "The Hudson Bay Company and Its Geographic Impress, 1670–1870." In Baker, *Geography and History: Bridging the Divide.* Cambridge: Cambridge University Press, 2003, 180.

Moore, Edwin Nisbet. *Our Covenant Heritage: The Covenanters' Struggle for Unity in Truth and the Sermons of John Nevay.* Ross-shire: Christian Focus, 2000.

Morrill, John. "The National Covenant in Its British Context." In *The Scottish National Covenant in Its British Context 1638–51,* edited by John Morrill. Edinburgh: Edinburgh University Press, 1990.

Mullan, David George. *Scottish Puritanism 1590–1638.* Oxford: Oxford University Press, 2000.

Murdoch, Steve. "The Scots and Ulster in the Seventeenth Century: A Scandinavian Perspective." Kelly and Young, eds., *Ulster and Scotland,* 85–104.

Murray, Douglas M. "Martyrs or Madmen? The Covenanters, Sir Walter Scot, and Dr. Thomas McCrie." *Innes Review* 43.2 (1992): 166–75.

Narne, William. *Christs Starre: Or, a Christian Treatise for Our Direction to Our Saviour, and for Our Conjunction with Him.* London, 1625.

Nash, Alanna. "Songs of Faith." *Country Weekly* (June 19, 2006): 36–40.

Naylor, Simon, and James R. Ryan. "The Mosque in the Suburbs: Negotiating Religion and Ethnicity in South London." *Social and Cultural Geography* 3.1 (2002): 39–50.

Nisbet, James. *The Private Life of the Persecuted.* Edited by William Oliphant. Edinburgh, 1827.

———. "A True Relation of the Life and Sufferings of John Nisbet in Hardhill." In *Select Biographies,* edited by William K. Tweedie. 2 vols. Edinburgh, 1845–47, 407–8.

Ogborn, Miles. "Historical Geographies of Globalisation." In *Modern Historical Geographies,* edited by Brian Graham and Catherine Nash. Harlow, Essex, England: Longman, 2000.

Ogilvie, J. N. *The Presbyterian Churches: Their Place and Power in Modern Christendom.* New York: Revell, 1897.

Ohlmeyer, Jane H. "Civilising those rude partes: Colonization within Britain and Ireland, 1580s–1640s." In *The Oxford History of the British Empire: British Overseas Enterprise to the Close of the Seventeenth Century: The Origins of Empire,* edited by Nicholas Canny. Oxford: Oxford University Press, 1998. 124–47.

Pacione, Michael. "The Geography of Religious Affiliation in Scotland." *Professional Geographer* 57 (May 2005): 235–55.

———. "The Relevance of Religion for a Relevant Human Geography." *Scottish Geographical Journal* 115 (1999).

Packer, J. I. *Knowing God.* Downers Grove, Ill.: Interversity Press, 1993.

Park, Chris C. *Sacred Worlds: An Introduction to Geography and Religion.* London: Routledge, 1994.

Parker, A. W. *Scottish Highlanders in Colonial Georgia: The Recruitment, Emigration, and Settlement in Darien, 1735–1748.* Athens: University of Georgia Press, 1997.

Parker, Geoffrey. *Empire, War, and Faith in Early Modern Europe.* London: Allen Lane, 2002.

Pattison, William D. "Four Traditions of Geography." *Journal of Geography* 63.5 (1964): 211–16.

Pearson, A. F. S. *The Origins of Irish Presbyterianism.* Carey Lecture pamphlet. Belfast: Irish Presbyterian Historical Society, 1947.

———. *Puritan and Presbyterian Settlements in Ireland, 1550–1650.* Belfast: Presbyterian Historical Society, 1947.

Peden, Alexander. *The Lord's Trumpet Sounding an Alarm against Scotland, by Warning of a Bloody Sword.* Edinburgh, 1739.

Pendergast, J. D. *Cromwellian Settlement in Ireland.* 2nd ed. Dublin, 1875.

Perceval-Maxwell, Michael. "Ireland and the Monarchy in the Early Stuart Multiple Kingdom." *Historical Journal* 34 (1991): 279–95.

———. *Scottish Migration to Ulster in the Reign of James I.* London: Routledge and Kegan Paul, 1973.

Perry, Arthur L. *Scotch-Irish in New England.* Boston: J. S. Cushing, 1891.

Phillips, Walter Alison. *History of the Church of Ireland, from the Earliest Times to the Present.* Oxford: Oxford University Press, 1934.

Philo, Chris. "History, Geography, and the Still Greater Mystery of Historical Geography." In Gregory, Martin, and Smith, *Human Geography,* 252–82.

Presbyterian Church, U.S.A. The Book of Confessions, Presbyterian Church U.S.A. Louisville: Office of the General Assembly, 1994.

Presbyterian Church in Ireland. "Presbyterian Principles and Political Witness in Northern Ireland." In *General Assembly Reports.* Belfast: Presbyterian Church in Ireland, 1993, 43–65.

Preyer, Norris W. *Hezekiah Alexander and the Revolution in the Backcountry.* Charlotte: Heritage Printers, 1987.

Ravenstein, E. G. "The Laws of Migration." *Journal of the Royal Statistical Society* 48 (1885): 167–227.

Ray, Celeste. *Highland Heritage: Scottish Americans in the American South.* Chapel Hill: University of North Carolina Press, 2001.

Register of the Privy Council of Scotland, 1604–7. Edinburgh, 1604–1607.

Register of the Privy Council of Scotland, 1622–25. Edinburgh, 1622–1625.

Register of the Privy Council of Scotland. 1st series, 7. Edinburgh, 1545–69.

Register of the Privy Council of Scotland. Vol. 8. Edinburgh, 1607–10.

Reid, A. G. *The Annals of Auchterarder and Memorials of Strathearn.* Perth: Perth-Kinross Library, 1989.

Reid, James Seaton. *History of the Presbyterian Church in Ireland.* Edited by W. D. Killen. 2 vols. Belfast: W. Mullan, 1867.

Renwick, James. *The Apologetical Declaration.* 1684.

Robinson, Philip. *The Plantation of Ulster: British Settlement in an Irish Landscape, 1600–1670.* Belfast: Ulster Historical Foundation, 1994.

Rogers, Richard. "The Diary of Richard Rogers." In *Two Elizabethan Puritan Diaries,* edited by M. M. Knappen. Chicago: American Society of Church History, 1933, 62.

———. *Seven Treatises.* 1603.

Rollock, Robert. *Certaine Sermons, upon Severall Texts of Scripture.* Edinburgh, 1634.

———. *Five and Twenty Lectures.* Edinburgh, 1616.

———. *Lectures upon the First and Second Epistles of Paul to the Thessalonians.* Edinburgh, 1598.

Ross, David. *Chronology of Scottish History.* New Lanark: Geddes and Grosset, 2002.

Rubenstein, James. *The Cultural Landscape: An Introduction to Human Geography Seventh Edition.* 7th ed. Upper Saddle River, N.J.: Prentice Hall, 2002.

Rutherford, Samuel. *The Divine Right of Church Government and Excommunication.* London, 1646.

———. *The Due Right of Presbytery.* London, 1644.

———. *Exercitationes Apologeticae.* Amsterdam, 1636.

———. *Fourteen Communion Sermons.* 1891. Edited by A. A. Bonar. Edinburgh: Banner of Truth Trust, 1973.

———. *Letters of Samuel Rutherford.* Edinburgh: Banner of Truth Trust, 1973.

———. *Lex Rex.* London, 1644.

———. *Rutherford Letters.* London, 1894.

Sauer, Carl O. "The Agency of Man on the Earth." In *Man's Role in Changing the Face of the Earth,* edited by Williams L. Thomas. Chicago, 1956, 49–69.

———. *Agricultural Origins and Dispersals.* Cambridge, Mass.: MIT Press, 1952.

———. "Forward to Historical Geography." *Annals of the Association of American Geographers* 31 (1941): 1–24.

Savage, M. "Spatial Differences in Modern Britain." In *The Changing Social Structure,* edited by C. Hamnett, L. McDowell, and P. Sarre. London: Sage Publications in association with the Open University, 1989. 244–68.

Schama, Simon. *A History of Britain: At the Edge of the World? 3000 BC–AD 1603.* New York: Hyperion, 2000.

———. *A History of Britain: The British Wars 1603–1776.* London: BBC Worldwide, 2001.

The Scots Confession, 1560. Edited by James Bulloch. Reprinted with translation by James Bulloch. Edinburgh: St. Andrew Press, 1960.

Scott, Hew. *Fasti Ecclesiae Scoticanae: The Succession of Ministers in the Church of Scotland from the Reformation.* Edinburgh: Oliver and Boyd, 1915.

Second Helvetic Confession. Zurich, 1561.

Seddall, Henry. *The Church of Ireland: A Historical Sketch.* Dublin: Hodges, Figgis, 1886.

Sefton, Henry. "Revolution to Disruption." In *Studies in the History of Worship in Scotland,* edited by Duncan Forrester and Douglas Murray. Edinburgh: T and T Clark, 1984, 47–63.

Semple, Ellen C. "The Anglo-Saxons of the Kentucky Mountains: A Study in Anthropogeography." *Geographical Journal* 17 (1901): 588–623.

Shapiro, Henry D. *Appalachia on Our Mind: The Southern Mountains and Mountaineers in the American Consciousness, 1820–1920.* Chapel Hill: University of North Carolina Press, 1978.

Shea, William L., and Earl J. Hess. *Pea Ridge: Civil War Campaign in the West.* Chapel Hill: University of North Carolina Press, 1992.

Shields, Alexander. *Hind Let Loose.* Cited in Gordon Donaldson, *Scotland: James V–James VII.* Edinburgh: Oliver and Boyd, 1965, 316.

Sibbald, James. *Diverse Select Sermons.* Aberdeen, 1658.

Sibbald, Robert. *Provision for the Poor in Time of Dearth and Scarcity.* Edinburgh, 1699.

Sinclair, John. *Analysis of the Statistical Account of Scotland.* Vol. I. Edinburgh, 1826.

Smout, T. C. *A History of the Scottish People 1560–1830.* London: Collins, 1998.

Smout, T. C., N. C. Landsman, and T. M. Devine. "Scottish Emigration in the Seventeenth and Eighteenth Centuries." In Canny, *Europeans on the Move,* 76–113.

Spatz, Chris. *Basic Statistics: Tales of Distributions.* 7th ed. Pacific Grove, Calif.: Brookcote Publishing, 2001.

Sprott, G. W. *The Worship of the Church of Scotland after the Covenanting Period 1638–61.* Edinburgh, 1893.

Sproul, R. C. *Faith Alone: The Evangelical Doctrine of Justification.* Grand Rapids: Baker, 1995.

———, ed. New Geneva Study Bible. Nashville: Thomas Nelson, 1995.

———. *Willing to Believe: The Controversy over Free Will.* Grand Rapids: Baker, 1997.

Steele, Phillip W., and Steve Cottrell. *Civil War in the Ozarks.* Gretna, La.: Pelican, 1993.

Stevenson, David. *The Covenanters: The National Covenant and Scotland.* Edinburgh: Saltire Society, 1988.

———. *Revolution and Counter Revolution in Scotland, 1644–51.* Edinburgh: John Donald, 1976.

———. *Scottish Covenanters and Irish Confederates: Scottish-Irish Relations in the Mid-Seventeenth Century.* Belfast: Ulster Historical Foundation, 1981.

———. *The Scottish Revolution, the Triumph of the Covenanters, 1637–44.* New York: St. Martin's, 1973.

Stevenson, John. *Two Centuries of Life in Down, 1600–1800.* Belfast: White Row, 1920.

Struther, William. *Scotland's Warning, or a Treatise of Fasting.* Edinburgh, 1628.

Stump, R. W. "The Geography of Religion—Introduction." *Journal of Cultural Geography* 7 (1986): 1–3.

Thomas, Colin. "Landscape with Figures: In the Steps of E. G. Bowen." *Cambria* 12 (1985): 24.

Thrift, Nigel. "Taking Aim at the Heart of Region." In Gregory, Martin, and Smith, *Human Geography,* .

Todd, Margo. *The Culture of Protestantism in Early Modern Scotland.* New Haven: Yale University Press, 2002.

Tonnies, Ferdinand. *Community and Society: Gemeinschaft und Gesellschaft.* Edited by Charles P. Loomis. East Lansing: Michigan State University, 1957.

Torrance, James B. "Covenant or Contract: A Study of the Theological Background of Worship in Seventeenth Century Scotland." Lecture notes, delivered about 1968–1969 at New College, University of Edinburgh. Archives of the Stewartry of Strathearn. Manse, Aberdalgie Perthshire, U.K.

———. *The Westminster Confession in the Church Today: Papers Prepared for the Church of Scotland Panel on Doctrine*. Edited by A. C. Herron. Edinburgh: St. Andrew Press, 1982.

Torrance, Thomas F. *Scottish Theology: From John Knox to John McLeod Campbell*. Edinburgh: T and T Clark, 1996.

Tracy, James D. *Europe's Reformations: 1450–1650*. Lanham, Md.: Rowan and Littlefield, 1999.

Tranter, Nigel. *The Story of Scotland*. Glasgow: Neil Wilson, 1987.

Tuan, Y. F. "Humanistic Geography." *Annals of the Association of American Geographers* 66 (1976): 266–76.

Turner, B. L., II. "Contested Identities: Human-Environment Geography and Disciplinary Implications in a Restructuring Academy." *Annals of the Association of American Geographers* 92 (2002): 52–74.

Tweedie, Steve. "Viewing the Bible Belt." *Journal of Popular Culture* 11 (1978): 865–76.

Tweedie, W. K. *Select Biographies*. 2 vols. Edinburgh, 1845–47.

Tyacke, Nicholas. *Anti-Calvinists: The Rise of English Arminianism c. 1590–1640*. Oxford: Oxford University Press, 1987.

Tyson, R. E. "The Population of Aberdeenshire 1695–1755: A New Approach." *North Scotland* 6 (1984–85): 113–31.

Ulster-Scots Agency. *The Ulster-Scot* (November/December, 2002).

United States Bureau of the Census. 1990 Census Report. Washington, D.C., 1990.

———. Statistical Abstract of the United States. 116th ed. Washington, D.C.: U.S. Department of Commerce, 1996.

Valins, Oliver. "Identity, Space, and Boundaries: Ultra-Orthodox Judaism in Contemporary Britain." Ph.D. thesis, University of Glasgow, United Kingdom, 1999.

Vallance, Edward. "An Holy and Sacramentall Paction: Federal Theology and the Solemn League and Covenant in England." *English Historical Review* 16 (February 2001): 50–75.

Vann, Barry A. "Irish Protestants and the Creation of the Bible Belt." *Journal of Transatlantic Studies* 5 (Spring 2007): 87–106.

———. "Learning Self-Direction in a Social and Experiential Context." *Human Resource Development Quarterly* 7.2 (1996): 121–30.

———. "Presbyterian Social Ties and Mobility in the Irish Sea Culture Area." *Journal of Historical Sociology* 18 (November 2005): 227–54.

———. *Rediscovering the South's Celtic Heritage*. Johnson City, Tenn.: Overmountain, 2004.

Walker, James. *Theology and Theologians of Scotland, 1560–1750*. 2nd ed. Edinburgh: John Knox, 1982.

Wandycz, Piotr. *The Price of Freedom: A History of East Central Europe from the Middle Ages to the Present.* London: Routledge, 1993.

Webb, James. *Born Fighting: How the Scots-Irish Shaped America.* New York: Broadway, 2004.

Weber, Max. *Protestant Ethic and the Spirit of Capitalism.* New York: Scribner, 1958.

Webster, Alexander. *Scottish Population Statistics: Including Webster's Analysis of Population, 1755.* Edited by James Gray Kyd. Edinburgh: Scottish Academic, 1975.

Weeks, John R. *Population: An Introduction to Concepts and Issues.* 8th ed. Belmont, Calif.: Wadsworth, 2002.

Weir, John. "Letter to the General Assembly, April 1644." In McCartney, *Nor Principalities Nor Powers,* 55.

Westerkamp, Marilyn. *The Triumph of the Laity: Scots-Irish Piety and the Great Awakening, 1625–1760.* Oxford: Oxford University Press, 1987.

Westminster Confession of Faith. London, 1643–47.

Whatley, C. A. *Bought and Sold for English Gold? Explaining the Union of 1707.* East Lothian, Scotland: Tuckwell, 2001.

Whyte, Ian D. *Migration and Society in Britain, 1550–1830.* Basingstoke, Hampshire, England: Macmillan, 2000.

———. *Scotland before the Industrial Revolution: An Economic and Social History, c. 1050–c. 1750.* London: Longman, 1995.

———. *Scotland's Society and Economy in Transition, c. 1500–c. 1760.* London: Macmillan, 1997.

Whyte, Ian D., and Whyte, K. "Geographical Mobility in a Seventeenth Century Scottish Rural Community." *Local Population Studies* 32 (1984): 45–53.

Williams, Cratis. "Who Are the Southern Mountaineers?" In *Voices from the Hills,* edited by Robert J. Higgs and Ambrose N. Manning. New York: F. Ungar, 1975, 493–506.

Williams, George H. *Wilderness and Paradise in Christian Thought: The Biblical Experience of the Desert in the History of Christianity.* New York: Harper, 1962.

Williams, Hank, Jr. Song. *America, the Way I See It.* 1990.

Wilson, John. *Dunning: Parochial History, with Notes, Antiquarian, Ecclesiastical, Baronial, and Miscellaneous.* Creiff, Scotland, 1906.

Witherow, Thomas. *Historical and Literary Memorials of Presbyterianism in Ireland.* London: William Mullan and Son, 1879.

Wokeck, M. S. "Irish Immigration to the Delaware Valley before the American Revolution." *Proceedings of the Royal Irish Academy* ser. C. (1996): 103–35.

Womack, Sarah. "Majority Do Not Feel British." *Daily Telegraph* (Belfast) December 18, 2002.

Woodburn, James B. *The Ulster-Scot: His History and Religion.* London: H. R. Allenson, 1914.

Woodward, D. "The Anglo-Irish Livestock Trade of the Seventeenth Century." Cited in R. Gillespie, *Colonial Ulster,* 72.

Wright, John K. "Terrae Incognitae: The Place of Imagination in Geography." In *Human Nature in Geography.* Cambridge: Harvard University Press, 1966, 68–88.

———. "Notes on Early American Geopiety." In *Human Nature in Geography*: Fourteen Papers, 1925–1965. Cambridge: Harvard University Press, 1966, 251–52.

Young, James. "Scotland and Ulster in the Seventeenth Century: The Movement of Peoples over the North Channel." In Kelly and Young, *Ulster and Scotland.*

———. *Life of John Welsh, Minister of Ayr.* Edinburgh, 1866.

Zakai, Avihu. *Exile and Kingdom: History and Apocalypse in the Puritan Migration to America.* Cambridge: Cambridge University Press, 2002.

Zelinsky, Wilbur. "An Approach to the Religious Geography of the United States: Patterns of Church Membership in 1952." *Annals of the Association of American Geographers* 51 (1961): 139–93.

———. *Cultural Geography of the United States.* Rev. ed. Upper Saddle River, N.J.: Prentice Hall, 1992.

———. "The Hypothesis of Mobility Transition." *Geographical Review* 61 (1971): 219–49.

INDEX

ABOUT THE AUTHOR

BARRY ARON VANN is an associate professor of geography at Lincoln Memorial University in Harrogate, Tennessee, where he also serves as the founding director of programs in Appalachian development studies, geography, and social studies. He is the author of *Rediscovering the South's Celtic Heritage*.